The *Criterion*
Cultural Politics and Periodical
Networks in Inter-War Britain

The *Criterion*

Cultural Politics and Periodical Networks in Inter-War Britain

JASON HARDING

OXFORD
UNIVERSITY PRESS

OXFORD

UNIVERSITY PRESS

Great Clarendon Street, Oxford OX2 6DP

Oxford University Press is a department of the University of Oxford.
It furthers the University's objective of excellence in research, scholarship,
and education by publishing worldwide in

Oxford New York

Auckland Bangkok Buenos Aires Cape Town Chennai
Dar es Salaam Delhi Hong Kong Istanbul Karachi Kolkata
Kuala Lumpur Madrid Melbourne Mexico City Mumbai Nairobi
São Paulo Shanghai Singapore Taipei Tokyo Toronto

and an associated company in Berlin

Oxford is a registered trade mark of Oxford University Press
in the UK and in certain other countries

Published in the United States
by Oxford University Press Inc., New York

© Jason Harding, 2002

The moral rights of the author have been asserted

Database right Oxford University Press (maker)

First published 2002

British Library Cataloguing in Publication Data

Data available

Library of Congress Cataloging in Publication Data

Harding, Jason
The Criterion: cultural politics and periodical networks in inter-war Britain/Jason Harding.
p.cm.
Includes bibliographical references (p.) and index

ISBN 0–19–924717–X

1. Eliot, T.S. (Thomas Stearns), 1888–1965 – Contributors in journalism. 2. Eliot, T.S.
(Thomas Stearns) 1888–1965 – Political and social views. 3. Culture – Political aspects –
Great Britain – History – 20th century. 4. Periodicals – Publishing – Great Britain –
History – 20th century. 5. Journalism – Great Britain – History – 20th century.
6. Criticism – Great Britain – History – 20th century. 7. Great Britain – Intellectual
life – 20th century. 8. Criterion (London, England: 1922). I. Title.

PS3509 L43 Z68158 2002   821′.912–dc21   2001059300

1 3 5 7 9 10 8 6 4 2

Typeset in Sabon
by Newgen Imaging Systems (P) Ltd., Chennai, India
Printed in Great Britain
on acid-free paper by
Biddles Ltd, Guildford and King's Lynn

In Memory of

LORNA SAGE

Acknowledgements

I WOULD LIKE to acknowledge a debt of gratitude to the following persons: Daniel Adamski, the late Sir Malcolm Bradbury, the late Janet Carleton (née Adam Smith), John Constable, Martin Dodsworth, Elsie Duncan-Jones (née Phare), the late David Gascoyne, the late Desmond Hawkins, David Holbrook, Sir Frank Kermode, Jim McCue, Wilfrid Mellers, Rod Mengham, John Ochsendorf, Ian Patterson, F. T. Prince, the late Anne Ridler (née Bradby), the late George Rylands, Derek Savage, Ronald Schuchard, Erica Schumacher (née Wright), Roger Scott, Sebastian Skeaping, John Sutherland, Robert Waller, and George Watson. I wish to express my deepest thanks to Stefan Collini for his guidance and encouragement on this project from beginning to end.

I owe a second set of debts to the following archivists and librarians: Rosalind Moad, Modern Archive Centre, King's College, Cambridge; Jacky Cox, Deputy Keeper of the University Archives, University Library, Cambridge; Richard Luckett, the Pepys Librarian, Magdalene College, Cambridge; Chris Fletcher, Manuscripts Department, British Library, London; Chris Petter, Special Collections Librarian, McPherson Library, University of Victoria; Lori Curtis, Associate Curator of Special Collections, McFarlin Library, University of Tulsa. Thanks are due to the staff of the following institutions: Universitäts und Landesbibliothek, Bonn University; Archive Centre, Churchill College, Cambridge; Downing College Library, Cambridge; Wren Library, Trinity College, Cambridge; Special Collections, St John's College, Cambridge; Brotherton Library, Leeds; Department of Manuscripts, Trinity College, Dublin; National Library of Scotland, Edinburgh; Keele University Library; Senate House, University of London Library; New York Public Library; Butler Library, Columbia University; Beinecke Rare Book and Manuscript Library, Yale University; Bodleian Library, Oxford. I am grateful to Jason Maloy and Anne Margaret Daniel for research assistance work at the Harry Ransom Humanities Research Center, University of Texas, and Princeton University Libraries respectively.

For permission to quote from copyright material, I wish to thank Ben Knights (L. C. Knights), Benedict Read and the Herbert Read Trust (Herbert Read), Andrew Roberts (Janet Adam Smith), Lady Natasha Spender and the Stephen Spender Trust (Stephen Spender). I am grateful to the editors of the *Times Literary Supplement* for permission to reprint material that first appeared as the 'Commentary' for 25 August 2000. Quotations from the published and unpublished writings of T. S. Eliot and *The Criterion* have been included by permission of the Eliot Estate and Faber and Faber Ltd.

J. H.

Contents

Abbreviations

References in the notes to articles in periodicals have been given in the form of date of issue (day, month, and year) and the page number(s); volume or part numbers have been omitted. *The Letters of T. S. Eliot*, i. *1898–1922*, ed. Valerie Eliot (London, 1988), has been abbreviated to *Letters*.

Details of manuscript collections have been abbreviated to the location of the repository:

Bonn	Universitäts und Landesbibliothek, Bonn
Cambridge (Churchill)	Archive Centre, Churchill College, Cambridge
Cambridge (King's)	Modern Archive Centre, King's College, Cambridge
Cambridge (Magdalene)	Old Library, Magdalene College, Cambridge
Cambridge (St John's)	Special Collections, St John's College, Cambridge
Cambridge (Trinity)	Wren Library, Trinity College, Cambridge
Dublin	Department of Manuscripts, Trinity College, Dublin
Edinburgh	National Library of Scotland, Edinburgh
Keele	Special Collections, Keele University
Leeds	Brotherton Library, Leeds University
London (British Library)	Department of Manuscripts, British Library, London
London (Senate House)	Special Collections, Senate House, University of London Library
New York (Public Library)	Berg Collection, New York Public Library
New York (Columbia)	Manuscript and Special Collections, Columbia University
Northwestern	Special Collections, Northwestern University Library, Evanston
Oxford	Bodleian Library, University of Oxford
Princeton	Firestone Library, Princeton University Libraries
Sussex	Manuscript Collections, University of Sussex Library

Texas   Harry Ransom Humanities Research Center, University of
              Texas, Austin
Tulsa   Department of Special Collections, McFarlin Library,
              University of Tulsa, Oklahoma
Victoria   Special Collections, McPherson Library, University of
              Victoria, British Columbia
Yale   Beinecke Rare Book and Manuscript Library, Yale
              University

The Criterion has brought me associations, friendships and acquaintanceships of inestimable value; I like also to think that it may have served contributors, by initiating friendships and acquaintances between those who might not otherwise have met, or known each other's work.

T. S. Eliot, 'Last Words', *Criterion* (January 1939)

Introduction

If we look for a mark of modernism's coming of age, the founding of the *Criterion* in 1922 may prove a better instance than *The Waste Land*, better even than *Ulysses*, because it exemplifies the institutionalization of the movement, the accession to cultural legitimacy.

Michael Levenson, *A Genealogy of Modernism*
(Cambridge, 1984), 213

I

Michael Levenson's challenging contention that the launch of the *Criterion* in 1922 marks a modernist 'coming of age' would require agreement about his definition and use of the nebulous terms 'modernism', 'institutionalization', and 'cultural legitimacy' to gain widespread assent. It does, all the same, neatly frame a number of methodological presuppositions raised in the study of the *Criterion* as a periodical text, and more broadly of literary journalism as a distinctive genre. In the first instance, consideration of the institutional role of the *Criterion* in the cultural and intellectual debates of the inter-war period necessitates constant attention to the periodical *qua* periodical; at the very least a more discriminating exploration of the *Criterion*'s contextual setting than has been the case in existing scholarship. Accounts of the *Criterion* hitherto have centred almost exclusively on Eliot, approaching the journal as a commentary upon his practice as a poet, his 'intellectual development', or his role as a political thinker. But it is as well to remember that every contribution to intellectual debate is conditioned by the means of its dissemination and reception: literary journalism is not a private speculation in a vacuum, rather an intervention in an ongoing cultural conversation, most immediately a dialogue with a shifting set of interlocking periodical structures and networks. Measured assessment of the *Criterion*, therefore, demands a high degree of historical specificity: not just that the critic should be *au fait* with contemporary cultural and intellectual debates (for instance regarding the formulation and impact of movements like 'modernism'), but, more teasingly, an awareness of how the journalistic *context*, witnessed in the distortions of public controversy or the potential dangers of collusion and vulgarization, may affect the substantive *content*. The proposition is stranger to modern academic critics, who habitually display a lofty distaste for minutiae relating to the commodification of writing in the market-place, than it was to T. S. Eliot, who as editor of the *Criterion* frequently worried over the commercial imperatives of finance and circulation: cultivating patrons, attempting to promote sales, struggling to reduce expenses, securing copy, and so forth. And yet, the *Criterion*, in its bulky and dignified format, as in the magisterial nature of its contents, strove to evade the built-in ephemerality of disposable periodical journalism. Today the eighteen hard-bound tomes, complete with index, exude an unmistakable aura of permanence, an 'organ of documentation' as Eliot hoped.

The question of what it is that gets documented and embalmed between the hardcovers requires careful consideration of the milieu of inter-war literary journalism. The *Criterion* provided Eliot with a public forum from which he could participate in the general cultural conversation: mediating authors and ideas to a variegated field of periodicals and more broadly to highly differentiated organizations and institutions in modern society. More responsive than the printed book, the subtle and intricate reciprocity of literary journalism allowed Eliot to address and even, upon occasions, to shape the agenda of inter-war cultural criticism. The centrality of print journalism as a locus of intellectual discussion is a notable feature of the period: one that requires the modern reader to develop an awareness of the complexity of the reception of these commonly hotly contested debates by multiple interpretative communities. The question of the reading patterns or the 'implied audience' of various inter-war periodicals, then, is a thorny and sometimes intractable problem that resurfaces at various points in this study. It is no simple matter to distinguish the distinctive profiles of the small, overlapping readerships of inter-war literary periodicals, drawn from an intelligentsia of writers, artists, and journalists, and a broader corpus of readers from the educated and professional classes. The task requires a sensitive ear for the allusions and references to the larger cultural conversation in which literary journalism is inescapably embedded.

It is easier to be more precise about the intellectual-social milieu of the various contributors to the *Criterion* and their connections to an almost exclusively male, upper-middle-class, metropolitan literary establishment. It has often been necessary in this study to decode the literary topography, social networks, and class-bound snobberies that criss-crossed literary London between the wars, perhaps to a degree that may appear like hair-splitting to non-British observers. Suffice it to say, that a sensitivity and consciousness of caste was a defining trait of the cadres, cabals, and coteries that coloured inter-war literary journalism. This study has drawn upon a wealth of unpublished correspondence and archive material, together with a systematic survey of the journals themselves, in an attempt to re-situate the *Criterion* within a structure or constellation of inter-war literary periodicals: its immediate social and institutional context. No straightforward linear narrative could attempt to convey the diversity and richness of the *Criterion* or the complexity of its relation to other inter-war literary periodicals. It is the aim of the tripartite structure of this book—three detailed cross-sections through the labyrinthine field of inter-war literary journalism—to delineate the periodical networks in which the *Criterion* existed. It is hoped that material from insufficiently known archive sources and from interviews with living witnesses to the period may provide a deepened understanding of the principles upon which Eliot solicited, accepted, rejected, and revised contributions.

The first section examines the *Criterion* in counterpoint with other influential literary journals: not those like the *Times Literary Supplement*, the *London Mercury*, or the *Nation and Athenaeum*, which operated on such a dissimilar conception of form and function, but rather those literary-cultural neighbours whose existence was predicated upon at least some minimal shared interests with the *Criterion* and from which intelligible and profitable commerce might proceed. In the 1920s, Eliot spoke of the 'common ground for disagreement' that the *Criterion* shared with the *Adelphi* and the *Calendar of Modern Letters*. The only excuse for retracing the well-worn tracks of the classicism and romanticism debate that took place in the pages of the *Criterion* and the *Adelphi* during the 1920s, is to demonstrate the extent to which the controversy was effected by the medium of its periodical publication.[1] The exchange with John Middleton Murry reveals the modulations of Eliot's 'printed voice' as a public intellectual and some of the rhetorical tactics and editorial manœuvres (in particular, a penchant for imprisoning opponents within dichotomizing *ad hominem* arguments) that characterized his forays into public controversy. A briefer exchange with the vigorous but short-lived *Calendar* highlights how Eliot was initially adept at responding to, and absorbing, new currents in metropolitan literary journalism; thereby advancing the *Criterion*'s position and standing in the field. The episode is also instructive in revealing how it is necessary to get back behind retrospective accounts of the putative 'success' or 'failure' of the periodicals in question and to bear in mind that periodical controversy can be manipulated as a saleable commodity and circulation builder.

A tone of embattled dogmatism came to characterize British intellectual debate in the 1930s. The pages of *New Verse* and *Scrutiny*, largely harvested from the fertile recruiting grounds of Oxford and Cambridge, displayed a curious mixture of antagonism and deference toward the *Criterion*, often regarded as the pre-eminent literary review of the decade. Both *New Verse* and *Scrutiny* are testimony of the regrettable tendency for *esprit de corps* to narrow into *esprit de clique*: accusations of cliquery and racketeering were prevalent throughout the 1930s. That said, F. R. Leavis's exaggerated and programmatic accounts of the *Criterion* as representative of a monolithic literary establishment *and* as a mouthpiece for a Marxist gang of authors, should not be taken at face value. *Scrutiny*, it will be seen, shared an overlap of contributors and concerns with the *Criterion*; in particular, both journals espoused an alarmist cultural pessimism in which the fate of civilization was linked to a tendentious version of English social history and the health of contemporary literary journalism. Similarly, *New Verse* may have printed a mock-obituary of Eliot and served as a showcase for the work of the Auden generation of poets, but it maintained closer links to Eliot in his roles as

---

[1] This controversy has been treated in David Goldie's *A Critical Difference: T. S. Eliot and John Middleton Murry in English Literary Criticism, 1919–1928* (Oxford, 1998). For my review of Goldie, see 'Doubting Thomist', *Cambridge Quarterly* (June 2000), 184–9.

publisher and periodical editor than might be expected. Geoffrey Grigson knew the commercial value of strong opinions pungently expressed, but he also knew when to practise diplomacy, sometimes even courtesy. The *Criterion*, it transpires, was a broader and more temperate church than most during the sectarian literary politics of Auden's 'low dishonest decade'.

The second section of this study shifts the focus from the *Criterion*'s engagement in a range of intertextual discourses occurring *across* the field of inter-war literary journalism, to a consideration of the intrinsic dynamics and tensions manifested *within* the journal. This section resists the temptation to offer blandly generalizing grand narratives about the *Criterion*, or to crystallize the character of the journal solely from Eliot's editorial pronouncements. A properly nuanced account of the *Criterion* must tease out the problematic multiple subject positions and interplay of voices often exhibited simultaneously in its pages. Although the names of the high peaks of the modern movement in English literature—D. H. Lawrence, Ezra Pound, Wyndham Lewis, I. A. Richards, W. H. Auden—frequently recur as points of reference in the wider terrain of this study, the emphasis here is on the undergrowth of metropolitan literary journalism, on four neglected 'men of letters' who were crucial in shaping the style and tone of the *Criterion*. Herbert Read and Bonamy Dobrée were Eliot's chief lieutenants on the *Criterion* during the 1920s. However, their professions of public loyalty masked, following Eliot's conversion to Anglo-Catholicism in 1927, an increasingly pronounced perception of aesthetic and ideological difference. The more religiously orthodox, if rather more opinionated and splenetic Montgomery Belgion was systematically employed by Eliot during the 1930s to stoke up the coals of controversy on carefully chosen topics. Ultimately, Eliot put his faith in Michael Roberts, ably seconded by his wife Janet Adam Smith, as the representative of the younger generation who best upheld *Criterion* policy. It was Roberts's principled Anglicanism, strange in the light of his subsequent reputation as an impresario of the proto-Communist Auden generation, which commanded Eliot's respect and support. That said, examination of Eliot's professional relationship with his four closest collaborators on the *Criterion* reveals the habitually cautious and at times calculating nature of his editorial directives.

The last section broadens the focus of enquiry in an attempt to situate the *Criterion* in a wider historical and intellectual context. Consideration of the *Criterion*'s excursions into politico-economic discourse, including some engagement with economic nostrums and with Christian sociological discussion groups, reveals a strain of Tory-Anglican conservatism as a defining feature of the journal. The *Criterion*'s 'disinterested' symposial treatment of some pretty unappealing right-wing causes has left it open, in recent debates, to slack charges of 'fascism' and 'anti-Semitism'. In truth, the *Criterion*'s largely dismissive treatment of the violent and abrasive *realpolitik* of inter-war foreign affairs is evidence of a rather painful inability to estimate contemporary social and political forces at their true strength. This failure is best understood in the context of the journal's self-appointed role as a guardian of European civilization. From its inception, the *Criterion* sought close links with cosmopolitan European periodicals, such as the *Nouvelle Revue française*, and with like-minded European men of letters, notably Ernst Robert Curtius. It was a connection that increasingly came to revolve around Hugo von Hofmannsthal's proclamation of a 'conservative revolution'; that is, nostalgia for the patrimony of a Latin-Christian tradition, an act of creative historical imagination that searched the past for continuity and order. This decidedly reactionary response to contemporary cultural and political developments, threatening an idealized 'mind of Europe', was enveloped by the wider apocalyptic 'myth of catastrophe' that coloured intellectual debate in the 1930s. More than that, it demonstrated just how far Eliot's ponderous quarterly review had fallen behind the more *engagé* intellectual weeklies, not to mention the alarming pace of political actualities, by the time of its demise in 1939.

Finally, this exploration of the milieu of inter-war British literary journalism must take as axiomatic the assumption of human agency. The distinctive contribution of this study is unintelligible without some notion of what D. F. McKenzie has called 'the sociology of the text': 'the human motives and interactions which texts involve at every stage of their production, transmission and consumption.'[2] In other words, a due emphasis on the *personalities* of editors and literary journalists, and on the serendipitous social connections by

---

[2] See D. F. McKenzie, *Bibliography and the Sociology of Texts* (London, 1986).

which periodical texts are structured, received, and contested, is treated as a *sine qua non* for a proper understanding of the *Criterion*. The overall profile of any periodical is a complex blend of the signatures of the individual contributors, ordered and articulated by innumerable editorial decisions. It is the contention of this study that the character of the *Criterion* cannot be divorced from the alliances and loyalties, rivalries, animosities, and friendships that mark all social relations as fully human. But before turning to the main body of this book it is necessary, first of all, to demarcate the field of inter-war literary journalism with a brief outline of the publication history of the *Criterion*.

II

In his May 1922 'London Letter' to the New York arts and literary monthly, the *Dial*, Eliot observed: 'Other cities decay, and extend a rich odour of putrefaction; London merely shrivels, like a little bookkeeper grown old.'[3] A large part of the problem was the demise of a number of varied and lively 'little' magazines—the *Egoist* in 1919, *Art and Letters* and *Coterie* in 1920, *Wheels* in 1921—forums and clearing houses for the work of London's literary avant-garde. Eliot had contributed poems, reviews, and critical essays to these journals; he had acted as the *Egoist*'s literary editor from 1917 until 1919, promoting the radical experimentation associated with the work of Pound, Joyce, Wyndham Lewis, and the Imagist poets. In 1921, Eliot's predecessor at the *Egoist*, Richard Aldington, complained to the poet and man of letters, Thomas Sturge Moore, a good friend of W. B. Yeats, that aside from the *Times Literary Supplement* there was a complete absence of serious periodicals to which one could contribute lengthy articles on literary matters: he added that the *London Mercury* was too dreadful.[4]

Eliot detested J. C. Squire's half-crown monthly magazine.[5] Launched in November 1919, the *London Mercury* quickly

---

[3] 'London Letter', *Dial* (May 1922), 510.
[4] Richard Aldington to Thomas Sturge Moore, 4 Jan. 1921. London (Senate House).
[5] See T. S. Eliot to John Quinn, 25 Jan. 1920: '[The *London Mercury*] is run by a small clique of bad writers. J. C. Squire, the editor, knows nothing about poetry; but he is the cleverest journalist in London.' *The Letters of T. S. Eliot, i. 1898–1922*, ed. Valerie Eliot (London, 1988), 358. Hereafter *Letters*.

found a niche in the popular book market, entertaining a broad and responsive audience in excess of 10,000 subscribers. With its reliance on well-established Edwardian and Georgian authors and given the lack of curiosity regarding modernist experimentation displayed in Squire's 'Editorial Notes', the keynote of the magazine, the *London Mercury* became a byword in advanced literary circles for the epithet 'middlebrow'. Certainly, by the end of the 1920s Squire must have come to rue his rude and uncomprehending dismissal of *The Waste Land* in its pages. On the other hand, the *Criterion* and the *London Mercury* were both created to meet the demands of a new reading public dissatisfied with the canons of taste dominant in the long established reviews of general culture. It is fair to say that the *Criterion* and the *London Mercury* differed in degree rather than in kind; they appeared to coexist amicably enough with discrete audiences and an intermittent but unmistakable overlap of contributors, until both collapsed on the eve of the Second World War.[6]

The standing of the *Times Literary Supplement* is harder to assess. In 1919, Aldington, a regular reviewer of French literature for the *TLS*, introduced Eliot to the non-contributing editor, Bruce Richmond. Thereafter, as a specialist on seventeenth-century literature, Eliot donned the mantle of institutional authority that characterized the anonymous pages of the 'Lit. Supp.' A recent anthology of contributions to the *TLS* highlighted the reviews of Virginia Woolf and T. S. Eliot as proof of the journal's engagement with the modern movement in literature. However, perusal of the marked 'contributors copy' reveals that the staple of *TLS* fare in the inter-war period was far more likely to come from the pen of a general journeyman of letters, such as Arthur Clutton-Brock, or salaried staff members of *The Times*. Elevated and patrician in tone and buttressed by a large and influential body of subscribers, usually above 20,000 throughout the inter-war years, the tightly packed columns of the *TLS* were, in truth, inveterately culturally conservative. Critics as different as George Gordon, Ezra Pound, and F. R. Leavis remarked with due emphasis how

---

[6] See Squire: 'Mr. Eliot's review has a distinct character and, consequently, there is a distinct place for it' (*London Mercury* (June 1927), 117).

the *TLS* stood as a bastion of the continuity of English criticism at a time when 'standards' had been shaken. Eliot described the *TLS* as the 'top rung of the ladder of literary journalism' and there is little doubt that his association with the journal was crucial in shaping a certain lapidariness of tone evident in his prose writings. Above all, the example of Richmond's amiable and unassuming editorship of the *TLS* was to cast a shadow over the *Criterion*.[7]

In the early 1920s, then, Eliot believed that it was necessary to establish a new literary periodical to consolidate the early groundwork of modernism and to combat the hostility or indifference of a highly commercialized industry of print journalism.[8] There was some talk that Eliot should act as the London editor of the *Dial*, edited and co-owned from New York by Scofield Thayer, a contemporary of his at Milton Academy and Harvard. However, in the summer of 1921, the novelist and wealthy patron of the arts, Sydney Schiff, introduced Eliot to the Viscountess Lilian Rothermere (the estranged wife of the newspaper magnate). She was keen to finance a London literary magazine that would have a social éclat among a select audience of writers, critics, and patrons of the arts. The business negotiations were put into abeyance in the autumn of 1921 when Eliot suffered a nervous breakdown and took three months' leave from Lloyds Bank (writing *The Waste Land* during his convalescence). However, by 1922 Eliot turned once more to the proposed magazine, informing the probable publisher, Richard Cobden-Sanderson, that he had been 'throwing out hooks to desirable contributors'.[9] Eliot's 'hooks' were carefully baited: a measure of his ambition and of his meticulous preparation.

Eliot's letter to Sturge Moore was particularly instructive in spelling out his aims:

I have undertaken the task of finding and selecting the contributors for a modest quarterly review which is subsidised to a moderate extent for three years. I propose that the quarterly should be simple and severe in

[7] See Eliot: 'To [Bruce Richmond] I owe a double debt, first for the work he gave me to do and for the discipline of writing for him, and second for illustrating, in his conduct of the weekly, what editorial standards should be—a lesson I tried to apply when I came to edit the *Criterion*' ('Bruce Littleton Richmond', *TLS* (13 Jan. 1961), 17).
[8] See T. S. Eliot to Sydney Schiff, 16 Jan. 1920, on the 'huge journalistic organism the "critical" or Review press' (*Letters*, 355–6). [9] Ibid. 511.

appearance, without illustrations, and my only ambition is that it should unite the best critical opinion in England, together with the work of the best critics whom I can find from other countries. Whilst I should admit other writing in very small quantity, I wish to make it primarily a critical review. To its ultimate financial success I am comparatively indifferent; but while it lasts, under my direction, I shall make its aim the maintenance of critical standards and the concentration of intelligent critical opinion; also, the diffusion of such funds as can be mustered, among the proper persons as contributors.[10]

Eliot's desire that the review should carry 'no illustrations' and should be concerned primarily with an austere 'maintenance of critical standards' uncovers fundamental differences from Lady Rothermere's conception of the journal. They shared, however, a belief that the journal should appeal to a tiny public, no more than 1,000 subscribers: as caviar to the general it should observe the law of the successful 'little' magazine and possess an influence on contemporary letters inversely proportional to its circulation. In other words, the magazine would provide a 'capital symbolique' (to appropriate Pierre Bourdieu's useful theoretical formulation), not governed by market principles of success, upon which Eliot's social and literary career could be advanced.

On 16 October 1922, Cobden-Sanderson published 600 copies of the 96 page octavo quarterly review: the plain beige cover sported the title, *The Criterion*, in red vertical typeface and in black type a table of contents. The *Criterion* was priced 3s. 6d. and there were no advertisements: in common with the *Nouvelle Revue française*, whom it resembled in appearance, experimental modernism was set inside the case of a great European review. At the centre of the first issue was *The Waste Land*—published without epigraph or explanatory notes—subsequently anthologized and studied in universities around the world as the epitome of modernist poetry. All the same, the contents of the first issue were eclectic: belletristic essays by Sturge Moore and George Saintsbury ('that genial *doyen* of English letters' as Eliot described him[11]), S. S. Koteliansky's translation of a plan of a novel from the recently opened Dostoevsky archive (polished stylistically by Virginia Woolf), a short story from the nearly 60-year-old author

---

[10] Ibid. 518.
[11] Preface to the *Criterion* reprint (London, 1967).

May Sinclair, and Valéry Larbaud's influential lecture on *Ulysses* translated from the *Nouvelle Revue française*. In the *TLS*, Harold Child commented with approval:

What literary school, then, does this new quarterly represent? It is a school which includes Saintsbury, Sturge Moore, and T. S. Eliot. There is no such school, obviously. It becomes apparent that the only school represented is the school of those who are genuinely interested in good literature.[12]

Eliot worried that the *Criterion* would appear too conservative to some, too radical to others. Lady Rothermere thought the first number 'dull'. Pound couched his praise to the New York lawyer and patron of the arts, John Quinn, in ambiguous terms: it was, he said, a wonderful piece of editing for the purpose of getting into the Athenaeum.

Eliot's fellow-travellers from his *Egoist* days, perhaps motivated by envy, proved querulous and troublesome. Aldington, initially the *Criterion*'s assistant editor 'at a very modest salary',[13] withdrew a solicited article after Eliot suggested some minor revisions. He added a characteristically spiteful remark about the quarterly's imperious title (apparently chosen by Eliot's wife, Vivien, although Pound had earlier proposed the title for a never realized review). Furthermore, although Eliot was keen to serialize the *Cantos* as they appeared, he complained that each one of Pound's quirky and truculent critical articles nearly sank the paper. Both Aldington and Pound complained that the *Criterion*'s rate of payment (£10 for 5,000 words and £1. 1s. per page of verse) was not worth their trouble. Less than a year after the launch of the *Criterion*, plagued by his wife's chronic ill health, financial worries, and overwork, Eliot sailed close to another nervous shipwreck. He wrote to John Quinn in near despair:

I wish to heaven that I had never taken up the *Criterion*. . . . It has been an evergrowing responsibility; It has been a great *expense* to me and I have not got a penny out of it; There is not enough money to run it and pay me too. . . . In order to carry on the *Criterion* I have had to neglect not only the writing I ought to be doing but my private affairs of every

---

[12] [Harold Child], 'Periodicals', *TLS* (26 Oct. 1922), 690.
[13] T. S. Eliot in Alister Kershaw and Frédéric-Jacques Temple (eds.), *Richard Aldington: An Intimate Portrait* (Carbondale, Ill., 1965), 24.

description which for some time past I have not had a moment to deal with. . . . I am worn out. I cannot go on.[14]

One can sympathize with Eliot's exhaustion and frustration, commuting home after a full day's work in the City before he could begin the arduous editorial routine of soliciting contributions and correcting proofs. Although aided by Vivien and his part-time secretary, Irene Fassett, who dealt with the voluminous correspondence, the *Criterion* must have seemed a thankless undertaking— an amateur venture, underpinned by capricious aristocratic patronage. As an employee of Lloyds Bank, Eliot was not permitted to draw a salary for the *Criterion*: his name did not appear on the magazine's masthead, although his editorship was an open secret in literary London. However, from 1924 the Eliots received payment for Vivien's short stories and reviews—written under various pseudonyms in order to keep Lady Rothermere in the dark as to their true authorship.[15] The contributions are notable for their echoes of Eliot's poetry and prose, as well as for their hints of marital tension; on another level, they are evidence of Eliot's determination to placate Lady Rothermere's craving for the clever, brittle conversation of fashionable society drawing-rooms. In 1924, he commissioned a satirical sketch of contemporary manners from Schiff (alias the novelist Stephen Hudson) described as the sort of thing the *Criterion* needed.[16] That sort of satirical, short sketch was supplied by Vivien, Stephen Hudson, Ada Leverson, and on one occasion by Aldous Huxley. Taken with further contributions on the Ballets Russes by Eliot and L. St Senan (the pen-name of Thomas MacGreevy), and on the fashion and theatre worlds by Lady Violet Ray and the actress Viola Tree, the *Criterion* may not have looked an out-of-place accessory in the 'correct' West End salons. Compared to these offerings of radical chic, the long and rambling diatribes from the self-styled 'exiles' and 'enemies'—Pound, Wyndham Lewis, and D. H. Lawrence— must have blown like an icy chill through a summer garden party.

---

[14] Cited in Donald Gallup, 'T. S. Eliot and Ezra Pound: Collaborators in Letters', *Atlantic Monthly* (Jan. 1970), 58.

[15] Vivien Eliot made 12 contributions to the *Criterion* between Feb. 1924 and July 1925. Payment was sent to a flat in Charing Cross Road and not to the Eliots' home address. Papers of Vivien Eliot, Oxford.

[16] T. S. Eliot to Sydney Schiff [1924]. London (British Library).

Standing somewhere between these extremes were the Sitwell and the Bloomsbury entourages who were both a growing force in literary London during the 1920s. Eliot solicited work from Osbert, Sacheverell, and Edith Sitwell, a trio of outspoken and eccentric aristocrats with whom he had collaborated on the avant-garde anthologies *Wheels* and on Frank Rutter's *Art and Letters*. The Bloomsbury set, an informal network of writers and artists, utilized the means of cultural production afforded by the Hogarth Press and the intellectual weekly, the *Nation and Athenaeum*, to promote their work. In 1923, probably at Vivien's behest, Eliot declined the literary editorship of the *Nation*, thereby turning his back on an opening into professional journalism.[17] He published work by Roger Fry, Clive Bell, Virginia Woolf, and E. M. Forster in the *Criterion* and he solicited contributions from Leonard Woolf, Lytton Strachey, and David Garnett. However, in September 1925, Virginia Woolf noted in her diary that Leonard, who had accepted the literary editorship of the *Nation*, referred to Eliot as that 'queer shifty creature'.[18] Eliot's connections with the progressive but snobbish Bloomsbury group were tinged by mutual suspicion.

In 1925, Eliot recruited the young Cambridge graduate, George Rylands, from Bloomsbury. Following the general rule, he received an enthusiastic review of his slim Hogarth poetry volume, *Russet and Taffeta*, before joining the reviewing ranks of the *Criterion* himself.[19] Thereafter, Rylands contributed witty and urbane reviews of Nöel Coward, Walter de la Mare, and Sacheverell Sitwell, before his rococo prose style occasioned a polite editorial reminder from Eliot about the more forthright approach appropriate to a 'serious' critical review.[20] In truth, Eliot's personal relations with the Bloomsbury group were often strained and there was certainly more than a touch of asperity in the *Criterion* reviews of works by Rylands's mentor, Lytton Strachey.[21] Nor was the *Criterion*'s treatment of

---

[17] For details see Valerie Eliot (ed.), *'The Waste Land': A Facsimile and Transcript of the Original Drafts* (London, 1971), pp. xxvi–xxviii.

[18] *The Diary of Virginia Woolf, iii. 1925–1930*, ed. Anne Olivier Bell and Andrew McNellie (London, 1980), 45.

[19] Eliot had wanted to print *Russet and Taffeta* in the *Criterion*. See George Rylands, 'Recollections', *Paris Review* (1988), 112.

[20] See T. S. Eliot to George Rylands, 27 Feb. 1926. Cambridge (King's).

[21] See Michael Holroyd, *Lytton Strachey, ii. 1910–1932* (London, 1968), 646–7.

the Sitwells lacking a slice of biting sarcasm. Wyndham Lewis's 'encyclical' to *The Apes of God*, published in the *Criterion* in 1924, castigated Bloomsbury and the Sitwells as 'those prosperous mountebanks who alternately imitate and mock at and traduce those figures they at once admire and hate'.[22]

However, Eliot was initially compromised in his selection and arrangement of the contents of the *Criterion* by an obligation to conciliate Lady Rothermere and to navigate a watchful and politic line through the social relations of the London literary world. Early in 1925, as Lady Rothermere's three-year contract with Cobden-Sanderson neared its expiry date, and with Vivien so alarmingly ill and distressed that Eliot feared that she might die, it appeared that the *Criterion* would itself expire.[23] In July 1925 Eliot informed Rylands that he was planning a new 60-page European quarterly review and that the autumn number of the *Criterion* would not appear (it did not).[24] For some time now, Eliot had felt desperately overworked: he wanted to leave Lloyds Bank and receive a salary and the time necessary to pursue a literary career.[25] His doctor advised a rest cure. Eliot left behind the *Criterion*'s uncertain future to enter a retreat near Lady Rothermere's cottage in the Alpes Maritimes. Fortunately, in the meantime, his name had been recommended to Geoffrey Faber as a literary adviser for the new publishing venture of Faber & Gwyer. Eliot joined the board of directors in September 1925 and although an issue of the *Criterion* had been lost, causing some consternation among his followers, a deal was struck with Lady Rothermere whereby the *Criterion* was reorganized on a business-like footing, with publication of the journal transferred to the more economical Faber imprint.

Eliot claimed that it was only from 1926 that the physiognomy of the inter-war period became clear. It has been customary to search for the meaning of this remark in public events, such as the General Strike, but it is also important to remember that in January 1926 Eliot launched the *New Criterion* with the institutional backing of Faber & Gwyer. A bumper 220-page issue selling at 5s. and

[22] 'The Apes of God', *Criterion* (Apr. 1924), 307.
[23] See T. S. Eliot to Bonamy Dobrée, 14 Mar. 1925. Leeds.
[24] T. S. Eliot to George Rylands, July 1925. Cambridge (King's).
[25] See T. S. Eliot to Richard Aldington, 8 Apr. 1924. Texas.

containing a smattering of up-market advertisements,[26] the first number carried work from, among others, D. H. Lawrence, Virginia Woolf, Aldous Huxley, and Gertrude Stein. In many ways, 1926 was a better marker of modernism's London 'institutionalization' and 'cultural legitimacy' than Levenson's *annus mirabilis*. From Faber's offices in Russell Square, Eliot could cast his net more widely, cultivating a myriad of social connections with the nearby bohemian purlieus of Soho and the Charing Cross Road, further afield to the more bourgeois intellectual communities in Hampstead, while still maintaining a foothold in the fashionable world of the Mayfair and Chelsea patron *salonniers*.

In his critical manifesto, 'The Idea of a Literary Review', Eliot rejected a sectarian programme or a mere literary miscellany in favour of a cryptic 'nice adjustment between editor, collaborators and occasional contributors.'[27] What this meant in practice can be seen from a series of weekly Thursday lunches at the Grove Tavern in Knightsbridge: a conclave of civil servants and men of letters. After Eliot's appointment at Faber, the Grove lunches became informal gatherings of the so-called 'Criterion group' where matters of finance and policy were discussed. They were attended by Herbert Read, Arthur Wheen and Willie Thorpe (Keepers at the Victoria and Albert Museum in Kensington), Frank Morley (an American-born literary man about town[28]), F. S. Flint (poet and civil servant), Bonamy Dobrée (university lecturer and drama critic), Harold Monro (poet, editor, and bookshop owner), Orlo Williams (author, civil servant, and Italian translator[29]), Richard Church (poet, novelist, and publisher[30]), Alec Randall (Foreign Office diplomat and reviewer of

---

[26] The *New Criterion* contained advertisements for P&O Cruises, Player's Cigarettes, and the publisher Jonathan Cape.

[27] 'The Idea of a Literary Review', *Criterion* (Jan. 1926), 3.

[28] During the 1920s, Frank Morley (b. 1899) acted as the London manager for the New York-based Century Company publishing house. In 1929 he joined the board of directors at Faber & Faber.

[29] Orlo Williams (1883–1967), Clerk of Committees at the House of Commons, educated at Eton and Balliol College, Oxford. Although Williams contributed 42 book reviews to the *Criterion*, Eliot did not consider him one of his most important reviewers. See T. S. Eliot to Herbert Read, 12 Aug. 1929. Victoria.

[30] Desmond Hawkins described Richard Church (1893–1972) as 'a timid, decent, worthy man who inspired in everyone a muted affection and a simultaneous desire to kick him' (*When I Was* (London, 1989), 139).

German literature), and J. B. Trend (freelance music journalist and expert on Spanish culture[31]). There were also longer and larger Friday night dinners in a private room at the Ristorante Commercio in Soho and more serious meetings at Monro's Poetry Bookshop in Great Russell Street. Over the years the personnel changed: Dobrée, Read, and Randall were absent from London for periods; the American poets John Gould Fletcher and Conrad Aiken attended when in town; Montgomery Belgion, Tom Beachcroft, and Geoffrey Tandy joined in the late 1920s; Harold Laski and Allen Tate were among a variety of distinguished guests. Eliot never distilled the editorial policy of the *Criterion* into a series of direct propositional statements, nevertheless the evolving and changing nucleus of writers who met weekly at the Grove consti-tuted, in his eyes, a 'phalanx' of critics whose beliefs were not antagonistic to his own. They represented, in effect, the editorial advisory committee of the *Criterion* and their influence upon the journal should not be discounted.

In August 1926, Monro, following the collapse of his own *Chapbook* magazine, sent Eliot a communiqué signed by the Criterion group. It urged that the *Criterion* be transformed from a quarterly into a 70-page monthly review, largely because it was felt that a quarterly could no longer keep pace with contemporary society. The proposed monthly would be made up of a regular editorial commentary, original creative writing, lengthy critical articles, chronicles of foreign literature, art, drama, and music, and an extensive review section, containing the best short reviews in Britain. It was suggested that the monthly should pay its way by carrying more advertising and that Faber should assign a business manager to oversee the running of the journal.[32] Eliot informed Herbert Read that although he agreed to the idea of the monthly *Criterion* in principle, he had two main worries: firstly, the monthly would require a much greater injection of capital from the spon-sors; secondly, he would require the services of a full-time editorial assistant.[33] Nevertheless, Eliot passed Monro's recommendation

---

[31] J. B. Trend (1887–1958) was the *Criterion*'s music critic from 1924 until 1932. In 1933 he took up a Chair of Spanish at Cambridge and was replaced as music chron-icler by Philip Radcliffe (1905–86), Fellow of King's College, Cambridge.

[32] Harold Monro to T. S. Eliot, 30 Aug. 1926. Victoria.

[33] T. S. Eliot to Herbert Read, 11 Aug. 1926. Victoria.

to Geoffrey Faber. The question of monthly versus quarterly publication was quite simply a financial one for Faber, who had relaunched the weekly *Nursing Mirror* in December 1925 as the firm's flagship periodical. That the monthly *Criterion* was seen as a viable undertaking was indicated by Eliot's remarks on the notional 'good literary review' in the January 1927 *Criterion*: 'To be perpetually in change and development, to alter with the alterations of the living minds associated with it and with the phases of the contemporary world for which and in which it lives: on this condition only should a literary review be tolerated.'[34] The following month, Eliot informed members of the Criterion group that the journal would become a monthly.[35]

The monthly *Criterion*, 'sicklied o'er with a bright cast of lemon', as J. C. Squire quipped, was launched in May 1927. The monthly format, of course, affected the character of the journal, speeding up the turnover of contributions, increasing the emphasis on up-to-date book reviews, and drawing the inner circle of contributors into closer collaboration. A necessary corollary was the financial imperative to promote sales, reflected in a series of laboured controversies that took place in the monthly *Criterion*, although they appear to have had a minimal effect on circulation (Eliot later claimed that the subscription list peaked at 800, which would put total sales not in excess of 1,000[36]). The controversies took up an inordinate amount of space in the monthly and created a logjam of contributions; even worse, they further alienated Lady Rothermere, who cannot have welcomed the great increase of expenditure required to subsidize a monthly. At the end of 1927, she summoned Eliot to Switzerland and informed him that she was withdrawing her support, plunging the *Criterion* into immediate financial crisis. On 5 December 1927, Irene Fassett informed Sturge Moore that 'owing to differences of opinion between the proprietors on matters of policy' the *Criterion* would cease publication.[37] Geoffrey Faber, however, had other ideas and

---

[34] 'A Commentary', *Criterion* (Jan. 1927), 1.
[35] See T. S. Eliot to Herbert Read, 1 Feb. 1927. Victoria. T. S. Eliot to Bonamy Dobrée, 28 Feb. 1927. Leeds.
[36] 'A Letter from T. S. Eliot, O. M.', *Catacomb* (Summer 1950), 367–8. Eliot claimed that most of the subscribers were unknown to him.
[37] Irene Fassett to Thomas Sturge Moore, 5 Dec. 1927. London (Senate House).

as the Estates Bursar of All Souls he was in a position to draw upon the 'old boy' network. After contacting Bruce Richmond (Winchester and Oxford) for the names of possible patrons, one week after the initial announcement Fassett cheerfully informed Sturge Moore that 'owing to certain concurrences of opinion' the *Criterion*'s immediate future was now secure.[38]

The *Criterion* was not yet out of the woods. In January 1928, the poet and Whitehall civil servant, Humbert Wolfe, an infrequent habitué of the Grove lunches, took Eliot to Cadogan Square to canvass the support of Arnold Bennett.[39] Author of a weekly review column, 'Books and Persons', in the high-circulation London *Evening Standard*, Bennett was an influential figure, not to mention a good friend of the paper's millionaire proprietor, Lord Beaverbrook. Eliot and Wolfe hoped that Bennett would put his full weight behind the *Criterion*. Unfortunately, Bennett was no admirer of the *Criterion* and he did not offer financial support or approach Beaverbrook, foisting *in lieu* the dubious gift of his lengthy 'Florentine Journal' (as arid as any Tuscan summer). The Grove meetings during the early months of 1928 were downbeat as the *Criterion* hovered on the verge of collapse. However, the need to secure sufficient financial guarantees was met by the support of private benefactors, including Eliot's friend, the scholar and journalist, Charles Whibley, and most generously from the Scottish barrister and historian, F. S. Oliver, who pledged £100 per year for three years. In April 1928, it was decided to continue the *Criterion* as a recruiting ground for Faber authors, reorganized as a more cost-effective quarterly and maintained on a subsidy of £750 per annum.[40] The oscillation from quarterly to monthly and back again was evidence, as astute contemporaries perceived, of financial instability. All the same, the success of the wide-circulation *Nursing Mirror*, packed with lucrative advertising, allowed Faber to gamble on the *Criterion* as a *succès d'estime*. A Faber author, Osbert Burdett, reassured Sturge Moore that the *Criterion*'s difficulties were not a sign of the financial instability of Faber & Gwyer for whom the publication of the *Criterion* was a secondary affair.[41]

---

[38] Irene Fassett to Thomas Sturge Moore, 12 Dec. 1927. London (Senate House).
[39] See Philip Bagguley, *Harlequin in Whitehall* (London, 1997), 265–6.
[40] See T. S. Eliot to Thomas Sturge Moore, 16 Mar. 1928. London (Senate House).
[41] Osbert Burdett to Thomas Sturge Moore, 9 Dec. 1927. London (Senate House).

Eliot would no longer harbour the illusion that the *Criterion* could make ends meet or survive without 'the aid of artificial respiration'.[42] In June 1928, the *Criterion* announced that 'in conformity with the preference of many supporters' the journal would revert to its original format.[43] The quarterly appeared for the remainder of its existence at what Hugh Gordon Porteus called the 'plutocratic' price of 7s. 6d., certainly an expense beyond the pockets of many impecunious young writers.[44] Eliot explained to Porteus that lowering the price of the *Criterion* would not have an appreciable effect on sales: the intended public had never been large and besides the journal needed to generate enough revenue to pay contributors.[45] It is usual to describe this last phase as the decline and fall of the *Criterion*. From 1928 onward the catalogue of public criticisms, many of the most damning from erstwhile *Criterion* contributors, was loud and long. During 1928, Eliot defended himself in the pages of the *New Statesman* against Desmond MacCarthy's complaint that the *Criterion* was a stronghold of 'Frenchified' neo-Thomism[46] and in the *Nation* against Edwin Muir's charge that there existed a powerful '*Criterion* school of criticism'.[47] In 1930, Eliot confided to Ada Leverson that the *Criterion* was losing vitality and had become, like its editor, middle-aged.[48] That year, Pound characterized 'Criterionism' as a 'diet of dead crow'. Two years later, Pound's protégé, Basil Bunting, classified the *Criterion* as 'an international disaster, since he [Eliot] began to love his gloom, and regretfully resigned to set about perpetuating the causes of it—kings, religion and formalism.'[49]

---

[42] 'A Letter from T. S. Eliot, O. M.', 367. In its last phase, the *Criterion* carried several exchange advertisements with like-minded periodicals.

[43] Advertisement in the *Adelphi* (June 1928). In his editorial commentary, Eliot claimed that the half-crown monthly was 'too heavy' for readers to digest (*Criterion* (June 1928), 289–90).

[44] Julian Symons wrote to Faber to ask for free specimen copies. See 'The Cri', *London Magazine* (Nov. 1967), 19.

[45] T. S. Eliot to Hugh Gordon Porteus, 17 Oct. 1933. Yale.

[46] Desmond MacCarthy, 'Frenchified', *New Statesman* (21 Jan. 1928), 460. For Eliot's reply see 'Correspondence' (4 Feb. 1928), 528–9.

[47] Edwin Muir, 'Past and Present', *Nation and Athenaeum* (14 Apr. 1928), 49. Eliot denied the existence of a *Criterion* 'school', see 'Letters' (21 Apr. 1928), 74.

[48] T. S. Eliot to Ada Leverson, 7 Jan. 1930. New York (Public Library).

[49] See Ezra Pound, 'Criterionism', *Hound and Horn* (Oct.–Dec. 1930), 113–16. Basil Bunting 'English Poetry Today', *Poetry* [Chicago] (Feb. 1932), 266. Bunting contributed a book review to the *Criterion* in Apr. 1938.

There were further criticisms of Eliot's public declaration of royalism, Anglo-Catholicism, and classicism in Aldington's mean-spirited *Stepping Heavenward* (1931) and in Thomas MacGreevy's early book-length study *Thomas Stearns Eliot* (1931). Porteus, who lent Eliot his copy of Wyndham Lewis's *Men Without Art* (1934), recounted that Eliot was so wounded by the satirical remarks on 'the Editor of *The Criterion*' that he considered folding the journal.[50]

The *Criterion* altered in accordance with changes in Eliot's public and private life. During his lecture tour of the United States in 1932–3, he permitted friends and his Faber colleagues to see the *Criterion* through the press—an indication that the journal no longer occupied a central place in his affairs. When Philip Mairet met Eliot in November 1934, he realized that Eliot was 'already disillusioned' and fatigued by the onerous duty of running the *Criterion*.[51] Eliot's Faber secretaries during the mid-1930s noted that he had begun to devote less care and attention to editorial duties.[52] In a 1936 letter to Bonamy Dobrée, Eliot jokily pencilled underneath the *Criterion* letterhead 'edited by T. S. Eliot' the epigraph 'without any help from his friends'.[53] A large part of the problem was the *Criterion*'s theological reorientation, a state of affairs that alienated some of the most important collaborators. Furthermore, Eliot's gloomy *ex cathedra* editorial pronouncements on political issues, such as the Spanish Civil War, appeared to a group of soi-disant Marxist editors and publishers in London as infuriatingly evasive, if not completely beside the point. Eliot's once authoritative 'Commentaries', whose subtlety and gravitas put Porteus in mind of 'those steam-hammers that are said to crack a filbert to perfection'[54] were by now habitually dismissed as sententious and priggish, grinding urgent public issues to the level of what Hugh Kenner has called 'a plane of desiccated urbanity'.[55]

---

[50] Unpublished memoir by Hugh Gordon Porteus. Yale.

[51] See Philip Mairet, 'Memories of T. S. E.', in Nevile Braybrooke (ed.), *T. S. Eliot: A Symposium for His Seventieth Birthday* (London, 1958), 36–44.

[52] See Brigid O'Donovan, 'The Love Song of T. S. Eliot's Secretary', *Confrontation* (Fall/Winter 1975), 3–8. Erica Schumacher, letter to Jason Harding, 1 Feb. 1999.

[53] T. S. Eliot to Bonamy Dobrée, 21 Nov. 1936. Cited in Allen Tate (ed.), *T. S. Eliot: The Man and His Work*, (London, 1967), 78.

[54] See 'Reviews', *New English Weekly* (11 Oct. 1934), 526.

[55] *The Invisible Poet* (London, 1960), 208.

In October 1938, in the wake of his profound 'depression of spirits' following the Munich pact between Hitler and Chamberlain, Eliot, in consultation with Geoffrey Faber, decided to suspend publication of the *Criterion*. Given the meagre subscription list of 600,[56] the prospect of war, and Eliot's mounting editorial fatigue, the quarterly slipped away peacefully—with a whimper and not a bang. The *Criterion*, as Auden observed of Yeats in his elegy, 'disappeared in the dead of winter' in January 1939. News of the decision to suspend publication was kept secret and indeed was not publicly announced until Eliot's valedictory 'Last Words' appeared in the final issue.[57] The closure of the *Criterion* naturally came as a shock in literary London and abroad, sparking a fusillade of respectful public obituaries and private professions of condolence. Pound spoke for many when he told Eliot that, in spite of the journal's shortcomings, its demise marked the end of an era in periodical publishing.[58] It is the aim of this study to provide a thickly textured account of the milieu of British interwar literary journalism necessary for measured assessment of the history and significance of the *Criterion*.

[56] T. S. Eliot in conversation with Malcolm Bradbury, Nov. 1954. Details confirmed by Malcolm Bradbury, letter to Jason Harding, 3 Nov. 1999.
[57] See T. S. Eliot to John Hayward, 20 Oct. 1938. Cambridge (King's).
[58] Ezra Pound to T. S. Eliot, 9 Jan. 1939. Yale.

PART I

Periodical Networks

I

The *Adelphi*
The Reaction against Romanticism

> Quarterlies, therefore, do not rival one another; one does
> not profit by another's loss, nor expand by its extinction.
> *The New Criterion* is opposed to *The New Adelphi*, it is
> true, but the opposition is on a plane where all must needs be
> friends. On this plane, to put it more truly, enemies are
> *necessary* to one another.
>
> John Middleton Murry, *Adelphi* (December 1929), 81

T. S. Eliot's editorial policy on the *Criterion* dictated that the
journal perform the office of a public platform upon which contributors and readers might come together and conduct debate
about 'fundamentals'. Examination of the prolonged classicism
and romanticism debate in the *Criterion* and the *Adelphi* has
become a *sine qua non* of studies of the intellectual development of
Eliot and Murry.[1] However, what accounts of this episode often
overlook is the extent to which the exchange was not simply a
contribution to intellectual debate, but an important means of
providing good copy for both periodicals. That is to say, the
controversy may be as interesting for the light it sheds on the specif-
ically journalistic context in which cultural debate was voiced in
the 1920s, as it is in terms of the substantive theoretical issues at
stake. Descending from the intellectual high ground into the

---

[1] For instance, see John Margolis, *T. S. Eliot's Intellectual Development,
1922–1939* (Chicago, 1972), 52–68; Malcolm Woodfield, 'Introduction', *Defending
Romanticism: Selected Essays of John Middleton Murry* (Bristol, 1989), 34–41; Paul
Kreller, 'Definitions of Classicism and Romanticism: Argumentative Strategies in the
Eliot–Murry Debate (1923–1927)', *Yeats Eliot Review* (Fall 1995), 63–70; David
Goldie, *A Critical Difference*, (Oxford, 1998) 96–166.

imbroglio of literary journalism unearths a complex exchange of viewpoints occurring both within and across the *Criterion*—a discourse in which Eliot's trenchant and timely editorial interventions could be decisive. There is little doubt that Eliot used Murry as he once urged Sturge Moore, 'as a sort of stalking horse'.[2] In short, Eliot carefully selected Murry as an antagonist in order to advance and develop his editorial goals; in particular, the movement he described in a wartime Extension lecture as the 'reaction against romanticism'. The classicism and romanticism controversy certainly reflected 'fundamentals', but its unfolding cannot be divorced from personal temperament and the politics of the literary market-place.

I

In June 1923, with £450 financial backing from Vivian Locke-Ellis, John Middleton Murry founded the *Adelphi*, a shilling monthly bound in yellow paper. Murry took no salary for his responsibilities regarding the running of the journal, but J. W. N. Sullivan[3] and H. M. Tomlinson[4] worked as his editorial assistants, and S. S. Koteliansky acted as the *Adelphi*'s business manager.[5] Appearing without a title-page or index and, unusually for a contemporary literary magazine, sporting a half-page cover advertisement—for the Remington Portable typewriter[6]—the *Adelphi* defined a sociology of taste distinct from the advanced modernism of Bloomsbury and other highbrow sections of the London literary intelligentsia. Murry claimed that the *Adelphi* would always appear 'lower grade' in the eyes of 'those who found the contents of the first number "lower grade" '.[7] In fact,

---

[2] *Letters*, 520.

[3] J. W. N. Sullivan (1886–1937), musician and reviewer of science books. In 1922, Eliot invited Sullivan to contribute to the *Criterion*, but he was unable to complete his article. See *Letters*, 603.

[4] H. M. Tomlinson (1873–1958), novelist and travel writer; a former war correspondent of the *Daily News* who contributed an article on 'War Books' to the *Criterion* (Apr. 1930), 402–19.

[5] S. S. Koteliansky (1882–1955) left the *Adelphi* in Nov. 1924 after an abortive attempt to wrestle control of the journal from Murry.

[6] See Murry: 'It is because it is far more important that *The Adelphi* should pay its way quickly than it should be beautiful to look at' ('A Month After', *Adelphi* (July 1923), 98). [7] Ibid. 98.

the first number went surprisingly well: it was reprinted three times and sold over 15,000 copies. Affordable and readable, the *Adelphi* could count upon a large readership outside London and was reputedly popular in Methodist and nonconformist communities in the north.[8] In August 1923, the *Adelphi* carried an advertisement for the *Criterion*, along with plentiful advertisements for, among other things, Luvisca pyjamas and Rowntree's chocolates. During its first year the circulation of the *Adelphi* dropped to 7,000; over the next four years it settled down to under 5,000, barely enough to secure the journal's existence.

There were a number of imperatives behind the founding of the *Adelphi*. It functioned, in part, as a memorial to Murry's first wife, Katherine Mansfield, who had died of tuberculosis in January 1923 (the opening number carried her photograph on the frontispiece).[9] Deeply distressed by her death, Murry underwent an emotional crisis that confirmed his 'deep dissatisfaction with prevailing modes of thought and an aversion from the attitude towards ultimate things implicit or explicit in most contemporary literature'.[10] Murry's accounts of the watershed conform to the paradigm of romantic spiritual autobiography: a journey through crisis to recovery. He claimed that his regeneration had been aided by reading D. H. Lawrence's *Fantasia of the Unconscious*, which the author had sent him in the spring of 1923. In the opening number of the *Adelphi*, Murry proclaimed himself 'only a *locum tenens* for a better man'. Although that man, Lawrence, whom Murry described as 'incomparably the most important English writer' following Mansfield's death, was singularly unimpressed by the *Adelphi*.[11] When Lawrence received the first issue in Mexico, he complained to Koteliansky: 'It seemed to me so weak, apologetic, knock-kneed, with really nothing to justify its existence'.[12] It soon became clear, in spite of generous references

---

[8] See F. A. Lea, *The Life of John Middleton Murry* (London, 1959), 11.

[9] Murry was Mansfield's literary executor. The *Adelphi* published several of her short stories, as well as extracts from letters and journals.

[10] Prospectus to the *New Adelphi* (Sept. 1927).

[11] 'Religion and Faith', *Adelphi* (Aug. 1923), 183.

[12] D. H. Lawrence to S. S. Koteliansky, 22 June 1923. *The Letters of D. H. Lawrence: iv. June 1921–March 1924*, ed. Warren Roberts, James Boulton, and Elizabeth Mansfield (Cambridge, 1987), 462.

to his collaborators, that the *Adelphi* was really launched to provide a means of self-expression for Murry.[13]

In his manifesto, 'The Cause of It All', Murry affirmed his faith in the romantic dictum 'a belief in life,' a position he sketched out with passionate conviction. There was much in Murry's chatty editorial that would have grated upon Eliot's fastidious intellectual sensibility. Recounting a glimpse of the bookmaker 'Fred Bacon of Putney' from the top of a London bus, Murry went on to consider what the two men shared in common. A 'faith' in life, it transpired, was the answer: the fundamental belief that apparently united all the contributors to the *Adelphi*. Murry justified this vague, existential credo in cadences and hortatory rhetoric that sounded, at times, like pulpit oratory: 'If you believe in them *passionately*, if you are prepared to make *sacrifices* for them, if, when the moment comes, you are prepared to *act* on their belief. . . .' (emphasis added).[14] When Murry confessed that his 'article, or homily, or outburst, or profession of faith' had 'given myself away pretty completely', it is hard not to think that the reserved editor of the *Criterion* (his name did not even appear on the front cover) interpreted Murry's evangelical zeal as anything other than exhibitionism.[15] At any rate, Murry continued to use the exploratory and ephemeral form of his monthly editorials as a vehicle to pursue a personal 'search for truth'.

The rivalry between Eliot and Murry, viewed by many contemporaries as the two most influential literary editors in London, intensified during the course of the 1920s.[16] The seeds of discord had been growing ever since their fruitful collaboration on the *Athenaeum*. Privately, Eliot told his mother:

I and Murry have fallen apart completely. I consider his verse quite negligible, and I don't like his prose style; his articles seem to me to

---

[13] See John Middleton Murry to S. S. Koteliansky, Oct. 1924: 'I am convinced that I have a work to do, a function to perform, in the world; and the *Adelphi* is the instrument.' Cited in John Carswell, *Lives and Letters* (London, 1978), 206.

[14] 'The Cause of It All', *Adelphi* (June 1923), 8. Cf. Murry: 'And anyone who starts a magazine, if he does not aim at personal profit and is not indulging his personal vanity, is just as surely as the New Adventist preacher at the street-corner, trying to establish a new Church' ('The Two Worlds', *Adelphi* (Mar. 1924), 865).

[15] Ibid. 10, 9.

[16] See G. Wilson Knight: 'During the years following the First World War London's more advanced literary thinking was dominated by John Middleton Murry and T. S. Eliot' (Allen Tate (ed.), *T. S. Eliot: The Man and His Work* (London, 1967), 245).

become more and more windy, verbose and meaningless. Personally, I think him a man of weak character and great vanity, and I do not trust him; I think he loves both money and being a public figure. He will become more and more a conventional and solemn pundit, quite insincere, hysterical and morbid.[17]

Nevertheless, when Eliot came to start the *Criterion* he informed Aldington that he did not wish to 'launch in a campaign' against Murry.[18] On the eve of publication, Eliot wrote to Murry to ask for his support: 'I think I am safe in believing that you will be in sympathy with the paper's aims'.[19] Eliot's appeal struck a conciliatory note which may have been partly strategic, for he believed that the terminally ill Katherine Mansfield was poisoning Lady Rothermere against the *Criterion* from their residence at the Gurdjieff Institute near Fontainebleau.[20] As it turned out, Eliot had good reason to be thankful for Murry's collaboration.

II

A sustained polemic between Murry and Eliot began, apparently accidentally, in September 1923. Murry took issue with Raymond Mortimer's remark in the *New Statesman* that the *Adelphi* was fighting 'the last stand' of romanticism.[21] He was willing to concur, given the proviso: 'In England there never has been any classicism worth talking about: we have had classics, but no classicism. And all our classics are romantic.'[22] Murry's claim that romantic individualism—a reliance upon the 'inner voice'—was *the* English literary tradition, constituted a deliberate provocation to Eliot, especially when Murry boasted that he could see no opponent worthy of debate.[23] The call to arms pleased Lawrence, who

Knight, an *Adelphi* contributor in the 1920s, recalled that Murry's articles 'acted on me like an avatar'. (*Neglected Powers* (London, 1969), 149).   [17] *Letters*, 432–3.

[18] Ibid. 537.   [19] Ibid. 581.

[20] In a short obituary, Eliot remarked: 'It had been hoped that Miss Mansfield would be a contributor to these pages' (*Criterion* (Apr. 1923), 307). However, Vivien Eliot satirized 'the semi-modern majority who still think that Katherine Mansfield's stories are "simply too marvellous for words" ' ([Feiron Morris] 'Books of the Quarter', *Criterion* (Jan. 1925), 326).

[21] 'New Novels', *New Statesman* (21 July 1923), 448.

[22] 'On Fear; and Romanticism', *Adelphi* (Sept. 1923), 274.

[23] See Murry: 'When a classicist comes along who knows as much about his own creed as I know about mine—then we may prepare for battle' (ibid. 277).

offered encouragement: 'Go for them amusingly like this. . . . I begin to see the *Adelphi* building up like a fortress.' He added: 'This classiosity is bunkum, but still more, *cowardice*.'[24] It must be stressed, however, that Lawrence's remark referred to Mortimer's formulation of classicism in the *New Statesman*, itself following close behind the publication of Herbert Grierson's 1923 Leslie Stephen Lecture, 'Classical and Romantic', and *not* to Eliot.[25]

In October 1923, Eliot picked up the gauntlet in his *Criterion* essay 'The Function of Criticism'; an Arnoldian plea for the social necessity of critical standards:

[Criticism] must always profess an end in view, which, roughly speaking, appears to be the elucidation of works of art and the correction of taste. The critic's task, therefore, appears to be quite clearly cut out for him; and it ought to be comparatively easy to decide whether he performs it satisfactorily, and in general, what kinds of criticism are useful and what are otiose. But on giving the matter a little attention, we perceive that criticism, far from being a simple and orderly field of beneficent activity, from which impostors can be readily ejected, is no better than a Sunday park of contending and contentious orators, who have not even arrived at the articulation of their differences. Here, one would assume, was a place for quiet co-operative labour. The critic, one would suppose, if he is to justify his existence, should endeavour to discipline his personal prejudices and cranks—tares to which we are all subject—and compose his differences with as many of his fellows as possible, in the common pursuit of true judgement. When we find that quite the contrary prevails, we begin to suspect that the critic owes his livelihood to the violence and extremity of his opposition to other critics, or else to some trifling oddities of his own with which he contrives to season the opinions which men already hold, and which out of vanity or sloth they prefer to maintain. We are tempted to expel the lot.[26]

Eliot's disdain for the dust and bustle of the journalistic arena, the 'literary whoring' of the popular press, was captured in the stylistic *hauteur* of his address.[27]

---

[24] D. H. Lawrence to John Middleton Murry, 17 Sept. 1923. *Letters of D. H. Lawrence*, iv. 500.

[25] The mistake is endemic in accounts of the classicism–romanticism debate, even though Lawrence's letter cites Mortimer and is dated *before* Eliot's intervention. See, for example, David Ellis, *D. H. Lawrence: Dying Game, 1922–1930* (Cambridge, 1998), 686 n. 33.   [26] 'The Function of Criticism', *Criterion* (Oct. 1923), 32–3.

[27] Cf. Eliot: 'But journalism begats [*sic*] journalism; only journalism can triumph over journalism. In such a debate as this the reader is only convinced of what he believed already' ('Recent Books', *Criterion* (May 1927), 254).

The distance, 'one would assume', between the Arnoldian higher journalism and Murry's popular critical journalism, divides wider than cloud-capped towers and a soap box placed in Hyde Park. It is signalled in the condescending tonal switch from words like 'otiose' and (elsewhere in the article) 'obnubilation' and 'regnant' to talk of expelling 'impostors'. Eliot's impatience arose from the pressing need, following the cataclysm of the First World War, to forge a new critical consensus—a question of the authority of tradition. Seizing upon Murry's remarks in the *Adelphi*, Eliot presented the issue as a stark choice between 'two antithetical views':

With Mr. Murry's formulation of Classicism and Romanticism I cannot agree; the difference seems to me rather the difference between the complete and the fragmentary, the adult and the immature, the orderly and the chaotic. But what Mr. Murry does show is that there are at least two attitudes toward literature and toward everything, and that you cannot hold both.[28]

If 'The Function of Criticism' gestured towards a transcendence of what Eliot called 'the most pretentious critical journalism', then it must be said that the sarcasm and ridicule he heaped upon Murry's 'inner voice'[29] might not have convinced all the readers of the *Criterion* that his own *parti pris* had risen above 'a Sunday park of contending and contentious orators'.[30]

In December 1923, Murry declared that he was glad to have found 'a real opponent in Mr T. S. Eliot, the gifted editor of *The Criterion*' adding: 'The debate, I profoundly believe, is concerned with fundamentals.'[31] Murry's tactic in 'More About Romanticism' was to introduce a historiographical dimension to the discussion. After the Reformation, he contended, the shackles of 'external spiritual authority' (ostensibly the medieval Catholic Church) had been discarded. Murry countered Eliot's objections against the 'Whiggery' of the 'inner voice' by claiming that his opponent was

---

[28] 'The Function of Criticism', 34.
[29] Cf. Eliot: 'The possessors of the inner voice ride ten in a compartment to a football match at Swansea, listening to the inner voice, which breathes the eternal message of vanity, fear, and lust' (ibid. 35.)
[30] By 1956, Eliot claimed to have forgotten 'what all the fuss had been about' ('The Frontiers of Criticism', *On Poetry and Poets* (London, 1957), 103).
[31] 'More About Romanticism', *Adelphi* (Dec. 1923), 557.

'an English Tory'—a revealing demarcation of the cultural politics underpinning the debate.[32] At Eliot's invitation, Murry continued his defence in 'the more leisurely and expansive pages of *The Criterion*'. Here Murry reiterated his belief 'that the tradition of Romanticism is just as lofty and august as the tradition of Classicism'.[33] However, his thunder was stolen by Eliot's introduction of an editorial (under the pseudonym 'Crites') praising the posthumous publication of T. E. Hulme's *Speculations* as a harbinger of the modern mind: 'classical, reactionary, and revolutionary . . . the antipodes of the eclectic, tolerant, and democratic mind of the last century.'[34]

On completion of the first volume of the *Criterion*, Eliot sought to define and defend 'The Function of a Literary Review'. It was clear from his remarks that Murry's effusions in favour of what he termed the 'insidious catchword "life" '[35] appeared, in his eyes, to tread the brink of absurdity; thereby precipitating the need for a running *Criterion* 'Commentary' to function as a competing form of cultural criticism. However, Eliot decided to withdraw temporarily from public controversy, choosing instead to permit Vivien to satirize Murry in the pages of the *Criterion*[36] and to publish the malicious fictional portrait of Murry, contained in Lawrence's 'Jimmy and the Desperate Woman'.[37] The next phase of the debate was subterranean and centred around tendentious readings of Hulme's call for a 'classical' revival. In March 1925, Murry chose to review *Speculations* in the *Adelphi*'s 'Contributors' Club'.[38] Under

---

[32] Cf. Eliot: '[If] a man's interest is political, he must, I presume, profess an allegiance to principles, or to a form of government, or to a monarch; and if he is interested in religion, and has one, to a Church' ('The Function of Criticism', 35).

[33] 'Romanticism and the Tradition', *Criterion* (Apr. 1924), 273.

[34] 'Crites' [T. S. Eliot], 'A Commentary', *Criterion* (Apr. 1924), 231.

[35] 'The Function of a Literary Review', *Criterion* (July 1923), 421.

[36] Cf. F. M. [Vivien Eliot]: 'Golly! as Mr J. Middleton Murry says in his last outcry but one, revealing his "sensitiveness to the living soul of language," and revealing to his readers how much better a Professor of Poetry he would make than that poor insensitive Mr Garrod' ('Letters of the Moment [II]', *Criterion* (Apr. 1924), 362). Her gibe referred to Murry's ejaculation in 'The Contributors' Club', *Adelphi* (Mar. 1924), 924.

[37] 'Jimmy and the Desperate Woman', *Criterion* (Oct. 1924), 15–42. The story satirized Murry's propensity to form relations with female readers of the *Adelphi*; although its edge owed something to the *ménage à trois* involving Freida Lawrence.

[38] 'The Contributor's Club' included offerings from Arnold Bennett and H. G. Wells, as well as articles from *Criterion* irregulars, John Shand and H. P. Collins. In 1927, Collins offered a critical account of 'The Poems of T. S. Eliot', *Adelphi* (Jan. 1927), 441–3.

the pseudonym 'Henry King', Murry complained that Hulme's 'keen and vigorous mind is, after all, not cutting very much ice'. He claimed that Hulme followed the aesthetic preferences of the royalist Action française movement, 'who want the Church without the religion, and the tradition without the sacrifice'. As for Hulme's programmatic opposition between the romantic and classical, which Murry rightly noted drew heavily on French antecedents, he commented: 'His essay on Romanticism and Classicism in English poetry only satisfies so long as you refuse to think about it.'[39] Eliot, on the other hand, planned a special T. E. Hulme number of the *Criterion*, including essays by Aldington and Ramon Fernandez.[40] Although it did not materialize, the *Criterion* published extracts from Hulme's uncollected writings as a leading article in July 1925.[41]

On the launch of the *New Criterion* in January 1926, Eliot's manifesto, 'The Idea of a Literary Review', articulated the journal's 'classical' sympathies:

I believe that the modern tendency is toward something which, for want of a better name, we may call classicism. I use the term with hesitation, for it is hardly more than analogical: we must scrupulously guard ourselves against measuring living art and mind by dead laws of order. Art reflects the transitory as well as the permanent condition of the soul; we cannot wholly measure the present by what the past has been, or by what we think the future ought to be. Yet there is a tendency—discernible even in art—toward a higher and clearer conception of Reason, and a more severe and serene control of the emotions by Reason. If this approaches or even suggests the Greek ideal, so much the better: but it must inevitably be very different.[42]

Eliot's recommended reading list of 'classical' texts, including *Speculations*, made it clear that the *Criterion* really had more in common with a neo-Thomist literary revival in France and with the twentieth-century 'reaction against romanticism' than with the Greek and Roman classics. It is little known that Eliot's manifesto took a consciously opposing line to the *Adelphi*; chastising

---

[39] 'Henry King' [John Middleton Murry], 'Contributors' Club', *Adelphi* (Mar. 1925), 848–51.
[40] For details, see Ronald Schuchard, *Eliot's Dark Angel* (Oxford, 1999), 65.
[41] See T. E. Hulme, 'Notes on Language and Style', *Criterion* (July 1925), 485–97.
[42] 'The Idea of a Literary Review', 5.

the 'amateur religions' of H. G. Wells (an *Adelphi* contributor) and George Bernard Shaw (*Saint Joan* was lavishly praised in the *Adelphi*[43]) and, in a footnote, 'the religion of Mr Middleton Murry, which I am totally unable to understand'.[44]

One of the works cited on Eliot's 'classical' reading list, Jacques Maritain's *Réflexions sur l'intelligence*, argued, in accordance with a number of contemporary French Catholics, for the importance of 'intelligence' as conceived by Thomist epistemology.[45] Eliot and Herbert Read agreed that Maritain's Thomism offered a useful template for the revival of European 'classicism'.[46] In 1925, Read used the *Criterion* to discuss 'the central problem of literary criticism—I mean the question of romanticism and classicism'[47] and in the opening number of the *New Criterion*, he adopted the editorial 'we' to pronounce: 'If we were required to point to a philosophy worked out in the terms of Western reality and consonant with our deepest instincts, we should turn to medieval philosophy and particularly to the thought of St Thomas'.[48] Meanwhile, in the January 1926 issue of the *Adelphi*, a depleted 60-page offering, Murry declared: 'it inexorably follows that the writer who slips back into the bosom of the Church today is, quite simply, an insignificant writer. It is a summary test, but quite infallible.' Eliot would doubtless have questioned the precise logical force of the locutions *inexorable, quite simply, insignificant,* and *quite infallible.*

Stung by the declarations made in 'The Idea of a Literary Review', Murry drafted a lengthy two-part rejoinder, 'The "Classical" Revival', which was sent to Eliot for his pre-publication comments.[49] Murry sketched out his opposition to the 'religious nullity' of Wells and Shaw, but more pointedly his opposition to

---

[43] Cf. 'The Journeyman' [John Middleton Murry]: 'I can spare Shaw, I can spare Wells—. . . but the sense that [Arnold] Bennett is past the best gives me a real pain' (*Adelphi* (Jan. 1926), 568).   [44] 'The Idea of a Literary Review', 6.

[45] Eliot enlisted Maritain, a philosophy professor at the Institut Catholique in Paris, as a contributor to the *Criterion*. Eliot introduced him as 'probably the most powerful force, in contemporary French philosophy' ('A Commentary', *Criterion* (Jan. 1927), 3).   [46] See T. S. Eliot to Herbert Read, 11 Dec. 1925. Victoria.

[47] 'Psychoanalysis and the Critic', *Criterion* (Jan. 1925), 221.

[48] 'Books of the Quarter', *Criterion* (Jan. 1926), 191.

[49] For an account of Eliot's annotations on the unpublished typescript, see Goldie, *A Critical Difference*, 156–62.

the sceptical 'classicism' of his former *Athenaeum* protégés, Eliot and Virginia Woolf, the prime culprits of what he saw as a modern confusion between theory and practice: 'As critical intelligences, they have, and have given utterance to, pro-classical velleities— for order and clarity and decorum; as creative writers they are, in spite of all the restraint they impose upon themselves, disordered, obscure, indecorous.'[50] Eliot, in particular, was charged with contradiction, if not quite hypocrisy, in having 'classicism for his wife and romanticism for his mistress': in having Charles Whibley and Gertrude Stein as *Criterion* bedfellows. For Murry, the nihilism of *The Waste Land* did not bespeak the order and restraint of classicism. With some percipience, he located Eliot's dilemma in a sort of aestheticized Catholicism; the dogma of the Church without the leap of faith.[51] To be true to himself, Murry concluded, Eliot should join the Catholic Church: 'there he will find an authority and a tradition.'[52]

Eliot invited Murry to contribute a further statement to the *Criterion*. It appeared under the curious title 'The Romantic Fallacy'. The 'fallacy', it turned out, was Tolstoy's emphasis on Christian values rather than purely aesthetic ones as the ultimate artistic touchstone. Murry offered the letters of John Keats—the subject of his 1924 Clark Lectures[53]—as a salutary example of the 'transcendental conception of the self-created soul'.[54] He discovered in Keats's letters some of his deepest needs, arguably because the poet's life and art gestured towards a triumphant transcendence of the tuberculosis and physical suffering that had ended Katherine Mansfield's life. But Murry's version of the romantic undissociated sensibility did not appeal to Eliot. In the course of a *Criterion* book review, discussing an anonymous *TLS* leading article on Herbert Read's *Reason and Romanticism* (1926)—Eliot knew it was written by Murry—he once more oversimplified Murry's position in order to discount it. 'The issue is', wrote Eliot, between those like Murry (quoted by name) who 'make *man the measure*

---

[50] 'The "Classical" Revival', *Adelphi* (Feb. 1926), 592.
[51] '[Eliot] lowers himself to the level of those "aesthetic" converts who are received into the Catholic Church, but whose lives are no more edifying afterwards than before' ('The "Classical" Revival [II]', *Adelphi* (Mar. 1926), 648–9).
[52] Ibid. 650.   [53] Murry nominated Eliot as Clark Lecturer in 1925.
[54] 'The Romantic Fallacy', *Criterion* (June 1926), 536.

of all things and those who find an extra-human motive'. Finding the formulation of 'intuition' advanced by 'the writer in the *Times*' confused, Eliot declared himself 'on the side of what we call intelligence'.[55] By introducing the binary opposition between 'intuition' and 'intelligence', he neatly framed the semantic wrangling that characterized the long drawn out endgame of this encounter.

It is important to recognize that Eliot's review consciously prepared the ground for an ensuing public controversy.[56] In 1927, both the *Criterion* and the *Adelphi* were troubled by commercial exigencies. The monthly *Criterion* needed to boost its circulation in order to cover greatly increased printing bills and production costs. The *Adelphi* was anxious to arrest its dwindling financial resources, following the exodus of many of its advertisers and leading contributors, including Lawrence.[57] In May 1927, the strain of editing the *Adelphi* proved too much for Murry and he threatened suspension from his coastal retreat in Dorset. His anxiety regarding the finances of the *Adelphi* was highly understandable bearing in mind that he had been bankrupted by a previous periodical venture. However, a donation of £300 from readers persuaded him to relaunch the journal as an austere quarterly review (the cover advertisement was dropped) selling at half a crown.[58] A resumption of the controversy between Eliot and Murry, therefore, gave a timely boost to both journals. The classicism and romanticism debate attracted a great deal of attention in the London literary world. Beyond that charmed circle, however, it is unlikely that it attracted many new subscribers to either periodical. A few years later, Queenie Leavis offered circulation figures for the *New Adelphi*—described as a 'much less uncompromising periodical' than the *Criterion*—which put

---

[55] 'Books of the Quarter', *Criterion* (Oct. 1926), 751–7.

[56] Conrad Aiken later described the controversy as a 'carefully picked quarrel' (*Ushant* (Boston, 1952), 233).

[57] In Jan. 1926, Murry wrote to Lawrence in an attempt to bolster the *Adelphi*. Lawrence rather unkindly advised: 'In short, shut up. Throw the *Adelphi* to the devil, throw your own say after it, say goodbye to J.M.M.' D. H. Lawrence to John Middleton Murry, 4 Jan. 1926, *Letters of D. H. Lawrence, v. March 1924–March 1927*, ed. James Boulton and Lindeth Vasey (Cambridge, 1989), 368.

[58] The new austerity of the *New Adelphi* was signalled by the reintroduction of *Criterion* advertisements from Sept. 1927 to Feb. 1930.

quarterly sales at 1,700.[59] Frank Morley claimed that Eliot's 'interminable' debates with Murry were 'not precisely popular'.[60]

Murry protested that he had been reluctantly 'compelled to become a controversialist'.[61] In December 1926, he recounted to Herbert Read the genesis of a conciliatory offering to the *Criterion*, optimistically entitled 'Towards a Synthesis'. He claimed that he had attempted to clear up the misinterpretations suggested by his and Eliot's recent reviews of *Reason and Romanticism*. He went on to explain that he had written an article for the *Criterion*. Eliot had agreed to read and comment upon the essay in draft, so that any misunderstandings could be cleared up before publication.[62] In spite of the behind-the-scenes collusion, Murry was frustrated in his attempt to 'clear up' the misconceptions. His essay, published in the *Criterion* in June 1927, expressed the wish: 'that we may advance a step nearer towards a less perplexing and wasteful distribution of intellectual forces.' That is, Murry attempted to reconcile Thomist 'intelligence' with Bergsonian 'intuition' in the Hegelian synthesis of 'reason';[63] in other words, a synthesis of classicism and romanticism. He concluded: 'The task of creating, or helping to create, a new synthesis is the most urgent business of criticism today.'[64]

Eliot mustered his forces in the *Criterion* during the latter half of 1927. Returning typescripts to Koteliansky and Gertrude Stein, he cited lack of space owing to the importance of the controversy with Murry.[65] In his September 1927 Commentary, Eliot welcomed further attention to 'classicism', preparing the ground for two critical responses to 'Towards a Synthesis'. Ostensibly *au dessus de la mêlée*, Eliot's guiding hand was evident in the rejoinders: from his personal translation of an essay by the French critic, Charles Mauron,

[59] Q. D. Leavis, *Fiction and the Reading Public* (London, 1932), 20.

[60] 'T. S. Eliot as a Publisher', in Richard March and Tambimuttu (eds.), *T. S. Eliot: A Symposium* (London, 1948), 62.

[61] 'Quo Warranto?', *Adelphi* (Aug. 1924), 190.

[62] John Middleton Murry to Herbert Read, 17 Dec. 1926. Victoria.

[63] 'Reason is as it were, generated by the friction between intuition and intelligence: therefore it is of extreme importance that reason should not be identified, or confused, with intelligence' ('Towards a Synthesis', *Criterion* (June 1927), 312–3).

[64] Ibid. 303. Murry's prospectus for the *New Adelphi* claimed that the magazine applied itself to creating a new synthesis.

[65] See T. S. Eliot to S. S. Koteliansky, 24 June 1927. London (British Library). T. S. Eliot to Gertrude Stein, Sept. 1927. Yale.

an affiliate of the Bloomsbury group, to his sponsorship of an article defending Thomist philosophy by the Jesuit, Father Martin D'Arcy, an English disciple of Maritain.[66] Both responses argued that Murry's lack of definition in defining the keywords 'intuition' and 'intelligence' undermined the efficacy of his synthesis. In fact, D'Arcy attempted to turn the tables on Murry by swallowing up his terms in his own Thomistic synthesis: 'All that Mr Middleton Murry includes in his two factors, intuition and reason, fall within the intelligence as understood by St Thomas, for the reason that the same problem confronted the medievals as tortures the modern lover of Synthesis'.[67]

Eliot informed Clive Bell that Lady Rothermere was becoming bored with the Murry debate, jeopardizing the financial stability of the *Criterion*.[68] However, he had already told Sturge Moore that he would contribute something to the debate.[69] In October 1927, he translated a further criticism of Murry by the *Nouvelle Revue française* polemicist, Ramon Fernandez.[70] The stage was now set for Eliot's intervention, 'Mr Middleton Murry's Synthesis', an attempt to wrap up the debate by an apparently fair-minded appeal that to be 'on the side of intelligence' is not to deny that 'intuition must have its place in a world of discourse'. The tonal qualities of Eliot's prose writings are invariably crucial in assessing their import. In the case of 'Mr Middleton Murry's Synthesis', Eliot modulated between condescension towards Murry's 'extremely interesting essay' and an unsympathetic, at times sarcastic, reluctance to entertain his opponent's position seriously:

I do not understand Mr. Murry's attitude toward 'faith', or his theory of 'reason', 'intelligence' and 'intuition', or his philosophy of history, with its sharp division between the Middle Ages and the Renaissance. . . . when Mr. Murry makes poetry a substitute for philosophy and religion—a higher philosophy and a purer religion, he seems to me to falsify not only religion but poetry too. . . . But what bothers me especially in Mr. Murry's

---

[66] In 1927 Eliot described Martin D'Arcy as 'one of the most brilliant young men in England'. Cited in Robert Sencourt, *T. S. Eliot: A Memoir* (London, 1971), 112.

[67] 'The Thomistic Synthesis and Intelligence', *Criterion* (Sept. 1927), 215.

[68] T. S. Eliot to Clive Bell, 29 Sept. 1927. Cambridge (King's).

[69] T. S. Eliot to Thomas Sturge Moore, 9 July 1927. London (Senate House).

[70] Jean Stewart recalled Ramon Fernandez (1894–1944) as 'a brilliant, aggressive and intolerant intellect' ('Recollections of Pontigny', *London Magazine* (Nov. 1954), 70).

fluid world is that Truth itself seems to change, either imperceptibly or by sudden mutations. That I simply cannot understand.[71]

It might be argued that Eliot could have tried harder. Certainly, the use of the first-person singular, a significant departure from the measured editorial 'we', signalled both an anxiety and a defensiveness ('what bothers me') towards some of the issues raised by Murry. In particular, the relation of poetic practice to religious belief was, in the light of Eliot's recent conversion to Anglo-Catholicism (not yet a matter of public knowledge), a sensitive issue. One may interpret Eliot's distaste for Murry's synthesis as a sign of personal animosity, but more plausibly as a determination to do less than justice to him in the pages of the *Criterion*.

Sturge Moore, a former adversary of Murry, added a florid and largely irrelevant contribution to the controversy in November 1927.[72] However, the debate had effectively ended with Eliot's carefully stage-managed intervention. Murry was permitted the last word, 'Concerning Intelligence', although it was hardly surprising that the essay betrayed a note of weariness, even pessimism. Murry confined his discussion to defending himself against accusations of vagueness and conceptual confusion. If his voice no longer carried the conviction that it might be possible to convert his *Criterion* interlocutors, he at least repeated the belief that the 'effort at syntheses may still be a pattern and an ideal'. Ostensibly cheerful about the fact that the editor of the *Criterion* had been 'pleasantly facetious about my "world"', Murry's closing remarks contained more than a trace of defiance.[73] Before Eliot's intervention, Murry had promised to keep readers of the *Adelphi* informed about the 'amicable discussion' of 'Towards a Synthesis'.[74] However, in December 1927, Murry informed his readers: 'The recent discussion in *The Monthly Criterion* has been interesting, but chiefly in a negative way. The real issue has not clearly emerged.'[75] Privately he told Eliot: 'All my hopeful feeling when I undertook that frightful

---

[71] 'Mr Middleton Murry's Synthesis', *Criterion* (Oct. 1927), 341, 344, 346.
[72] Eliot held back Moore's essay to November since he considered it a free-standing essay merely occasioned by Murry. See T. S. Eliot to Thomas Sturge Moore, 9 July 1927. London (Senate House).
[73] 'Concerning Intelligence', *Criterion* (Oct. 1927), 532.
[74] 'Notes and Comments', *Adelphi* (Sept. 1927), 1.
[75] 'Notes and Comments', *Adelphi* (Dec. 1927), 102.

essay ['Towards a Synthesis'] has evaporated. It seems that there is really some sort of abyss between us—not humanly thank goodness—but in respect of our ideas and convictions.'[76]

III

Murry was persuaded to appear in a further extended public debate in the *Criterion*, occasioned by another of Eliot's exemplary 'classical' texts, Irving Babbitt's *Democracy and Leadership*.[77] In June 1928, Eliot expressed reservations about Babbitt's 'humanism' in the monthly New York periodical the *Forum*. Eliot believed that the efforts of his former Harvard teacher to construct a system of ethical values was laudable, but that the self-discipline of Babbitt's 'inner check' amounted to a poor substitute for religious doctrine.[78] The essay provoked a considerable amount of resistance from Babbitt's supporters in the United States and when Norman Foerster's *American Criticism* (containing what Eliot called an 'authoritative' exposition of the 'new humanism'[79]) came up for review, Eliot sensibly passed the volume to Herbert Read, who had earlier expressed 'dissatisfaction with the whole tradition of humanism'.[80] Very much in the spirit of Eliot, Read claimed that Thomism was precisely the sort of supernatural revelation, validated by reason, that the new humanists sought to resuscitate.[81] In February 1929, Eliot solicited a contribution to the debate from Allen Tate, with whom he had begun to discuss Babbitt's humanism nearly three years earlier.[82]

Working up humanism in the *Criterion* meant rounding up the usual suspects: Murry, Read, Fernandez, and Foerster were canvassed for their opinions, along with Philip Richards, who had written on American humanism in *Twentieth Century* and

[76] John Middleton Murry to T. S. Eliot, 22 Sept. 1927. Cited in Lea, *John Middleton Murry*, 151–2.

[77] *Democracy and Leadership* was the subject of a long essay-review in the *Criterion* by Gorham Munson, the American editor of *Secession*. See 'The Socratic Virtues of Irving Babbitt', *Criterion* (June 1926), 494–503.

[78] See 'Can Humanism Replace Religion?', *Forum* (July 1928), 37–44.

[79] 'American Criticism', *TLS* (10 Jan. 1929), 24.

[80] 'Foreign Periodicals', *Criterion* (Jan. 1927), 169.

[81] 'Humanism and the Absolute', *Criterion* (Dec. 1928), 275.

[82] T. S. Eliot to Allen Tate, 11 Feb. 1929. Princeton. Eliot had corresponded with Tate since Mar. 1926. They first met at a Grove lunch in Oct. 1928.

G. K. Chesterton, in the guise of a Catholic apologist.[83] Murry's contribution, his last *Criterion* article, contained a barbed aside on Eliot's 'Christian religion'.[84] One might have expected Murry to deliver a passionate defence of humanism, or offer a repudiation of Eliot's Christianity. Instead, both he and Eliot now seemed to believe that the humanism and religion debate, like the earlier controversy over romanticism and classicism, had become subject to the law of diminishing returns.[85] At any rate, Eliot did not really want to use the *Criterion* as a platform to espouse Christian doctrine. In 1929, he thanked Paul Elmer More for his article dealing with the presumption of Papal Infallibility.[86] It was an essay that Eliot claimed might be 'taken as the Criterion *position* on the question', adding 'a paper under my own name would have given too distinct a theological cast to the *Criterion* itself'.[87] It was noticeable that Eliot's 'Second Thoughts about Humanism' did not appear in the *Criterion* but in Murry's *Adelphi*.[88] Otherwise, it seems clear that Tate's astringent essay 'The Fallacy of Humanism' (July 1929), which proposed that 'religion is the sole technique for the validating of values', expressed the *Criterion* 'position' on humanism.[89]

In 1930, Murry relinquished the editorial reins of the *Adelphi* to Max Plowman and Richard Rees. Eliot wrote to Murry asking for an introduction to Rees, a wealthy old Etonian who had taken over financial control of the *Adelphi*, in the hope that he could bring the two journals into some kind of solidarity regarding the current politico-economic crisis.[90] However, under the direction

---

[83] The debate is well treated in Margolis, *T. S. Eliot's Intellectual Development*, 110–28.

[84] 'The Detachment of Naturalism', *Criterion* (July 1930), 642–60. Richard Rees recognized that the article was 'primarily addressed to T. S. Eliot'. See *A Theory of My Time* (London, 1963), 81.

[85] See T. S. Eliot to Herbert Read, 12 Aug. 1929. Victoria. T. S. Eliot to I. A. Richards, 9 Aug. 1930. Cambridge (Magdalene).

[86] See 'An Absolute and an Authoritarian Church', *Criterion* (July 1929), 616–34.

[87] T. S. Eliot to Paul Elmer More, 30 Dec. 1929. Cited in Margolis, *T. S. Eliot's Intellectual Development*, 134–5.

[88] 'Second Thoughts about Humanism', *Adelphi* (June–Aug. 1929), 304–10. The article was also published in the Harvard quarterly, *Hound and Horn* (July–Sept. 1929).

[89] 'The Fallacy of Humanism', *Criterion* (July 1929), 661–81. Eliot thought the article was brilliant. See T. S. Eliot to Allen Tate, 5 Mar. 1929. Princeton.

[90] See T. S. Eliot to John Middleton Murry, 20 Oct. 1931. New York (Public Library).

of Rees, a committed member of the Labour Party, the *Adelphi* reverted to monthly publication and began openly to take up the cause of socialism. It was unlikely, given the circumstances, that the journals could find much common ground. In 1932, after what Eliot termed Murry's 'religious' conversion to Communism, the old adversaries were back to public intellectual controversy. Once again, Eliot's editorial tone slipped from his usually finely balanced irony to the condescending sarcasm he reserved for Murry: 'One must admire the skill with which Mr Murry, here, as elsewhere, envelops every utterance with his familiar odour of sanctity; not even the dearest of old ladies could be upset by such sentiments, Mr Murry puts things so nicely'.[91] The old dears, presumably, preferred the *Adelphi* to the *Criterion*. In 1935, they may have been upset when Eliot objected to Murry's search for a synthesis between Marxism and social aspects of Christianity, a synthesis he contrasted unfavourably with similar efforts made by John Macmurray, a philosophy professor at London University.[92] Throughout the 1930s, Eliot publicly scolded Murry as a religious heretic. Privately they remained friends. Eliot continued to commission book reviews from Murry, if no longer *causeries*: he reviewed Murry's studies of Lawrence and Shakespeare enthusiastically in the *Criterion*.[93] Only a few years before his death, Murry noted in his journal that for all his differences with Eliot there was 'a strange feeling of kinship between us'.[94]

The controversies between Eliot and Murry are notable for the lack of any real contestatory interaction, largely a consequence of their dissemination and reception in the arena of metropolitan literary journalism. Classicism defined as the antithesis of romanticism was a matter of personal taste and rhetorical tactics, not prima facie a question of ineluctable substantive differences. In fact, the classicism and romanticism debate appeared to debase the currency of these critical terms. Eliot admitted as much in *After Strange Gods*(1934) when he described the terms as 'temporary

[91]   'A Commentary', *Criterion* (Apr. 1932), 469.
[92]   See 'A Commentary', *Criterion* (Apr. 1935), 431–6.
[93]   Eliot described the critical biography of Lawrence, *Son of Woman*, as 'the best piece of sustained writing that Mr Murry has done' ('Books of the Quarter', *Criterion* (July 1931), 771). He also claimed that Murry's *Shakespeare* was 'a very good book indeed' ('Books of the Quarter', *Criterion* (July 1936), 708).
[94]   Cited in Lea, *John Middleton Murry*, 72.

and political'.[95] Moreover, the exclusive and rigid dichotomy Eliot erected between the 'inner voice' and 'external authority' made it difficult to arrive at a commensurating middle-ground, even the possibility of sympathetic disagreement. Ultimately, Eliot's refusal to take a more charitable view of the semantic boundaries of Murry's synthesis was symptomatic of the conservative cultural politics underlying his position. It is no exaggeration to say that Eliot detested Murry's romantic individualism, whose potentially harmful social consequences he derided as 'Whiggery'.

The *Criterion* and the *Adelphi* were not really in direct competition and aimed, for the most part, at discrete audiences. They did, however, propound rival cultural politics, capitalizing upon the existence of the other as a catalyst, or as a foil, to issue an opportunistic *prise de position* or to boost flagging fortunes. Whatever the precise details of the sociology and economics of the rivalry, Eliot's argumentative strategies in the *Criterion* reveal that he could be a subtle and successful periodical controversialist (notwithstanding certain 'errors of tone' he would later come to regret), deftly putting his editorial thumb in the scales of weighty intellectual matters. Or, as he grudgingly conceded, he had 'some skill in the barren game of controversy'.[96] In this respect, the appearance of the *Adelphi* had been extremely useful. It was as if, to adapt a cadence from *Four Quartets*, the *Criterion* and the *Adelphi* were united in the periodical controversy that divided them. Or as Murry put it: on the plane of serious literary journalism, 'enemies are *necessary* to one another'.

[95] *After Strange Gods* (London, 1934), 25.
[96] T. S. Eliot to Paul Elmer More, 20 June 1934. Cited in Margolis, *T. S. Eliot's Intellectual Development*, p. xv.

2

The *Calendar*

Standards of Criticism

> In reviewing we shall base our statements on the standards
> of criticism, since it is only then that one can speak plainly
> without offence, or give praise with meaning.
>
> 'Comments and Reviews', *Calendar of Modern Letters*
> (March 1925), 71

John Gross was correct to question respectfully the 'underground reputation' enjoyed by the *Calendar of Modern Letters*.[1] The origins of that reputation can be traced to F. R. Leavis's admiring introduction to his 1933 selection of critical essays and reviews from the *Calendar*. Comparing the *Calendar* to the *Criterion*, he spoke of its 'superior liveliness' and of 'its great critical superiority'.[2] In 1961, Malcolm Bradbury, who had interviewed Eliot, Leavis, and the *Calendar*'s chief editor, Edgell Rickword, described the journal as 'in many ways' the best literary review of the 1920s.[3] A few years later, on the reception of the Frank Cass three-volume reprint of the *Calendar* (with Bradbury's essay as introduction), it looked as if the journal had levitated out of the 1920s altogether and become, in the words of Frank Kermode, a 'paragon': 'No other review in English has come anywhere near it.'[4] And yet, it is essential to recontextualize the *Calendar* within the milieu of inter-war literary journalism. For careful examination of the 'episode of *The Calendar*' (as Leavis was fond of calling it) reveals

---

[1] *The Rise and Fall of the Man of Letters* (London, 1969), 271–2.
[2] 'Introduction', *Towards Standards of Criticism* (London, 1933), 9.
[3] See 'A Review in Retrospect', *London Magazine* (Oct. 1961).
[4] 'The Calendar of Modern Letters', *New Statesman* (2 Sept. 1966), 320.

an overlap of substantive concerns with the *Criterion*, acknowledged by Eliot as a matter of 'common ground'. That terrain was reflected in a co-operative drive to reform standards of metropolitan literary reviewing; in the difficulty, even impossibility, of teasing out an active and responsive readership; in the brushes both journals had with the touchy and hypersensitive egos of established writers. Most interestingly of all, the journals engaged in a lengthy and sometimes acrimonious critical exchange, cut short by the sudden demise of the *Calendar*, which sheds a fascinating light on the cultural politics espoused by both journals. In short, the *Criterion* was an evolving critical organ, responsive to a generation of critics disturbed by the immense cultural upheaval following the First World War.

I

Invalided out of the Royal Berkshire Regiment, with a glass eye and the Military Cross, Edgell Rickword went up to Oxford in October 1919 to read French literature.[5] Like many of the ex-officers who crowded Oxford in the years immediately following the war, he was impatient with academic mores and regulations and left after four terms without graduating.[6] All the same, Rickword and his close friend, the Australian Bertram Higgins, encountered a lively circle of writers in Oxford. They contributed to *Oxford Poetry 1920*, a grouping of ex-soldiers such as Robert Graves, Edmund Blunden, and L. P. Hartley, and tyros like Roy Campbell and Richard Hughes. Rickword gravitated to London using his Oxford connections to carve out a living as a literary journalist, predominantly on the *New Statesman* under the tutelage of Desmond MacCarthy, but also as a regular reviewer for the *TLS*, where he could earn up to £20 a month. Rickword's traumatic war experience permeated his poetry and his reviewing. There was a strain of morbidity informing his reviews of work on Donne and the Elizabethan dramatists, as well as his admiration for the *poètes maudits*, Baudelaire and Rimbaud. In 1924, after some encouragement from MacCarthy, Rickword published a

---

[5] Rickword's left eye was removed in Jan. 1919 after the onset of septicaemia. For biography see Charles Hobday, *Edgell Rickword: A Poet at War* (Manchester, 1989).
[6] See Rickword's farewell to Oxford, 'Complaint of a Tadpole Confined in a Jam-Jar', *Behind the Eyes* (London, 1921), 22–3.

pioneering study *Rimbaud: The Boy and the Poet* which received lukewarm reviews from Sir Edmund Gosse in the *Sunday Times* and F. S. Flint in the *Criterion*.[7] The unsatisfactoriness of the reviews of Rickword's study of Rimbaud (the *Criterion* managed to misspell the author as 'Rickward'), were symptomatic of a growing rift between an Edwardian generation of critics, whose tastes and style of reviewing were essentially gentlemanly and impressionistic, and a younger generation who had returned from the trenches filled with a profound disenchantment with the *de haut en bas* pronouncements of mandarins, like Gosse, who presided over literary London.

In the autumn of 1924, Roy Campbell introduced Rickword to his brother-in-law, Douglas Garman, the son of an affluent doctor from the industrial West Midlands. After graduating from Cambridge, Garman had turned his back on a conventional middle-class career in order to devote more time to writing poetry. Rickword, Garman, and Higgins met frequently to discuss the possibility of starting a literary magazine with systematic and uncompromising standards of reviewing. Rickword later described the triumvirate as 'a sort of discontented club, discontented with all the established novelists and the literary cliques'. Although Rickword admired Eliot's achievement as a poet and critic, he numbered the *Criterion* among those cliques.[8] There was some justice in this opinion, for when Eliot introduced a 'Books of the Quarter' section in 1924 it did not begin auspiciously: there were perfunctory reviews by Eliot, Vivien (under various pseudonyms), his secretary Irene Fassett (who dismissed Forster's *A Passage to India*), together with the verse reviews of Harold Monro and F. S. Flint, who were largely unsympathetic to the younger generation of poets.

By March 1925, having received assurances of work from a wide range of authors,[9] and with financial backing from Garman

---

[7] See F. S. Flint, 'Books of the Quarter', *Criterion* (Jan. 1925), 329–30. In a slashing 1920 *Daily Herald* review of Flint's *Otherworld*, Rickword had attacked Flint's abandonment of poetic metre. See Edgell Rickword, *Essays and Opinions, 1921–1931*, ed. Alan Young (Manchester, 1974), 313–14.

[8] See Alan Young and Michael Schmidt, 'A Conversation with Edgell Rickword', *Poetry Nation* (1973), 78.

[9] Among the writers the *Calendar* advertised as forthcoming were Richard Aldington, Edmund Blunden, Roy Campbell, A. E. Coppard, E. M. Forster, Robert Graves, Aldous Huxley, D. H. Lawrence, Wyndham Lewis, Desmond MacCarthy, Peter Quennell, Bertrand Russell, Siegfried Sassoon, and W. J. Turner.

and his wealthy brother-in-law, Ernest Wishart, the *Calendar of Modern Letters* was launched: an attractive literary monthly priced 1s. 6d., containing original fiction, poetry, critical essays, and short book reviews. It was a family affair. Rickword's cousin, Cecil, acted as business manager and Garman's brother was the advertising manager, a role he performed with little efficiency. The *Calendar* arrived virtually unheralded into the London literary world.[10] What is more, a wilful disregard for the economic realities of the literary market-place characterized the publication history of the *Calendar*. By the end of the first year the original print-run of 7,000 had dwindled to a modest 2,000 copies, too small it appears to sustain a monthly periodical with considerable overheads. The *Calendar* paid a competitive rate of £3. 3s. for 1,000 words, helping to draw impecunious writers, like D. H. Lawrence, whose livelihood depended on revenue from periodical publication. The *Calendar* paid Lawrence a princely sum of £53. 11s. for the novella 'The Princess', serialized in the opening three issues, considerably more than the £18 the *Criterion* paid for 'Jimmy and the Desperate Woman' in October 1924 (although Eliot had exceeded the standard rate for contributions[11]).

The *Calendar*'s willingness to attract writers with a following in advanced literary circles effectively put the journal in competition with the *Criterion*; indeed, the organization of a fruitful relationship with an appreciative and discriminating readership was a frequent topic for the journal's editorial team. And yet, the *Calendar* displayed an intransigent disdain for the taste and opinions of the reading public, declaring in the opening number: 'The reader we have in mind, the ideal reader, is not one with whom we share any particular set of admirations and beliefs.'[12] Ideal readers do not sustain literary periodicals. Beyond Rickword's bohemian acquaintances who frequented the Fitzroy Tavern in Charlotte Street, it is not clear that the *Calendar* was received in the smoking-rooms of Pall Mall clubs or among the louche 'bright young things' whom Aldous Huxley depicted as the intellectual shakers and movers of the 1920s. The *Criterion*, unlike the self-consciously iconoclastic *Calendar*, possessed closer links to gentlemanly, long

[10] Although the first number was noted favourably in the *TLS* (5 Mar. 1925), 158.
[11] See *The Letters of D. H. Lawrence*, v. *March 1924–March 1927*, ed. James T. Boulton and Lindeth Vasey (Cambridge, 1989), 180 n. 1 and 86 n. 1.
[12] 'Comments and Reviews', *Calendar* (Mar. 1925), 70.

established quarterlies and monthlies and was not averse to the occasional contribution from an illustrious Edwardian bookman (for instance, George Saintsbury, Ford Madox Ford, or Thomas Sturge Moore). Nor, as Eliot told Herbert Read in October 1924, was the *Criterion* against a little fashionable window-dressing.[13]

Rather than appeal to an existing body of readers, the *Calendar* chose to please itself, indulging a misty-eyed nostalgia for Dr Johnson's 'common reader', that ideal reader 'uncorrupted with literary prejudices'. The appeal to a small but choice eighteenth-century audience was not really helpful. More pointedly, the *Calendar* looked at the break-up of the late-Victorian reading public as the defining moment of modern culture. Reviewing the first series of Virginia Woolf's *Common Reader* essays, Rickword observed caustically:

Since [the Victorians] then, the reading-public has split. We have the small body of educated sharp-witted readers from whom a small spark of intelligence sometimes flickers, but being passionate, if at all, only about values and not experience, ultimately uncreative; and themselves so frequently practitioners as to be unsatisfactory as audience. Beyond lies the vast reading-public which is led by the nose by the high-class literary-journalist-poet type and its tail tweaked by the paragraphist with pretensions not rising above personal gossip.

Rickword believed that it was necessary for the *Calendar*, if it was to perform the function of criticism, to resist the commercial obligation to appeal to popular taste or to follow the latest fads of the metropolitan literary world. The *Calendar*'s readership, it could be argued, was still in the process of being forged in the aftermath of the First World War; that such a journal could pay its way was something Rickword scarcely dared to hope:

Modern work appeals necessarily to a restricted audience, of no particular class but with a common sensibility, and there is no object in trying to expand this audience artificially. It is certainly to the advantage of literature, now, to fall below commercial standards of value.[14]

Not that there was anything particularly new in this complaint. It has been customary for anxious young writers to bemoan the hostility and insensitivity of the literary market-place.

---

[13] T. S. Eliot to Herbert Read, 18 Oct. 1924. Victoria.
[14] 'Comments and Reviews', *Calendar* (June 1925), 321, 322.

A few months later, Garman's jeremiad on the subject of 'Audience' spoke of the decline in terms of bourgeois propriety:

There is no longer a body of opinion so solid as that represented by *The Quarterly, The Edinburgh*, and *Blackwood's*. The fact that they pronounced a vigorous aesthetic creed, and were, therefore, of the greatest benefit to a lively interest in poetry, is forgotten because they were sometimes ungentlemanly. Their place has been taken, but not filled, by the torrential journalistic criticism which is poured out daily, weekly, and monthly, and is so enlightened and refined that the fulfilment of its obvious function is overlooked in its effort to be open-minded and polite. There has never been such a rubbishy flow of poetry as that which is vomited by contemporary publishers, yet the reading public has never expressed its opinion through such mealy-mouthed critics. . . . But the part to be played by the audience is as important as the poet's, and it is possible that a regeneration of intelligent sensibility may only be possible after a devastating and bloody revolt against the sickly, bourgeois, animal consciousness of our age.[15]

For all the revolutionary grumbling, the *Calendar* remained vague about the proposed restorative, rejecting the idea of a preconceived 'editorial doctrine' in favour of 'the value of spontaneous growth.'[16] Many years later, Rickword recalled: 'There was a committee of the whole house. We agreed about most things, I think. We talked a lot together and got an arrived at consensus.'[17] That consensus was tangible, reflected in the tone of the *Calendar*'s 3,000 word critical articles and in the punchy fifteen or so pages devoted to short book reviews. In fact, the *Calendar* exhibited a degree of uniformity and singleness of purpose that was impossible in a journal of the size and scope of the *Criterion*.

A new generation of critical malcontents, dissatisfied with the apparently capricious nature of contemporary reviewing, a diagnosis echoed in academic literary theory,[18] made it possible for Rickword to assemble a team of critics sharing similar aims and aspirations. In the summer of 1925, the *Calendar* was strengthened by the appearance of the poet and translator, Edwin Muir, and his

---

[15] 'Audience', *Calendar* (Sept. 1925), 48, 49.
[16] 'Comments and Reviews', *Calendar* (Mar. 1925), 70.
[17] Young and Schmidt, 'A Conversation with Edgell Rickword', 78.
[18] Reviewing I. A. Richards's *Principles of Literary Criticism*, Rickword praised his 'lucid' theory of literary criticism 'as a sort of colophon to an appreciation which is far from exhaustive' (*Calendar of Modern Letters* (Apr. 1925), 162–4).

friend John Holms.[19] Allied with Rickword, Garman, and Higgins, they proved a discerning, trenchant, and refreshingly original group. From unpublished correspondence, it is clear that Eliot discussed the *Calendar* with Herbert Read. Eliot's brief comments on the *Calendar* critics—they were unknown to him, with the sole exception of Muir, whom Sydney Schiff had introduced to him in 1924[20]— give the impression that he hoped that some of their number (in particular, Muir and Holms) would be drawn into the *Criterion* camp.[21] However, it appears that various talented freelance literary journalists found the *Calendar* a more hospitable, not to say a more lucrative, outlet for articles and reviews.

II

The reviewing policy of the *Calendar* was notable for its public demolition of inflated literary reputations. Humbert Wolfe, a regular reviewer for the *Saturday Review, Vogue*, the *Observer*, and (in spite of a complete insensibility to *The Waste Land*)[22] a *Criterion* poetry reviewer, was a familiar whipping boy. The mere mention of Wolfe's name stood as a sort of shorthand for the deleterious state of the metropolitan literary world.[23] According to Rickword, the Edwardian malaise in contemporary reviewing required some plain speaking: 'Toleration or indifference has gone so far, and prostituted the terms of praise, that it is impossible to tell from an ordinary review whether a book of poems contains really original work or if it just avoids the more obvious commonplaces.'[24] The assertion of 'standards' was forcibly advanced in the *Calendar*'s series of bracing critical articles entitled 'Scrutinies'. Rickword later described the task: 'We started out with this idea of a clean break, or whatever you like to call it, and we wanted to say why

---

[19] After public school and war service, John Holms (1897–1934), made an unsuccessful attempt to become a novelist.

[20] Muir contributed a review to the *Criterion*. See 'Books of the Quarter', *Criterion* (July 1925), 583–4.   [21] See T. S. Eliot to Herbert Read, 17 Oct. 1925. Victoria.

[22] See 'Books of the Quarter', *Criterion* (Jan. 1926), 206.

[23] Rickword described Wolfe's dramatic sequences, *Humoresque*, as 'frustrated by an ingrained banality of style' ('Notes and Reviews', *Calendar* (July 1926), 159). F. S. Flint was more forgiving: '[Wolfe] is so deft with his versification, that if you but give him half a chance, he takes you with him' ('Books of the Quarter', *Criterion* (June 1926), 602).   [24] 'Reviews', *Calendar* (Aug. 1925), 482.

these figures needed shifting so we had to criticise them. I mean they were just taken for granted by the public.'[25]

In the opening salvo, Rickword directed a withering attack upon Sir James Barrie; next month Garman decried the 'falsity of the values' exhibited in the work of Walter de la Mare; the following month Higgins lambasted John Masefield's 'downright bluff'.[26] The recurrent complaint, delivered with a shrill insistence, was the lack of a mature intelligence exhibited by these writers, where 'maturity' (also an important word in Eliot's critical lexicon) implied full cognizance of the 'negative emotions', as Rickword called them, unleashed by the First World War. In subsequent 'Scrutinies', Muir, Holms, and Cecil Rickword sought to undermine the reputations of further eminent Edwardians—Bennett, Shaw, and Wells—although the aggressive tone and force of these essays perhaps too readily dismissed any suggestion of merit in these literary forebears. In 1927, Rickword commissioned a 'Scrutiny' of the novelist John Galsworthy by D. H. Lawrence, candidly described by Lawrence as 'not very nice to Galsworthy'.[27]

Lawrence was a contributor to the *Criterion* and the *Calendar*. The dynamics of various influential writers—Lawrence, Wyndham Lewis, Robert Graves—who failed to maintain solidarity with the *Criterion* and appeared in the pages of the *Calendar* is worth examining for the pointers they provide towards the relations between the journals. Interestingly, the trajectories, if less than straightforward, suggest that human motives and interactions (for instance, wrangling over payment) often outweighed the 'symbolic capital' afforded by publication in Eliot's prestigious quarterly review. Although Lawrence was happy to place his work in the *Criterion* (he did not deal directly with Eliot) his stories, essays, and travelogues often went to the highest bidder.[28] After the appearance of 'The Princess', Lawrence contributed two essays to the *Calendar*. He did not know the *Calendar* team personally and received some

---

[25] Young and Schmidt, 'A Conversation with Edgell Rickword', 81.
[26] See 'Scrutinies', Edgell Rickword (Mar. 1925), 38–43; Douglas Garman (Apr. 1925), 133–8; Bertram Higgins (May 1925), 219–25.
[27] D. H. Lawrence to Nancy Pearn, 28 Feb. 1927. *Letters of D. H. Lawrence, v.* 649.
[28] See D. H. Lawrence to Richard Cobden-Sanderson, 1 Dec. 1924: 'I am so relieved that *The Criterion* has got some guts, and isn't another *Adelphi* or *London Mercury*' (ibid. 181).

biting reviews of his work in the journal.[29] In November 1926, he informed his literary agent:

The Calendar, like most other little magazines, seems to have a swelled head and a shrivelled pocket. I don't care a button whether I do review for them or not: I call it charity work, at the price, and with all the pompous conditions. But if they send a book along, I'll review it, *if it interests me*. That's my only condition.[30]

However, Rickword was anxious to secure Lawrence as a regular contributor and he eventually overcame his misgivings. Lawrence's reviews in the Calendar were an important gesture of support (he did not review for the Criterion) and did much to sustain the journal through difficult times. He continued to sell pieces to the Criterion, but he described the journal privately as 'that expensive and stewed T. S. Eliot quarterly'.[31]

Eliot described Wyndham Lewis as 'the most brilliant journalist of my generation' and considered his support essential to the success of the Criterion.[32] Eliot wanted a contribution from Lewis for each issue and he was prepared to pay above the standard rate to secure his work. He persuaded a reluctant Lewis to serialize fragments of his sprawling, satirical overview of literary London in the Criterion and praised the extracts in glowing terms.[33] However, the seeds of discord were present from the beginning. Lewis, hard upon the collapse of his own journal, the Tyro, had attempted to persuade Sydney Schiff to fund a rival magazine to the Criterion. Lewis was really only interested in voicing his own rapidly evolving critical opinions and not in providing tailor-made copy for another editor: he was erratic and unreliable as a contributor. Eliot was forced to turn to Clive Bell (and later Roger Hinks)[34] when it became clear that Lewis could not be relied upon to contribute a regular 'Art

---

[29] See H. C. Harwood on *St Mawr*: 'On the whole, the bosh predominates' ('Comments and Reviews', *Calendar* (June 1925), 327). See also Cecil Rickword, 'Notes and Reviews', *Calendar* (Apr. 1926), 77–9.

[30] D. H. Lawrence to Nancy Pearn, 11 Nov. 1926. *Letters of D. H. Lawrence*, v. 570–1.

[31] D. H. Lawrence to Earl and Achsah Brewster, 7 Feb. 1929. *The Letters of D. H. Lawrence*, vii. *1928–1930*, ed. Keith Sagar and James T. Boulton (Cambridge, 1993), 170.   [32] *Charles Whibley: A Memoir* (London, 1931), 8.

[33] See *The Letters of Wyndham Lewis*, ed. W. K. Rose (London, 1963), 140 n. 1.

[34] Roger Hinks (1903–63), Assistant Keeper in the Department of Greek and Roman Antiquities at the British Museum from 1926 until 1939.

Chronicle'. Furthermore, the work that Lewis sent to the *Criterion* was invariably overlong and undigested portions of books in progress. Eliot, who generally disliked splitting contributions into instalments, was presented with some difficulty in settling on the contents of each issue.

In January 1925, Lewis and Eliot quarrelled over 'The Perfect Action', a 20,000-word essay advertised as forthcoming in the *Criterion*. When Eliot enquired if it might be possible to break up the essay into manageable portions, Lewis angrily withdrew the essay and all other contributions to the magazine. Affecting to be insulted by Eliot and the appearance of his Bloomsbury *bête noire*, Clive Bell, in the *Criterion*, he darkly warned Eliot against future 'treachery'.[35] In truth, Lewis was suffering from extreme financial hardship and needed to sell the essay for ready money. He sold the article to the *Calendar*, pruned to 12,000 words and retitled 'The Dithyrambic Spectator' for £40 (three times the *Criterion* rate), and defended his decision to Eliot:

Yesterday Monro said that in selling something to a paper called the Calendar I was associating myself with a rival venture to yours and his [the *Chapbook*]. . . . I don't consider that a paper like the Calendar will harm your paper. . . . The Calendar had already Lawrence, Huxley and so on as its contributors, with Joyce benevolently in the background.[36] I think that, unless the editors have a great deal of personal merit themselves, that these well-known names will limit the nature of their enterprise, rather than confer it with any special character, which you are eminently able to give yours.[37]

It is not clear that Eliot was inclined to agree with Lewis's characterization of the relation between the journals. The *Calendar* was undoubtedly taking potential contributions from the hand of the *Criterion*. Eliot was resigned to losing Lewis. He expressed his disappointment, although he told Read that Lewis's petulance

[35] Wyndham Lewis to T. S. Eliot, 30 Jan. 1925. *Letters of Wyndham Lewis*, ed. Rose, 149.
[36] The appearance of a section from Joyce's 'Work in Progress' was advertised in the *Calendar* (Sept. 1925), but it did not appear after the printers objected on the grounds of obscenity. See James Joyce to Harriet Shaw Weaver, 6 Sept. 1925. London (British Library). The *Criterion* had published Joyce's 'Fragment of an Unfinished Work' (July 1925), 498–510.
[37] Wyndham Lewis to T. S. Eliot, Mar. 1925. *Letters of Wyndham Lewis*, ed. Rose, 152.

made the breach difficult to patch up.[38] Not surprisingly, Rickword also found Lewis a difficult contributor. He was soon irritated by Lewis's tongue-in-cheek praise of Mussolini in the *Calendar*.[39] In January 1927, after securing a subsidy from Lady Waterhouse, Lewis launched the aptly titled, *The Enemy*, described as 'merely a person; a solitary outlaw and not a gang'.[40] Although Eliot was one of only a handful of contributors to this journal, he did not escape satirical treatment as the 'dry' Mr Horty in Lewis's *The Apes of God* (1930), where he appeared alongside unflattering portraits of the *Calendar* editors, Rickword, Garman, and Higgins.[41] Cecil Gray, the *Calendar*'s forthright music critic, remarked of Lewis: 'All of his friends and collaborators have, sooner or later, come under the lash of his pen, and have been led in a tumbril to the guillotine in his books.'[42]

Robert Graves maintained equally precarious relations with the *Criterion* and the *Calendar*. Graves had known Rickword at Oxford and contributed poetry to the opening number of the *Calendar*. He also attempted to interest Rickword and Eliot in the work of his partner, Laura Riding. The *Calendar* printed ten pages of Riding's poetry in 1925, but she did not appear in the *Criterion*. However, when the cover of the *Calendar* advertised Graves and not Riding as the author of their collaborative attack on poetry anthologies, they impetuously withdrew their support.[43] Graves turned to the *Criterion*, contributing a review defending the posthumous reputation of his friend, W. H. R. Rivers.[44] This connection was short-lived. In 1927, John Gould Fletcher, in a *Criterion* batch review of recent poetry, praised Graves's *Poems 1914-1926* but described Riding's *The Close Chaplet* as 'borrowed threads'. Worse, Fletcher suggested that Riding's poems were derivative of Graves (an assessment that undoubtedly caused friction between the couple).[45] Graves sent a furious letter to Eliot,

---

[38] T. S. Eliot to Herbert Read, 13 Mar. 1925. Victoria.

[39] See 'The New Roman Empire', *Calendar* (Feb. 1926), 411-20.

[40] Wyndham Lewis, *Enemy* (Jan. 1927), p. ix.

[41] Hedgepinshot Mandeville Pickwort, Siegfried Victor, and Bertram Brown, respectively. *The Apes of God* was not reviewed in the *Criterion*.

[42] *Musical Chairs* (London, 1985), 274.

[43] See Laura Riding and Robert Graves, 'The Anthologist in Our Midst', *Calendar* (Apr. 1927), 22-36.   [44] 'Recent Books', *Criterion* (May 1927), 247.

[45] 'Recent Books', *Criterion* (Aug. 1927), 170.

denouncing Fletcher, Wolfe, and Flint as 'literary politicians' and accusing the *Criterion* of pandering to the tastes of the market. Against his native caution, Eliot printed Graves's intemperate 'object lesson' on the politics of literary reviewing.[46] He attempted to conciliate Graves by offering to publish his poetry in the *Criterion*, but was informed: 'Let's nod and walk on'.[47] Riding later dismissed the *Criterion* as an 'exclusive Thomist club'.[48]

In general, American poets and critics, such as Riding, found a more welcoming home in the *Calendar* (which was distributed in Boston, New York, and San Francisco) than in Eliot's Eurocentric *Criterion*.[49] John Crowe Ransom, who had misgivings about Eliot's influence, found a platform for his critical principles in the *Calendar*.[50] So, too, did Gorham Munson for his early study of the New York literary journalist Kenneth Burke.[51] Reviewing *The Selected Poems of Carl Sandburg* (it was not noticed in the *Criterion*), Rickword observed:

real American poetry free from the traditions of what, for propaganda purposes, was called the English tradition, but which was really the mannerism of a small colonial clique. . . . our idioms are distinct, and it is through the realisation of its automatic uniqueness that American literature is coming into existence.[52]

Harbingers of that new American poetry, Hart Crane and Allen Tate, shared the experience of having their poetry accepted by the *Calendar* but rejected by the *Criterion*.

The case of Crane, a poet deeply influenced by *Prufrock and Other Observations*, but not the crumbling imperial towers of *The Waste Land*, is instructive. Crane celebrated the debaucheries and soaring skyscrapers of roaring jazz age New York. It was the Dionysian energies of Crane's work, the willingness to succumb to

---

[46] See 'Correspondence', *Criterion* (Oct. 1927), 357–9.
[47] See *In Broken Images: Selected Letters of Robert Graves, 1914–1946*, ed. Paul O'Prey (London, 1982), 177–9.
[48] See *Anarchism is Not Enough* (London, 1928), 90.
[49] The *Criterion*'s relations with the *Dial* worsened after 1926 when Marianne Moore rejected a submission from Vivien Eliot. See Papers of Vivien Eliot. Oxford.
[50] Ransom outlined his critique of Eliot in *The New Criticism* (Norfolk, Conn., 1941). See also Allen Tate, *Memories and Essays Old and New: 1926–1974* (Manchester, 1976), 41–4.
[51] 'In and about the Workshop of Kenneth Burke', *Calendar* (July 1926), 129–41.
[52] 'Notes and Reviews', *Calendar* (Apr. 1926), 75–6.

Faustian damnation, that appealed to Rickword.[53] The *Calendar* published the syncopated sensuality of 'Three Songs' ('Outspoken buttocks in pink beads/Invite the necessary cloudy clinch') from *The Bridge*. Crane wrote to thank Rickword for his editorial 'kindness'.[54] A month after the demise of the *Calendar*, however, he was considerably more enthusiastic when Eliot accepted the purgatorial 'Tunnel' section of *The Bridge* for publication in the *Criterion*.[55] In a similar vein, Tate's pride at the publication of his essay on American humanism in the *Criterion* surpassed any pleasure he derived from his association with the *Calendar*. For all the *Calendar*'s sensitivity to new currents in contemporary literature, Eliot's reputation among young poets and critics lent publication in the *Criterion* a prestige that the *Calendar*, with its little-known editorial team, could not hope to emulate.[56] Many writers, who perhaps should have identified themselves more closely with the skirmishing tactics of the *Calendar*, found themselves hankering after a berth in the *Criterion*'s imperious pages.

III

The *Calendar* did not immediately tackle the reputation of the *Criterion* head on. Muir's even-handed review of *Homage to John Dryden* set the tone for later developments. Applauding the essays as 'probably the most penetrating body of observation on the metaphysical poets that has yet appeared in English', he regretted that Eliot's 'derangement of values' had helped to bring about an unwarranted foreshortening of the critical reputations of Milton and Wordsworth. Muir believed that Eliot's slender volumes of collected journalism, although acute and insightful, were not the last word on literary matters.[57] Rickword applied

[53] Both Crane and Rickword wrote poems on the Marlovian theme of Faustus's damnation at the hands of a simulacrum of Helen of Troy.

[54] See Hart Crane to Edgell Rickword, 7 Jan. 1927. *Letters of Hart Crane, 1916–1932*, ed. Brom Weber (Berkeley, 1965), 283.

[55] Cf. Hart Crane to Otto Kahn, 12 Sept. 1927: 'I have been especially gratified by the reception afforded me by *The Criterion*, whose director, Mr T. S. Eliot, is representative of the most exacting literary standards of our times' (ibid. 308). See also T. S. Eliot to Hart Crane, 16 Aug. 1927. New York (Columbia).

[56] The New York *Nation* described the *Criterion* as 'the most interesting clearing-house of literary ideas that we now have' ((22 Sept. 1926), 259).

[57] See 'Comments and Reviews', *Calendar* (May 1927), 242. After revising the review for book publication, Muir wrote to Sydney Schiff: 'I sincerely hope that [Eliot]

the same clear-sighted judgement to Eliot's *Poems, 1909–1925*. One of a handful of contemporaries to appreciate the originality and scope of *The Waste Land*, he observed that Eliot was unrivalled as the modern poet who 'has most effectively upheld the reality of the art in an age of preposterous poeticising'. According to Rickword, the triumph was partly a matter of idiom and rhythm, partly a matter of the urgency of the poet's personality showing through the occasionally threadbare tissue of allusion. *The Waste Land* exemplified a contemporary sense of cultural fragmentation, compelling reading to an army of soldier poets struggling to find an appropriate form in which to articulate their war experience. However, Rickword condemned Eliot's obscurity and concluded that his poetry ultimately failed to satisfy, even if he had been a great example to a generation 'for whom all the romantic escapes had been blocked'.[58]

By the time this review appeared, the *Calendar* was in severe financial difficulties. In January 1926 the back cover announced:

After the February number, the *Calendar* will enter the second phase of its development. As a monthly it has done the best it could to distil some unity out of the prevailing chaos, by analysing present conditions and giving examples of contemporary work.

But, the Re-action having been exposed, it remains to illustrate more fully than we have yet been able to do, the new Action. We find that this can be done more economically (for the resources of a literary paper are necessarily limited) by quarterly than by monthly publication, and we have been at some pains to ensure a certain run.

The appeal to potential subscribers in a society in 'chaos', an attempt to circumvent reliance upon distribution through booksellers, exposed the failure of the journal to market and promote itself effectively. Publication as a quarterly was an admission that the *Calendar*, like the *Criterion*, could only appeal to a tiny public of at most 1,000 readers. In addition, the *Calendar* was not only short of subscribers but of contributors. As a direct consequence of a lack of advertising revenue, payment was reduced to £2. 2s.

himself will not feel hurt by it; the effect of all criticism such as this which is perfectly sincere and disinterested should be ultimately to help a writer, make him reconsider himself and be prepared against his deficiencies' (*Selected Letters of Edwin Muir*, ed. P. H. Butter (London, 1974), 52).

[58] 'Notes and Reviews', *Calendar* (Dec. 1925), 278–81.

per 1,000 words, making it harder for the magazine to attract copy of the desired quality. The second volume of the *Calendar* shrank from 80 to 72 pages. It became increasingly necessary for the editors to fill the empty *Calendar* hull with pseudonymous offerings. Subscribers could justifiably complain that the sharp increase in price to half a crown was accompanied by only a modest increase in size to 88 pages.

It was highly understandable that the *Calendar* should cast an envious eye on the *Criterion*, recently rejuvenated by Faber & Gwyer. The editors displayed irritation with what they took to be the *Criterion*'s lack of a coherent direction: 'not even the bulkiest review can be boundlessly eclectic, and as soon as the element of choice is introduced the question of a principle or a programme becomes paramount.' Eliot's editorial manifesto had, of course, spoken of the tendency of 'classicism'. The *Calendar* expressed dissatisfaction with the *Criterion*'s classicism: 'we do not find much of Mr Eliot or of his tendency, in this number, high as it is above the level of the ordinary literary review.'[59] The charge was difficult to refute: the *Criterion* certainly exhibited a bewildering variety of creative and critical approaches, possessing some of the traits of a miscellany. It was not always easy to discern the 'classicist' pattern in the *Criterion* carpet, let alone 'a more severe and serene control of the emotions by Reason' (Eliot's critical epitome of the classical tendency), in, say, the experimentalism of Gertrude Stein's wilfully oblique 'The Fifteenth of November'.[60] It was not clear to the *Calendar* team that Eliot had the right to use the term 'classicism' at all.

In July 1926, in an unsigned note, the *Calendar* laid claim to its own formulated aesthetic of classical discipline:

The characteristics of a healthy criticism are invariably 'classic,' tending towards an ever greater rigidity of principle, organisations more explicit, and the canalisation of the wide, shallow stream of taste.[61]

---

[59] 'Notes and Reviews', *Calendar* (Feb. 1926), 432.

[60] See 'The Fifteenth of November', *Criterion* (Jan. 1926), 71–5. The piece was apparently named after the day Eliot had commissioned an 'up-to-date' contribution from Stein.

[61] 'Euthanasia: or the Future of Criticism', *Calendar* (July 1926), 152. Malcolm Bradbury ascribed the article to Bertram Higgins.

In April 1927, Higgins appended a footnote to his article 'Art and Knowledge' intended to signal a clear breach between the *Calendar* and certain reactionary, albeit unspecified, proponents of 'Neo-Classicism':

the literary version of a reactionary Latin philosophy which is being adapted, in one or two English reviews, into a repressive instrument of literary criticism. . . . the verbal sobriety which disguises its positivism, its calm and socialized demeanour in the midst of the revolutionary concepts by which we are surrounded, and its genuine but exaggerated docility to the world of learning.[62]

Eliot was not amused: taking the comments as an attack on his recent publication of several Catholic intellectuals in the *Criterion* he mounted the editorial platform in a pontifical humour:

We have used, and shall continue to use the word 'classicism', unsatisfactory as it is. . . . The term 'neo-classicism' is not ours, and is not particularly commendable; for all 'neos' indicate some fad or fashion of the moment, and it is not our concern to be fashionable.

Eliot felt impelled to offer readers of the *Criterion* a public refutation of the *Calendar*'s veiled slur on his editorship. What, in particular, appeared to have upset him was the accusation of 'repression':

In what way is the 'instrument of literary criticism', called neo-classicism, so repressive? What testimony of 'repression' of anything valuable can be advanced? If this reproach is addressed to us—and at whom else can it be levelled?—it reads more like the cry of a muddled neo-communist against what he believes to be, to adopt his own jargon, a form of neo-fascism. We have always assumed that certain men of genius, such as Mr. D. H. Lawrence, were simply irrepressible and therefore not to be repressed, and we have printed them without attempting to repress them.[63]

Douglas Garman expressed the *Calendar*'s indignation at Eliot's 'unconsidered, semi-political jeer' of 'neo-communism' (a jeer presumably directed at Garman who had just returned from the Soviet Union). Sensitivity to political allegiances and class-based nuances of 'tone' were highly charged in the aftermath of the General Strike, and further embittered by the prolonged coal

---

[62] 'Art and Knowledge', *Calendar* (Apr. 1927), 58–9.
[63] 'A Commentary', *Criterion* (June 1927), 284–5.

strike. The suggestion that Eliot might actively repress Lawrence, the coalminer's son contributing to the *Calendar*, touched a raw nerve. According to Garman, the repression entailed by the *Criterion* was disseminated by means of 'an over-insistence or an undue appreciation of the dogmas which support neo-classicism'. He continued:

The stately editorial 'We', in many cases so justly inspiring confidence, has sometimes introduced judgements of a less indisputable nature, and Mr. Higgins has reason for his fear that such judgements, acquiring prestige from the same 'calm and socialized demeanour', should delude both their writer and reader.[64]

This verdict appeared in the last issue of the *Calendar* (July 1927). The court of appeal moved to the *Criterion*, where Higgins launched a guerrilla raid from the correspondence columns. Few of his points were well made and Higgins's facetiousness pointed towards a deterioration in the level of discussion.[65] Eliot defended the *Criterion* once more in his Commentary, although it was hard to forget that the *Calendar* no longer possessed full rights of debate. Eliot's solemnity, bordering upon pomposity, really did amount to a mildly authoritarian form of repression. His defensiveness confirmed a residual anxiety:

We could only 'repress' a writer of genius by influencing him, and the repression consequently would take the form of the writer's criticism of his own work. If there is any other repression, it is only in the sense in which Mr. Jack Dempsey is anxious to repress Mr. Gene Tunney.[66]

The wounded air was disingenuous: the editor of the *Criterion* was shrewd enough to know that editorial commission and omission was a more sophisticated instrument of restraint than any heavyweight boxing glove.

In their defiant 'Valediction Forbidding Mourning', the editors of the *Calendar* uncharitably adduced: 'we shall not be surprised to observe more satisfaction than dismay among our contemporaries since the fact [of the *Calendar*'s demise] approves them relatively more seaworthy.' The *Calendar* used its dying breath to fire a barely disguised parting shot at the *Criterion*: 'One can have

---

[64] 'Notes and Reviews', *Calendar* (July 1927), 155.
[65] See 'Correspondence', *Criterion* (Sept. 1927), 258–9.
[66] 'A Commentary', *Criterion* (Sept. 1927), 194.

little respect for the periodical which flaunts a pretension to philosophic righteousness and yet makes as many blunders with regard to the actual works of poetry or literature before it as the most unenlightened of its Georgian predecessors.'[67] Eliot, on the other hand, graciously acknowledged a debt to the *Calendar*:

We take the opportunity of expressing regret at the suspension of *The Calendar*. Were the demise of one literary review useful to the success of another, we should assume no mask of hypocrisy; but this is not at all the fact. Our complaint against most of our contemporaries is that they are so little interested in ideas that it is never worth while either to agree or disagree with them; but in *The Calendar* and *The Adelphi* we have sometimes found, at least, a common ground for disagreement.[68]

The *Calendar*'s 'Valediction' spoke of the exigencies of the 'present literary situation' that required 'a different organization', presumably referring to the reorganization of the *Calendar* team on the editorial staff of Wishart & Company. Nevertheless, in the year in which Humbert Wolfe's *Requiem* went into multiple impressions,[69] the howl of hostility that greeted Wishart's publication of *Scrutinies by Various Writers* (1928)—predominantly 'Scrutinies' reprinted from the *Calendar*—was an index of the great resistance the *Calendar* had faced in attempting to emerge from the literary underworld.[70] The *Calendar* numbered the *Criterion* among the London literary cliques who had marginalized them.[71]

The appearance of the *Calendar*, although Rickword and his team remained personally unknown to Eliot,[72] significantly affected the *Criterion*. For one thing, the stringency of the *Calendar*'s reviewing of contemporary work gave a salutary jolt to the *Criterion* and set the yardstick by which Eliot measured some of his own editorial standards. In the prospectus for the *Monthly Criterion*, Eliot followed the *Calendar*'s example and told readers that the review section did not intend to be comprehensive, rather

---

[67] 'Valediction Forbidding Mourning', *Calendar* (July 1927), 176.

[68] 'A Commentary', *Criterion* (Sept. 1927), 194.

[69] See Philip Bagguley, *Harlequin in Whitehall* (London, 1997), 247.

[70] 'Terror of emotion and dismay before any constructive ideal or effort of intelligence chiefly mark these critics' (*TLS* (10 May 1928), 362). The volume was not reviewed in the *Criterion*.

[71] John Holms scolded 'the school to which Mr. Read belongs' ('Notes and Reviews', *Calendar* (Oct. 1926), 251).

[72] See T. S. Eliot to Thomas MacGreevy, 6 Sept. 1927. Dublin.

to appraise carefully selected books with greater care than the
weeklies. The review section of the *Criterion* continued to grow in
length and prestige, eventually taking up one-third of the magazine
and employing a distinguished array of reviewers.[73] In the longer
term, the shock waves sent out by the *Calendar*, for all the animosity they initially engendered, helped to clear the literary terrain of
moribund writing, preparing the ground for a wider critical reception of many of the young talents sponsored in the *Criterion*. By the
appearance of a second volume of *Scrutinies* (1931), made up of
essays on Eliot and other post-war writers (some from *Criterion*
hands), the reorientation was more readily accepted. In the *Criterion*, H. P. Collins greeted the collection as representative of
'a group of critical writers, most of them almost unknown, who
possess a detachment and a capacity for subtle differentiation
and analysis that would have been incomprehensible a dozen years
ago. . . . as isolated fruits in the wilderness of contemporary journalism they would afford a tonic, if bitter, stimulus'.[74]

In 1932, F. R. Leavis described the *Calendar* as 'that uniquely
intelligent review which, from 1925 to 1927, was, it is hardly exces-
sive to say, the critical consciousness of the younger adult genera-
tions'.[75] Leavis, who had tasted the bitter stimulus of the Western
Front, took many of his critical valuations (for instance, his admiration for T. F. Powys and disapproval of Humbert Wolfe) from the
Calendar. In his influential introduction to the Wishart selection of
criticism from the *Calendar*, he claimed that the journal had 'laid
down the grounds of criticism upon which T. S. Eliot was to be duly
appraised, so that recognition of his significance came as a matter of
course'.[76] At this time, Leavis's programmatic account of the *Calendar* had more to do with preparing the entry of *Scrutiny* into the
London literary world, than with any deep engagement with the
current work of Rickword and Garman, whom he quickly found
were too maverick, politically radical, and indeed hostile to Eliot,
for prolonged collaboration.[77] By the end of the 1930s, it was

---

[73] From Apr. 1931, Edwin Muir contributed 12 book reviews, 2 poems, and a
translation (with his wife Willa) of Hermann Broch.

[74] 'Books of the Quarter', *Criterion* (July 1931), 745–6.

[75] *New Bearings in English Poetry* (London, 1932), 1.

[76] 'Introduction', *Towards Standards of Criticism*, 22.

[77] Edgell Rickword and Douglas Garman contributed to *Scrutiny* from Sept. 1932
until Sept. 1933. In 1938, F. R. Leavis told L. C. Knights that he was surprised that
Garman remembered him with anything but a puzzled hostility. Private collection.

clear that Rickword, the author of Popular Front editorials in *Left Review* and the satirical poem 'To the Wife of a Non-Interventionist Statesman', shared little common ground with the author of non-interventionist *Criterion* Commentaries.[78] Rickword and Garman joined the Communist Party in the 1930s, although it must be recalled that the *Calendar* had no prescribed doctrinal basis.[79] Its real mission was a cultural regeneration brought about by a new system of literary values: the consolidation of authoritative 'standards' in the wake of the First World War. The brief episode of the *Calendar*, then, was an illustration and inspiration to the founders of *Scrutiny* of the cultural aspirations of a literary magazine.

The difference was that the Leavises went to considerable pains to enlist a vigorous and committed body of readers, a 'saving remnant' of loyal subscribers, who would keep the journal afloat in the stormy waters of periodical journalism. Frank Kermode's remark that the *Calendar* was 'rather too good for any possible audience'[80] begs its own questions, just as Malcolm Bradbury's eulogy in the Cass reprint did not escape the pitfalls of hindsight. Accepting Leavis's valuation of the *Calendar* almost uncritically, Bradbury failed to appreciate that the magazine's small band of admirers were not so much few and fit but posthumous, prepared by a sea-change in the world of literary journalism after the Second World War. It is important not to exaggerate the detachment of the *Calendar* from the milieu of metropolitan literary journalism, nor exaggerate its difference from the *Criterion*, with whom it shared contributors, readers, and even an opportunistic appeal for 'classical' standards. The achievement of the *Calendar* depended on a mixture of reciprocity and rivalry with the *Criterion*, illustrated by an extended public debate regarding the function of a literary review. This complex, contested, and at times acrimonious relationship can perhaps be best understood in the dialectical terms advanced by Rickword and Garman: Action to Re-action.

---

[78] Rickword wrote progressively more hostile reviews of Eliot's works during the 1930s in *Scrutiny, Left Review*, and the *Daily Worker*. See *Literature in Society: Essays and Opinions II, 1931–1978*, ed. Alan Young (Manchester, 1978).

[79] Two contributors to the *Calendar*, Wyndham Lewis and Cecil Gray, were bitterly anti-communist.   [80] 'The Calendar of Modern Letters', 320.

3

Scrutiny
Critics from Cambridge

> In the light of modern research, it is becoming clear that we
> may talk about society as an organism, and do more than use
> a metaphor. And we see the part that journalism might play
> in such an organism.
>
> F. R. Leavis, 'The Relationship of Journalism to Literature'
> (1924), cited in Ian MacKillop, *F. R. Leavis: A Life in
> Criticism* (London, 1995), 123

A considerable amount of light is shed on the *Criterion*'s place
within the field of inter-war literary journalism by considering its
relations with *Scrutiny*. Eliot's poetry and critical theories were
nowhere more influential than in an undergraduate Cambridge
dominated by the followers of I. A. Richards and F. R. Leavis. In
particular, Leavis's generalizations of the implications of Eliot's
early critical pronouncements shaped many of the crusades and
battles fought by *Scrutiny* during its formative years. Looking
back at Leavis's self-congratulatory 'Retrospect' for the 1963
Cambridge University Press reprint of *Scrutiny*, however, it is
remarkable to note just how far he had come to repudiate the
social and cultural values promulgated by the *Criterion*. But there
is a danger in taking Leavis's exaggerated post-war accounts of
the antagonism between the respective journals at face value: a
reading complicated by the similarity of their pessimistic diagnosis of cultural decline, in the appeal to Arnoldian minority 'standards', and in the relations that various Cambridge critics, most
importantly L. C. Knights, maintained with both journals. These
details suggest closer connections and less direct rivalry than are
commonly assumed. The tangled interplay of running relations

between the *Criterion* and *Scrutiny* is a sensitive recorder of the extent to which mutations in a specific cultural milieu could determine the agenda of inter-war literary journalism.

I

In 1926, on the strength of the growing reputation of *The Sacred Wood* and *Homage to John Dryden*, Eliot delivered the Clark Lectures at Cambridge. They were attended *en masse* by the newly developing English School.[1] At a series of informal weekly coffee-circles Eliot met promising undergraduates. One of those undergraduates, William Empson, kept Cambridge informed about the *Criterion* in his capacity as the literary editor of the student magazine *Granta*. In November 1927, Empson praised the first five volumes of the monthly *Criterion* for their coverage of European literature and for their elaboration of 'intelligence' as a critical touchstone. However, by February 1928 he was less impressed and concluded: 'I am afraid the *Criterion* has been rather dull lately.'[2] In October 1928, Empson's successor at *Granta*, T. H. White, complained that the *Criterion* was now regrettably old-fashioned.[3] If undergraduate Cambridge began to display a note of caution towards the *Criterion*, then Eliot's example as a modernist poet was still in the ascendant. Two rival student magazines, the *Venture* and *Experiment*, launched in November 1928, displayed a marked preoccupation with Eliot and aside from much incidental comment, published essays on his poetry by Empson, Martin Turnell, and Elsie Phare.[4]

I. A. Richards's crowded Cambridge lectures had performed the necessary groundwork for the academic study of Eliot. His role as chief apologist for this disconcertingly modern poet was soon seconded, even superseded, by another Cambridge lecturer. In 1929, Richards informed Eliot that F. R. Leavis, a probationary lecturer in the Faculty, was 'a good supervisor on literary and general critical matters'.[5] It was Leavis's lectures on contemporary poetry, building

---

[1] For details see George Watson, 'The Cambridge Lectures of T. S. Eliot', *Sewanee Review* (Fall 1991).

[2] See *Empson in Granta* (London, 1993), 25–6 and 43.

[3] 'Crites' [T. H. White], *Granta* (12 Oct. 1928), 25.

[4] See my '*Experiment* in Cambridge', *Cambridge Quarterly* (Dec. 1998), 287–309.

[5] *Selected Letters of I. A. Richards*, ed. John Constable (Oxford, 1990), 49.

on the repudiation of romantic and Georgian aesthetics outlined in Eliot's volumes of collected journalism that did much to establish his cult status at Cambridge. In February 1929, Leavis's article 'T. S. Eliot: A Reply to the Condescending' in the *Cambridge Review* fired a broadside at 'condescending' remarks made in a *New Statesman* review of *For Lancelot Andrewes*.[6] Leavis mistakenly believed that the review had been written by a member of the Cambridge English Faculty, F. L. Lucas, a poet and critic with Bloomsbury connections and 'openly hostile' to Eliot.[7] In the *Cambridge Review* in March 1929, Lucas expressed his dislike of the Eliot 'contagion' infecting Cambridge and he certainly wrote condescendingly about Eliot in Desmond MacCarthy's monthly *Life and Letters*: 'I would far rather a young man spent his time reading *The Earthly Paradise* on his back in a punt (I do not say he could not do better) than stewing over the *Criterion*.'[8] All the same, the young men (and women) continued to stew over the *Criterion*. Eliot's influence was analysed by Leavis, in its positive and negative manifestations, in reviews of two Hogarth volumes of *Cambridge Poetry*.[9] In short, in the Cambridge English School *c*. 1930, it was impossible *not* to have an opinion on Eliot: 'the man really responsible', according to E. M. W. Tillyard, Secretary of the Faculty Board of English, 'for introducing into Cambridge a set of ideas that both shocked and satisfied'.[10]

By the spring of 1931, the *Venture* and *Experiment* had folded. Furthermore, Leavis lost his foothold in the donnish and semi-institutional *Cambridge Review*, complaining to his friend Ian Parsons (a former *Cambridge Review* editor) that his proffered reviews were 'put in the waste-paper basket'.[11] He suspected the machinations of Tillyard, although the breach is more simply

[6] See [R. Ellis Roberts], 'For T. S. Eliot', *New Statesman* (29 Dec. 1928), 387–8, and F. R. Leavis, 'T. S. Eliot: A Reply to the Condescending', *Cambridge Review* (8 Feb. 1929), 55–71.

[7] See E. M. W. Tillyard, *The Muse Unchained* (London, 1958), 98–9.

[8] See the *Cambridge Review* (26 Apr. 1929), 395, and 'Criticism', *Life and Letters* (Nov. 1929), 462. It is worth pointing out that Eliot had been critical of Lucas's edition of *The Complete Works of John Webster* in the *Criterion* (June 1928), 443–6.

[9] See 'Cambridge Poetry', *Cambridge Review* (1 Mar. 1929 and 16 May 1930). Sherard Vines noted the volumes of *Cambridge Poetry* in the *Criterion*.

[10] *The Muse Unchained*, 98.

[11] F. R. Leavis to Ian Parsons, 25 Aug. 1931. Cited in G. S. Singh, *F. R. Leavis: A Literary Biography* (London, 1995), 264–5.

explained by the departure of his former pupil, Geoffrey Rossetti, as the editor of the review.[12] Leavis compensated for his increasing isolation in Cambridge by organizing Friday tea-parties at his home in Chesterton Hall Crescent, overseen by his wife Queenie Roth—a brilliant English graduate now researching a doctoral thesis on fiction and the reading public—and attended by other promising graduates, including L. C. Knights, Denys Thompson, and Muriel Bradbrook. Leavis also published a few pamphlets under the imprint of Gordon Fraser's Minority Press.[13] The most influential of these, *Mass Civilisation and Minority Culture* (1930), was a diagnosis of a perceived cultural crisis in England and its effects upon an oppositional and dissident 'small minority' resisting the standardization of culture in a mass civilization. According to *Mass Civilisation and Minority Culture*, in the field of the serious critical review: 'The *Criterion* carries on almost alone.'[14] The pamphlet was sent to Eliot, who approved of its thesis. In October 1931, Leavis was invited to Russell Square.

As an attentive reader of the *Criterion*, Leavis would have liked to find a place in Eliot's quarterly. He travelled to London in the hope of securing permission to review T. F. Powys's *Unclay*, but the commission was not forthcoming.[15] Instead, Eliot asked Leavis to write a successor to *Mass Civilisation and Minority Culture* for the Criterion Miscellany pamphlet series. However, when Leavis read the *Criterion* during the train journey to London he was annoyed by F. S. Flint's 'Verse Chronicle'. Flint had noticed the appearance of *The Loosening and Other Poems* by Ronald Bottrall but passed it over without comment. Leavis had a special interest in Bottrall, a Cambridge graduate teaching in Finland who had appealed to him for advice and support. He had counselled Bottrall

---

[12] Geoffrey Rossetti and Ian Parsons each contributed a single article to the *Criterion*. In the *Cambridge Review* 'D.M.' complained of the *Criterion*'s 'growing pompousness', adding 'old age is freezing the *Criterion*'s blood; however, it remains pre-eminent' ((30 Oct. 1931), 74).

[13] Fraser was an enterprising undergraduate at St John's College, Cambridge, supported financially by his father.

[14] *Mass Civilisation and Minority Culture* (Cambridge, 1930), 19.

[15] Leavis had submitted an essay on Powys to the *Criterion*, although he confided to Parsons: 'I often suspect (and seeing the average quality of it, hope) that [Eliot] hasn't much to do with the running of the "Criterion".' F. R. Leavis to Ian Parsons, 25 Aug. 1931. Cited in Singh, *F. R. Leavis*, 265.

to send his poems to Faber and after Eliot declined to publish them, he secured publication of *The Loosening* by the Minority Press. On Christmas Day 1931, Leavis wrote a deferential, almost obsequious, letter to the editor of the *Criterion*, pointing out Flint's shortcomings as a reviewer. Eliot printed the letter in January 1932; it was to be Leavis's only contribution to the *Criterion*.[16] The pamphlet commissioned for the Criterion Miscellany, a sweeping indictment of the alleged superficiality and corruption of the metropolitan literary world, including Bonamy Dobrée, Desmond MacCarthy, and the Royal Society of Literature, could not possibly appear under Eliot's patronage.[17] Eliot was a member of the Royal Society of Literature and an acquaintance of Dobrée and MacCarthy. He toyed with the idea of revising Leavis's essay, but he eventually chose not to publish the pamphlet: the tone of Leavis's jeremiad would have proved an embarrassment for him. Leavis later claimed that Eliot's decision pointed to an 'editorial determination to maintain a solidarity' with the metropolitan literary world, 'plain to see, once one's eye had lost its respectful innocence'.[18]

In February 1932, Chatto & Windus published Leavis's *New Bearings in English Poetry*—a book that helped to consolidate the modernist movement in poetry. According to Leavis, Eliot and Pound exemplified the disintegration of the 'modern sensibility' and, although both Americans by birth, were the best models for the contemporary English poet. *New Bearings* closed with a short 'Epilogue' praising the poetry of Bottrall and Empson—Leavis's standard-bearers for the post-Eliot tradition.[19] In April, Chatto published Queenie's *Fiction and the Reading Public*, the fruits of her doctoral dissertation. Her supervisor, I. A. Richards, advised caution and a wholesale revision of the thesis before publication, but she was reluctant to wait.[20] The book contains all that is best and worst about Queenie's trenchant prose style; characterized by Muriel Bradbrook as a 'St.Trinian style, with such vigorous and

[16] See 'Correspondence', *Criterion* (Jan. 1932), 509–10.
[17] For Leavis's reworked version of the projected Criterion Miscellany pamphlet, see 'What's Wrong With Criticism?', *Scrutiny* (Sept. 1932), 132–46.
[18] 'A Retrospect', *Scrutiny* (Cambridge, 1963), 3.
[19] 'Epilogue', *New Bearings in English Poetry* (London, 1932), 144–57. Chatto & Windus did not send a review copy of *New Bearings* to the *Criterion*. It was not noticed.
[20] See I. A. Richards to Q. D. Leavis, 27 Nov. [1931]. Cambridge (Magdalene).

well aimed thumping and jumping'.[21] In fact, the sociological (or as the Leavises preferred to describe it 'anthropological') approach of *Fiction and the Reading Public*, served to reconnoitre the potential readership of a serious critical review. In brief, Queenie claimed to trace the 'disintegration' of the reading public into stratified levels: subscribers to the *Criterion* represented the 'highbrow' élite, whereas the readers of the contemporary bestseller or the commercial popular press a deplorably 'lowbrow' mass consumer.[22] She looked nostalgically at the readership of Francis Jeffrey's *Edinburgh Review*—reputedly 13,500 in 1818—and compared it with the exiguous circulation that had brought about the collapse of the *Calendar*.[23] She concluded on a defiant note:

If there is any hope, it must lie in conscious and directed effort. All that can be done, it must be realised, must take the form of resistance by an armed and conscious minority. . . . There might be such people, if rallied, to support a periodical and provide a sure public for a publisher.[24]

And that public, it was implied, could be rallied in Cambridge.

II

In July 1932, the *Criterion* Commentary noted the appearance of *Fiction and the Reading Public*. Eliot expressed his belief that it was 'a useful book' and that he shared Queenie's conclusions 'up to a certain point'. That said, Eliot found the martial histrionics of the 'armed and conscious minority' alarmist and indicative of a lost cause. Moving on to the ecclesiastical higher ground, he observed: 'anyone who is committed to religious dogma must also be committed to a theory of art which insists upon the permanent as well as the changing.'[25] Talk of religious dogma, as well as of the transitory and the permanent, may have been Eliot's way of throwing down a challenge to a new competitor in the

[21] 'Queenie Leavis: The Dynamics of Rejection', *The Collected Papers of Muriel Bradbrook* (Brighton, 1982), 127.
[22] '*The Criterion* will review only those novels which have some pretensions to literary merit and can be criticised by serious standards' (*Fiction and the Reading Public*, 19–20).
[23] *Scrutiny* published Denys Thompson's article on the nineteenth-century 'higher journalism' (June 1935) and extracts from Gordon Cox's doctoral thesis on the Great Reviews (June and Sept. 1937).   [24] *Fiction and the Reading Public*, 270, 272.
[25] 'A Commentary', *Criterion* (July 1932), 676–9.

quarterly periodical market. For by this time the Leavises had ended up in control of *Scrutiny* by virtue of a state of affairs something akin to the determination of the cuckoo to take over the nest. Early in 1932, Knights and Donald Culver had approached the Leavises for assistance with a faltering student magazine and found them eager to give direction to the venture, pledging capital and rallying support.[26] When the first number of the review appeared in May 1932, it sported a pearl-grey cover and a format redolent of the *Calendar*. More than that, Leavis had chosen the title in homage to the scrupulous critical 'Scrutinies' sponsored in the *Calendar*.

Although Leavis's name did not initially appear on the editorial masthead, owing to mysterious 'politic reasons'[27] that were symptomatic of his rather cloak-and-dagger relationship with the literary and academic worlds (some called it persecution mania[28]), he carefully proof-read Knights and Culver's editorial manifesto. It contained the requisite smattering of Arnoldian keywords: namely, a concern for 'standards of living' and the function of a 'serious critical review'. Outlining the journal's *raison d'être*, Knights and Culver felt obliged to acknowledge the prior existence of the *Criterion*, albeit tucked away in a footnote:

There is of course *The Criterion*, of which it is difficult to speak without respect. It is still the most serious as it is the most intelligent of our journals. But its high price, a certain tendency to substitute solemnity for seriousness, and, during the last two years, a narrowing of its interests, prevent it from influencing more than a small proportion of the reading public. It is necessary, but not the *unum necessarium*.[29]

By December 1932, in the course of a principled objection to the current vogue of intellectual Marxism, Leavis felt confident enough to reject outright the *Criterion* 'philosophy':

The effective particularity we can fairly demand would involve maintaining in *The Criterion* high standards of thinking and of literary criticism.

---

[26] For details of the setting up of *Scrutiny*, see L. C. Knights, 'Remembering Scrutiny', *Sewanee Review* (Fall 1981), 560–85.

[27] F. R. Leavis to Ian Parsons, 9 Feb. 1932. Cited in Singh, *F. R. Leavis*, 266.

[28] Leavis claimed that *Scrutiny* was 'an outlaw enterprise' in Cambridge, pointing out that when the journal was launched in 1932 neither he nor Queenie held a college fellowship or was a full-time lecturer in the English Faculty. However, it would be impossible to describe such early contributors as Goldsworthy Lowes Dickinson, Herbert Butterfield, Joseph Needham, Michael Oakeshott, I. A. Richards, or L. C. Knights and Muriel Bradbrook, as 'outlaws' in Cambridge.

[29] 'Scrutiny: A Manifesto', *Scrutiny* (May 1932), 3 n. 1.

The point that it is necessary to make is, in view of our own enterprise, a delicate one, but only the more necessary for that. Let us suffer the retort when, and as much as, we may deserve it, and express now the general regret that the name of *The Criterion* has become so dismal an irony and that the Editor is far from applying to his contributors the standards we have learnt from him.

The relevance of the point may be enforced by remarking the particular weakness of *The Criterion* for the dead, academic kind of abstract 'thinking', especially when the 'thinker' (incapable of literary criticism) stands in a general, abstract way for 'order,' 'intelligence' and other counters, all of which are worth less than nothing if not related scrupulously to the concrete.[30]

For all Leavis's tortuous self-justifications, spiced with taunts of 'academic', *Scrutiny* sought an intellectual audience contiguous with that of the *Criterion*. The difference was demarcated partly in terms of price—*Scrutiny* at 2s. 6d. (10s. per annum) was certainly much cheaper than the *Criterion* at 7s. 6d. (30s. per annum). *Scrutiny*'s original print-run of 500 began to sell out regularly and the journal soon printed 750 copies per issue, quite possibly higher than the circulation of the *Criterion*. Reliable information about the respective readerships of both journals is difficult to obtain, although it is possible to infer from editorial comments, lists of contributors, and published correspondence, that *Scrutiny* circulated more widely among professional English teachers and readers from a provincial or a lower-middle-class background. A cross-section of the *Criterion*'s 'intellectual minority' (as Denys Thompson described it) was more metropolitan and ecclesiastical. *Scrutiny* could not afford to pay contributors and did not have a salaried editorial staff (it had no business manager; Queenie—to the detriment of her health and her own writing career—bore the brunt of the secretarial duties), but, in time, a committed body of subscribers, the mainstay of any unsubsidized small circulation magazine, was established allowing the journal to escape early financial ruin.[31]

[30] 'Under Which King, Bezonian?', *Scrutiny* (Dec. 1932), 213.

[31] From Sept. 1932, *Scrutiny* carried a subscription form inside the back cover. Editorials made impassioned appeals for 'all buyers to become subscribers'. See 'Appeal to Readers', *Scrutiny* (Mar. 1933), 314.

By the end of 1933, Culver had left Cambridge for Paris and Leavis, together with Denys Thompson[32] and D. W. Harding[33] joined Knights on the editorial board of *Scrutiny*. Following a period of intense strain and overwork, especially for Knights and the Leavises, *Scrutiny* found its feet and commanded a loyal and enthusiastic public interest.[34] In 1933, Eliot declined Knights's invitation to contribute to *Scrutiny*, although in the following year the journal began to carry a regular full-page advertisement for the *Criterion*.[35] For an initial period the advertisement enticed readers of *Scrutiny* with a free 'specimen copy'. The *Criterion*, secure in the knowledge of Faber's financial backing, had no reason to feel unduly threatened by *Scrutiny*. The Leavises, on the other hand, bitterly bemoaned Eliot for not supporting *Scrutiny* with some favourable publicity in his well-established quarterly. It should not be forgotten, however, that Eliot personally subscribed to *Scrutiny* or that the *Criterion* regularly advertised Leavis's journal in its pages. More than that, *Scrutiny* was even conscious of *gaining* a portion of its readers from the *Criterion*: the 'Notes on Contributors' for March 1933 introduced James Smith and A. L. Morton as 'familiar' and 'known' to readers of the *Criterion*, respectively.

In the summer of 1934, Leavis assembled a series of early critical articles from *Scrutiny* under the rubric *Determinations*, including essays from three *Criterion* contributors—Knights, Smith, and Empson—and with an epigraph taken from Eliot's *Criterion* essay 'The Function of Criticism'. The volume was sold outright to Chatto to generate extra revenue for *Scrutiny*. It also served to spell out what Leavis called 'a clear and full conception of literary criticism, its function, its scope and responsibilities'.[36] The

---

[32] Denys Thompson was the co-author with Leavis of the pedagogic handbook *Culture and Environment*. The French poet, Marcel Aurousseau, reviewed *Culture and Environment* in the *Criterion*. He suggested many of the critical passages were 'unworthy of the critical gift of Mr. Leavis' and that the remarks on the 'organic community' exaggerated the evils of modern education and entertainment. See 'Books of the Quarter', *Criterion* (Oct. 1933), 136–7.

[33] Leavis described D. W. Harding as 'the most intelligent of all my pupils'. Cited in Knights, 'Remembering *Scrutiny*', 562.

[34] See Q. D. Leavis to L. C. Knights, Oct. 1933. Private collection.

[35] See T. S. Eliot to L. C. Knights, 8 Oct. 1933. Texas. Apart from the *Criterion*, the only other regular advertisers in *Scrutiny* during the 1930s were the journal's printers, S. G. Marshall, and a few Cambridge booksellers.

[36] F. R. Leavis, 'Introduction', *Determinations* (London, 1934), 1.

distinctive nature of 'Cambridge Criticism' (a title Leavis initially proposed for *Determinations*) tacitly defined itself in opposition to the *Criterion*, so that the *New English Weekly* felt the critical standpoints of the two journals worthy of comparison.[37] When *Determinations* came up for review in the *Criterion*, Eliot generously passed the volume to a regular *Scrutiny* contributor, Frank Chapman, a secondary school teacher and former literary editor of *Granta*. Hardly surprisingly, Chapman commented upon the 'admirable proof of the validity of *Scrutiny*'s aims' and 'the positive achievement of the group'—a glaring example of the sort of back-slapping *Scrutiny* deplored as 'clique-puffery'.[38]

Determinations exhibited the first fractures of a subsequent full-scale schism within Cambridge English. In the *Criterion*, Chapman had praised 'two admirably reasoned essays': critical revaluations of the work of I. A. Richards and his collaborator C. K. Ogden, written by Harding and the Cambridge political philosopher Michael Oakeshott.[39] Both essays were judicious and closely argued, but their double inclusion in a volume of 'Cambridge criticism' would not have gone unnoticed by supporters of Richards. Knights attempted to keep Richards on board by inviting him to respond in the pages of *Scrutiny*.[40] However, when Knights took up a full-time position at Manchester University, editorial control of *Scrutiny* resided firmly within Chesterton Hall Crescent.[41] A definite breach with Richards was made in 1935, in the course of a long 'diagnostic' review of *Coleridge on Imagination*.[42]

---

[37] 'Ille Ego' noted that *Scrutiny* 'obviously derives from T. S. Eliot', but was 'dissatisfied with Eliot'. He attempted to distinguish *Scrutiny*'s literary-critical mission from the *Criterion*'s religio-cultural credo: 'The *Criterion* judges; *Scrutiny* scrutinises. Compared to judgement, scrutiny is a non-committal occupation' ('Readers and Writers', *New English Weekly* (5 Jan. 1933), 282). Leavis replied that the *Criterion*'s standards of 'intelligence, tradition and orthodox Christianity' could lead to 'negation', 'nullity', and 'impotent abstraction' ('Restatements for Critics', *Scrutiny* (Mar. 1933), 316).

[38] 'Books of the Quarter', *Criterion* (Oct. 1934), 125–8.

[39] Harding recalled: 'Leavis did suggest that I should write on Richards, at a time when he was disappointed in hopes for Richards's personal support and knew that my admiration of Richards's early work was tempered by a sense of its limitations.' Cited in Denys Thompson (ed.), *The Leavises* (Cambridge, 1984), 197. Leavis thought Harding's critique of Richards was 'extraordinarily well done'. Cited in Singh, *F. R. Leavis*, 50.

[40] Richards responded to Oakeshott in 'Bentham's Theory of Fictions', *Scrutiny* (Mar. 1933), 406–10.

[41] Harding was a lecturer on psychology at the London School of Economics and Thompson a schoolteacher at Gresham's in Norfolk.

[42] 'Dr. Richards, Bentham and Coleridge', *Scrutiny* (Mar. 1935), 384–400.

Leavis argued that *Coleridge on Imagination* demonstrated that Richards had abandoned the true function of literary criticism for a crude 'Benthamite' theory of value. He complained that the author of *Practical Criticism* displayed little aptitude for the rigorous close reading of poetry. Reading the attack in *Scrutiny*, Eliot speculated upon the causes of Leavis's bad temper.[43] Richards could only surmise: 'I suppose it was just my turn (as his last friend here in the Faculty!). You mind what you do, it will be your turn before long!'[44]

When William Empson visited Russell Square, Eliot apparently told him that he thought Leavis's review was 'disgusting'.[45] The animus seems exaggerated and was perhaps designed for the benefit of Richards's star pupil (Eliot, after all, was praised in Leavis's review and would have had some sympathy with the broad outline, if not the tone, of Leavis's critique[46]). After consultation with Richards, Eliot passed a review copy of *Coleridge on Imagination* to Empson, who noticed it favourably in the *Criterion*.[47] Empson prefaced his comments by drawing attention to 'a review of this extremely good book which gave much space to complaints about its arrogance', a reference which greatly angered Leavis.[48] Empson also sent a spirited defence of *Coleridge on Imagination* to *Scrutiny*, expressing some consternation about 'the feverish atmosphere of Dr. Leavis's quarrels'. The letter was printed with extreme reluctance. Leavis appended a laconic editorial footnote: 'No comment on the above seems necessary. Mr. Empson is referred back to his texts.'[49] One of the more unfortunate consequences

[43] T. S. Eliot to I. A. Richards, 16 May 1935. Cambridge (Magdalene).

[44] *Selected Letters of I. A. Richards*, ed. Constable, p. xli.

[45] See 'The Hammer's Ring', in Reuben Brower, Helen Vendler, and John Hollander (eds.), *I. A. Richards: Essays in His Honor* (New York, 1973), 74–5.

[46] The extant correspondence between Eliot and Leavis held at Texas suggests cordial relations during 1934–6. However, Eliot did express some irritation to third parties. On 12 Feb. 1934, Dorothy Richards recorded in her diary that Eliot had described Leavis as a, 'little dog who chases after motorbikes'. See John Constable, 'Introduction', *I. A. Richards and his Critics: Selected Reviews and Critical Articles* (London, 2001), p. lxi. See also T. S. Eliot to Ezra Pound, 19 Dec. 1934. Yale. T. S. Eliot to Stephen Spender, 9 May 1935. Northwestern.

[47] T. S. Eliot to I. A. Richards, 19 Nov. 1934. Cambridge (Magdalene). Charles Madge and Elsie Phare were mooted as possible reviewers.

[48] See 'Books of the Quarter', *Criterion* (Apr. 1935), 482. Leavis described Empson's review as 'downright stupid'. Cited in Ian MacKillop, *F. R. Leavis: A Life in Criticism* (London, 1995), 206.   [49] See 'Correspondence', *Scrutiny* (June 1935), 65–7.

of this bruising encounter over *Coleridge on Imagination* was Empson's withdrawal from *Scrutiny*—a significant loss for any project of 'Cambridge criticism'.[50]

Empson had returned from Tokyo in the summer of 1934, keen to make a living as a freelance writer in London but also eager to interest *Scrutiny* in essays that had appeared in Japanese journals. Leavis did not like Empson's post-Cambridge development. He decided not to publish Empson's Freudian analysis of *Alice in Wonderland* in *Scrutiny* and described the essay on Marvell included in *Determinations* as the 'least of anything in the book'.[51] He was equally critical of what he believed to be Empson's lack of poetic development.[52] Privately, the Leavises mourned Empson's reluctance to break free from what they saw as Richards's inhibiting influence. It was left to H. A. Mason, a forthright young critic recruited from Oxford, to deliver the inevitable *Scrutiny* 'placing' of Empson in limiting valuations of *Some Versions of Pastoral* and *Poems* (both 1935). The tone of Mason's comments may be summarized by his remark on the dangers implicit in Empson's precocious brilliance: 'the exhibition of a fine intelligence applied and misapplied.'[53] Thereafter, Empson published poems, reviews, and his dense theoretical explorations of the structure of 'complex words' in the *Criterion*; no doubt, further evidence to the acutely class-conscious Leavis that this well-bred Wykehamist (as Leavis occasionally referred to Empson) had betrayed the mission of Cambridge criticism for the modish metropolitan literary world.

In fact, Richards was correct about the subsequent focus of *Scrutiny* invective. In the essay 'Religion and Literature' (1935) Eliot had declared: 'literary criticism should be completed by criticism from a definite ethical and theological standpoint.'[54] The remark was anathema to Leavis. In June 1936, he delivered a

[50] Leavis greatly admired the poetry and criticism Empson had written at Cambridge. In particular, he praised *Seven Types of Ambiguity* as 'simply the appropriate, critical, and very unusually efficient application of intelligence to poetry' ('The Literary Mind', *Scrutiny* (May 1932), 23).   [51] Cited in Singh, *F. R. Leavis*, 50.

[52] 'The uneasiness that qualified the interest one took in Mr. Empson's work long before he became a New Signature is settling into sad recognition that he is becoming less and less likely to develop. He seems no nearer than before to finding a more radical incitement to the writing of poetry (or of criticism) than pleasure in a strenuous intellectual game' ('This Poetical Renascence', *Scrutiny* (June 1933), 67).

[53] See 'William Empson's Verse' (Dec. 1935) and 'Mr. Empson's Criticism' (Mar. 1936).   [54] *Selected Essays* (London, 1951), 388.

disdainful, at times downright rude, estimation of Eliot's *Essays Ancient and Modern* (1936). The essay 'Modern Education and the Classics' convinced Leavis that 'we cannot take [Eliot's] interest in education very seriously' and he described the generally appreciative essay on Tennyson as 'the worst essay in literary criticism that Mr. Eliot has yet published'.[55] Such details form the background to Stephen Spender's *Criterion* review of *Revaluation: Tradition and Development in English Poetry* (1936), a collection of *Scrutiny* essays in which Leavis traced the development of English poetry from Donne to the point at which *New Bearings in English Poetry* had begun. The 'tradition' was heavily indebted to Eliot, although Leavis studiously avoided his *New Bearings* prefatory genuflection to 'a certain critic and poet',[56] acknowledging instead a debt to 'discussions' and 'collaboration' with his Cambridge students.[57] Spender's review, however, left little doubt about the provenance of many of the ideas expressed in *Revaluation*. Nevertheless, he sharply questioned Leavis's credentials to speak as a critic of poetry, pointing to his 'dull and cumbrous' prose style (a rather unsympathetic response to Leavis's convoluted but expressive syntax) as evidence of the academic's envious appropriation of the 'creative function'.[58]

Leavis's biographer, Ian MacKillop, has suggested that there was nothing 'mischievous' about Eliot's choice of reviewer for *Revaluation*, claiming that it was simply bad luck that the review went to Spender rather than Dobrée, Mario Praz, or James Smith. However, MacKillop underestimates the care with which Eliot apportioned *Criterion* reviews. Unlike Spender, neither Smith nor Praz was a regular reviewer. In point of fact, Smith did not review for the *Criterion* after the launch of *Scrutiny* and Praz reviewed for the *Criterion* only once after he accepted the chair of English Literature at Rome University in 1934. Dobrée, who did not care for *Scrutiny*, had already reviewed *Revaluation* in the *Spectator*.[59] His lukewarm

---

[55] 'Mr. Eliot and Education', *Scrutiny* (June 1936), 84–9.

[56] 'Prefatory Note', *New Bearings in English Poetry*, 9.

[57] 'Introduction', *Revaluation* (London, 1936), 16. The volume was dedicated 'To Downing College' where Leavis had been Director of Studies in English since 1932.

[58] See 'Books of the Quarter', *Criterion* (Jan. 1937), 350–3.

[59] See 'I don't think you are quite fair to my "school" when you say that we (I suppose the people who write for *Scrutiny*) neglect "form" ' (L. C. Knights to Bonamy Dobrée, 30 Sept. 1937. Leeds).

review was evidence of some residual support for Richards over *Coleridge on Imagination*.[60] Spender's review copy of *Revaluation* offers tantalizingly few clues to either his or Eliot's motivation. However, in November 1936, Eliot wrote to express his agreement with several remarks Spender had made about Leavis's limitations as a critic.[61] Many years later, Spender recalled that 'my reasons for being hostile to Leavis were perhaps that he had from the publication of my *Poems* (1933) onwards been completely contemptuous of my poetry in *Scrutiny*'.[62]

It would be possible to assemble a litany of abuse directed at Spender from the pages of *Scrutiny*. In 1933, Leavis ridiculed the praise accorded Spender as the 'lyric poet' of 'this poetical renascence' by the blurb on the dust-jacket of *Poems*: 'whoever was allowed to write it knew nothing about poetry' commented Leavis archly.[63] Since Eliot was Spender's *Criterion* patron, his Faber publisher, and almost certainly the blurb writer for *Poems*, it is highly improbable that Leavis's remarks would have escaped his attention.[64] Bearing in mind Eliot's response to Leavis's treatment of *Coleridge on Imagination* and the increasingly snide remarks about his failing powers as a critic—what author would relish such comments?—MacKillop's interpretation of the *Criterion*'s apparently innocent demolition of *Revaluation* sounds unconvincing. After all, Eliot had the *Criterion* example of Auden's treatment of Elsie Phare's book on Hopkins as an instance of the uneasy tension between Oxford poets and Cambridge critics.[65]

From 1936, *Scrutiny* increasingly took on the appearance of an isolated and sectarian publication preaching to the converted. Morton Dauwen Zabel, the editor of *Poetry* (Chicago) who had

[60] Bonamy Dobrée, 'The Aeolian Harp', *Spectator* (23 Oct. 1936). His sympathy with Richards is recounted in the introduction to the Dobrée Papers, Brotherton Library, Leeds.

[61] T. S. Eliot to Stephen Spender, 5 Nov. 1936. Northwestern.

[62] Cited in MacKillop, *F. R. Leavis*, 429 n. 21. Spender's review copy of *Revaluation* is in the possession of Lady Natasha Spender.

[63] 'This Poetical Renascence', 70.

[64] Leavis conceded as much in 'Keynes, Spender and Currency Values', *Scrutiny* (June 1951), 49–50.

[65] Auden praised Phare's study as 'very intelligent' but ultimately damned it as 'academic' ('Books of the Quarter', *Criterion* (Apr. 1934), 497). Phare was wounded by the criticism, which she believed to be unjust. Elsie Duncan-Jones in conversation with Jason Harding, 15 Dec. 1997, Cambridge.

arranged the exchange of review copies and advertisements with *Scrutiny*, observed: 'Unfortunately, *Scrutiny* suffers—doubtless through economic stringency—by an excess of concentration, shown chiefly by an undeviating sameness of contributors' names in issue after issue.'[66] The loss of Richards, Empson, and Muriel Bradbrook[67] from the original team of contributors was hardly offset by the appearance of young 'Downing men'—Gordon Cox, Geoffrey Walton, Boris Ford, and Wilfrid Mellers.[68] There were still, however, significant lines of affiliation between *Scrutiny* and the *Criterion*. The key figure was L. C. Knights, an important contributor to both journals on Shakespearean criticism. If developments in Shakespeare studies have often been regarded as prototypical of literary criticism *in esse*, then examination of the range of writing on Shakespeare in the *Criterion* and *Scrutiny* may help to differentiate 'the function of criticism' as conceived in these journals.

III

The *Criterion*'s coverage of Shakespeare was initially characterized by the contributions of W. J. Lawrence, a historian of Elizabethan stage conditions,[69] and Eliot's acquaintance, J. M. Robertson, a Liberal politician and the most eminent 'disintegrator' of the Shakespearean canon.[70] In 1926, Eliot commissioned the textual scholar John Dover Wilson, co-editor of the New Cambridge Shakespeare, to write a review of Robertson's *The Problems of the*

---

[66] 'Recent Magazines', *Poetry* [Chicago] (Apr. 1936), 54.

[67] In Oct. 1933 Queenie Leavis told L. C. Knights that *Scrutiny* should no longer publish essays by Bradbrook (private collection). *Determinations* did not contain an essay by her.

[68] Wilfrid Mellers lodged with the Leavises and wrote copiously on music for *Scrutiny* while an undergraduate at Downing College. He has recalled that he had little knowledge of the *Criterion* during the 1930s. Wilfrid Mellers, letter to Jason Harding, 6 Feb. 1999.

[69] See Eliot: 'The name of Mr. W. J. Lawrence stands very high in contemporary scholarship of Elizabethan drama' (*TLS* (8 Dec. 1927), 927).

[70] Although Eliot professed to write on Shakespeare as a literary critic and not as a scholar, he claimed: 'I have always agreed (in the rough) to Mr. Robertson's "disintegration" of the Shakespeare canon.' See the *Nation and Athenaeum* (12 Feb. 1927), 664. In 1936, commenting upon Robertson's hypothesis that *Hamlet* reworked an earlier play by Kyd, Eliot claimed he had now 'come to doubt my own additions to that theory'. See 'Books of the Quarter', *Criterion* (July 1936), 710.

Shakespeare Sonnets for the *Criterion.*[71] Dover Wilson continued to offer his urbane observations to 'the most serious literary review of our day', including polemical exchanges with Robertson; although the two critics masked fundamental methodological differences under good-natured references to 'my friend Professor J. Dover Wilson' or 'my dear Robertson'.[72] The *Criterion*'s coverage of Shakespeare became less mealy-mouthed after Eliot accepted a portion of L. C. Knights's doctoral thesis on the socio-economic background of Jacobean theatre for publication in the *Criterion*. What is more, Eliot asked Knights to review G. Wilson Knight's *The Imperial Theme*. Knights had been led to Wilson Knight's quasi-mystical 'spatial' interpretation of Shakespearean drama through Eliot's introduction to *The Wheel of Fire* (1930), expressing approval for the 'search for the pattern below the level of "plot" and "character"'.[73] For Knights, Wilson Knight's attention to the rhythm, imagery, and poetic symbolism of Shakespeare's plays was a breath of fresh air in a discipline that had for too long become accustomed to the character analysis exemplified by A. C. Bradley's massively influential *Shakespearean Tragedy* (1904).

Knights determined the *Criterion*'s approach to Shakespearean studies during the 1930s. In brief, that direction involved a devaluation of the work of followers of Bradley, together with qualified praise for the work of those Shakespearean critics whom he believed had shown the way forward—Wilson Knight, Bradbrook, and the American scholar E. E. Stoll.[74] Reviewing Anne Bradby's *Shakespeare Criticism 1919–1935*, published in the Oxford World's Classics series, Knights observed that the only justification

[71] T. S. Eliot to John Dover Wilson, 23 Nov. 1926. Edinburgh. Eliot reviewed Robertson's *The Problems of the Shakespeare Sonnets* for the *Nation and Athenaeum*.

[72] Robertson forewarned Eliot of the polemical nature of his *Criterion* essay 'Shakespearean Idolatry' (Jan. 1930), 246–67. However, it was not until after publication that Eliot invited a reply from Dover Wilson. See 'Idolatry and Scepticism in Shakespeare Studies', *Criterion* (July 1930).

[73] See 'Introduction', in G. Wilson Knight, *The Wheel of Fire* (Oxford, 1930), p. xviii. Wilson Knight submitted an essay on *Hamlet* to the *Criterion*. It did not appear, although the *Criterion* did publish his 'note' on *Henry VIII* ((Jan. 1936), 228–36).

[74] Knights drew upon his *Criterion* book reviews for ammunition in his influential pamphlet attacking Bradley, *How Many Children Had Lady Macbeth?* (Cambridge, 1933).

for an anthology of modern Shakespearean criticism was a program-matic selection of the post-Bradleyan reorientation. Knights criti-cized Bradby for her eclecticism and for including extracts from George Rylands's *Words and Poetry*,[75] while omitting the work of Empson and Bradbrook.[76] If Knights was for a time a formative influence on Shakespeare criticism in both the *Criterion* and *Scrutiny*, then the difference in context was tangible and illuminat-ing. In the *Criterion*, Knights's unfussed likes and dislikes were diluted by the breezy reviews of Dobrée, who might let slip the odd word of praise for Bradley or 'Dr Tillyard's erudition'. In *Scrutiny*, Shakespearean criticism was inescapably affected by Leavis's search for the elusive quintessence of Shakespearean 'genius' and his monomania regarding the exaggeratedly malign influence of Bradley. As the decade wore on, Leavis began to favour Derek Traversi's moralizing literary-critical approach to Shakespeare at the expense of Knights's semi-sociological intellectual history.[77]

It is natural to ascribe some of the contextual differences between the *Criterion* and *Scrutiny* to the personal temperaments of the respective editors as well as to subtle, if palpable, differences in their interpretation of seventeenth-century English social history. The *locus classicus* here was Eliot's celebrated *TLS* review of Herbert Grierson's *Metaphysical Lyrics* anthology, in which he diagnosed the so-called 'dissociation of sensibility': a catastrophic division of thought and feeling which 'set in' around the time of the Civil War and was 'aggravated' by the bad influence of John Milton.[78] In December 1925, Eliot informed Herbert Read that his forthcoming

[75] Knights found Rylands's prose style in *Words and Poetry* 'exasperating'. See *Scrutiny* (Dec. 1934), 309. The Leavises were hostile to Rylands after some confusion over the authorship of Geoffrey Rossetti's testy review of *New Bearings in English Poetry* in the *Cambridge Review* (signed 'GWR'). See Q. D. Leavis and F. R. Leavis to George Rylands, 18 May 1932. Cambridge (King's). Rylands dismissed the misunder-standing as a 'storm in a tea-spoon'.

[76] See 'Books of the Quarter', *Criterion* (Apr. 1937), 576–7. Bradby suspected that Knights's response would be 'unfavourable'. Anne Ridler, letter to Jason Harding, 28 Sept. 1998. Knights reviewed Bradbrook's *Elizabethan Stage Conditions* in the *Criterion* (Oct. 1932), 115–18.

[77] Traversi contributed a leading article on Dostoevsky to the *Criterion* (July 1937), 585–602.

[78] 'The Metaphysical Poets', *TLS* (20 Oct. 1921), 669–70. Frank Kermode offers a convincing critique of Eliot's tendentious historiography in *Romantic Image* (London, 1957), 158–77.

Clark Lectures would look beyond the 'English Renaissance' for evidence of a unified sensibility:

> The idea is briefly this: to take the XIII century—in its literary form, Dante—as my *point de repère*, to treat subsequent history as the history of the disintegration of that unity—disintegration inevitable because of the increase of knowledge and consequent dispersion of attention, but bringing with it many undesirable features.[79]

It was left to Eliot's Cambridge followers, such as Basil Willey, who had attended his Clark Lectures, to ransack seventeenth-century intellectual history in an attempt to substantiate the 'dissociation of sensibility' as an historical fact.[80] The *Criterion* published Willey's essay examining the effects of the seventeenth-century 'new philosophy' on Wordsworth's beliefs.[81] But Eliot's academic disciples left out the theological inflection of his cultural pessimism: nostalgia for Elizabethan Anglicanism and for a pan-European Catholic Christendom. The *Criterion* gradually softened its line on Milton, publishing Grierson's substantial and discriminating appreciation of the poet.[82] In *Scrutiny*, Leavis kept to the letter of Eliot's review of Grierson's anthology, crediting it with the 'dislodgement' of Milton from the canon. He remorselessly rebuked any backsliding on the matter.[83]

Scrutiny's version of the 'dissociation of sensibility', its elaboration and dissemination, was the hallmark of the journal. Countless essays and reviews codified the stages of English cultural decline: the break-up of the 'organic community' and traditional popular culture after the reign of Elizabeth; the rise of modern scientific empiricism and utilitarianism leading to (in Leavis's unlovely formulation) the 'technologico-Benthamite civilization'; the decisive impact of the Industrial Revolution and capitalism; finally, the parlous state of modern society, cheapened by the homogeneous

---

[79] T. S. Eliot to Herbert Read, 11 Dec. 1925. Cited in *The Varieties of Metaphysical Poetry*, ed. Ronald Schuchard (London, 1993), 10.

[80] Willey later claimed that he was influenced less by Eliot's 'dissociation of sensibility' than by A. N. Whitehead's *Science and the Modern World*. See *Cambridge and Other Memories, 1920–1953* (London, 1968), 60.

[81] Basil Willey, 'Wordsworth's Beliefs', *Criterion* (Jan. 1934), 232–51. Leavis described Willey's *The Seventeenth-Century Background* (London, 1934) as 'that very useful book'. See 'Education and the University', *Scrutiny* (Sept. 1940), 114.

[82] See 'John Milton', *Criterion* (Sept. 1928), 7–26 and (Dec. 1928), 240–57.

[83] See 'Milton's Verse', *Scrutiny* (Sept. 1933), 123.

'levelling-down' process of the commercially motivated mass media, advertising, and the bestselling novel. *Scrutiny*'s prelapsarian 'organic community' was reflected in the cultural achievements of the Tudor period—a schematic and rose-tinted picture of an age when popular culture (broadly conceived) could boast among its achievements the drama of Shakespeare, the journalism of Thomas Nashe, and the splendours of English folk song.

Knights's *Criterion* essay, 'Education and Drama in the Age of Shakespeare', suggested that the rise of Tudor grammar schools had underpinned the 'organic community',[84] one of the underlying assumptions behind *Scrutiny*'s programmatic restoration of an 'educated reading public'. *Scrutiny* was a real force for educational reform: it had come into existence with the aim of establishing strong links between schools and universities. In the summer of 1933, the journal carried a propagandist 4-page leaflet proclaiming 'The *Scrutiny* Movement in Education'. Led by the editors, Leavis, Knights, and Thompson, and seconded by practising English teachers, Raymond O'Malley, Frank Chapman, and Bruce Pattison, the journal examined all aspects of English studies; from the school-leaving certificate to the Cambridge tripos, from teacher-training colleges to the possibilities of 'education for living' in the universities (Leavis's idealized vision of the Cambridge English School was the yardstick here[85]). If the *Scrutiny* 'movement' in education remained joylessly high-minded in conception and somewhat vague in practice (it was given more substance when Thompson left the editorial board of *Scrutiny* in 1939 to found *English in Schools*), its self-professed 'missionary' ardour[86] attracted a loyal following in grammar school sixth forms and exploited a contemporary crisis of faith, attested to throughout the decade, in the English public school system.

The *Criterion* also numbered several schoolteachers among its ranks, but its treatment of education was piecemeal and uncoordinated: a Janus-faced mixture of Eliot's reactionary misgivings

[84] 'Education and Drama in the Age of Shakespeare', *Criterion* (July 1932), 599–625.
[85] See 'Education and the University: Sketch for an English School', *Scrutiny* (Sept. 1940), 98–120.
[86] See Queenie Leavis: 'They [English teachers] may even be filled with a missionary spirit' (*Fiction and the Reading Public*, 271).

about the benefits of 'popular education'[87] and the progressive theories of teachers who took a special interest in the teaching of poetry in schools; including W. H. Auden and John Garrett, co-editors of the widely praised school anthology *The Poet's Tongue*.[88] Eliot had argued in 'Modern Education and the Classics' that English literature was not well suited to university education. Instead, he offered a half-hearted defence of the public school admixture of Christian doctrine and the Classics. *Scrutiny*'s wholehearted commitment to the centrality of the study of English literature—in particular, the analytical tools of discrimination, sensibility, and critical judgement it fostered—was seen as an essential prophylactic against the mass standards of consumer capitalism. As Denys Thompson put it, the aim of education was to produce 'misfits' in a modern commercialized society. Put another way, *Scrutiny* and the *Criterion* promoted different forms of cultural élitism: the *Criterion* the preservation of an intellectual-ecclesiastical Coleridgean clerisy and *Scrutiny* the creation of an Arnoldian 'saving remnant' of liberal educationalists. Although both élites divided along broadly class lines (appealing to either end of the spectrum of educated middle-class taste), they were certainly not so far apart as Leavis's retrospective valuation of the 'achievement' of *Scrutiny* (weighed in the balance with the *Criterion*'s implied 'failure') suggested.

Looking back on the London literary world of the 1930s, Leavis habitually returned to Spender's hostile review of *Revaluation* as evidence that the *Criterion* had abandoned its reviewing pages to the Auden–Spender group:

Anyone who investigates the back files [of the *Criterion*] will see that, from the outset steadily onwards, the review pages of that Classicist, Anglo-Catholic, and Royalist organ were as unmistakably as those of the *New Statesman* (socialist and egalitarian) at the disposal of the 'gang' for its own purposes.[89]

---

[87] 'Unless popular education is also moral education, it is merely putting firearms into the hands of children' ('A Commentary', *Criterion* (Jan. 1931), 309).

[88] Among the schoolteachers who contributed to the *Criterion* were S. L. Bethell, Frank Chapman, John Garrett, Frank McEachran, James Reeves, Philip Richards, and Michael Roberts. Auden was a teacher at the Downs School during his period as a *Criterion* reviewer.

[89] 'T. S. Eliot as Critic', *'Anna Karenina' and Other Essays* (London, 1967), 192.

It was a reductive, self-serving estimation that passed into *Scrutiny* folklore, to be repeated with animus, some thirty years after Spender's review, by card-carrying Leavisites.[90] But Leavis did not mention that the reviewing pages of the *Criterion* were also at the disposal of various *Scrutiny* regulars; for example, Knights, Chapman, and E. W. F. Tomlin (an Oxford undergraduate whom Eliot had introduced to Leavis[91]). Nor did he recall that the *Criterion* had stood in solidarity with *Scrutiny* against what he called the 'general taboo' on Ronald Bottrall.[92] Bottrall later claimed that it was Eliot rather than Leavis who had been his most loyal supporter throughout the 1930s (the *Criterion* also published work by his wife Margaret).[93] Whatever the truth, Leavis's most damaging assertion about the *Criterion* was made in his 1940 'Retrospect of a Decade': 'a little research in the back-files will reveal the young, predominantly Left-inclined, *élite* incongruously cocking their snooks at *Scrutiny* from the pages of *The Criterion*—the only attention *Scrutiny* ever got in that promisingly-styled organ.'[94] His memory was short. The *Criterion* displayed a sustained interest in the work of *Scrutiny*'s editorial team. When Hugh Gordon Porteus, a former *Scrutiny* contributor, began a survey of English periodicals in the *Criterion*, *Scrutiny* received coverage as favourable as any of the magazines under consideration.[95] In April 1938, Porteus remarked that the

---

[90] See John Peter, 'Eliot and the *Criterion*', in Graham Martin (ed.), *Eliot in Perspective* (London, 1970), 264, and G. S. Singh, 'Il *Criterion* di T. S. Eliot', *Il Verri* (1978), 54.

[91] See Frederick Tomlin, *T. S. Eliot: A Friendship* (London, 1988), 24.

[92] Eliot thought that Bottrall's verse was more mature than the poetry of the Auden group. See T. S. Eliot to I. A. Richards, 24 Feb. 1934. Cambridge (Magdalene).

[93] See Ronald Bottrall, 'Reflections on the Nile', *TLS* (24 Oct. 1980). Bottrall explained that he met Leavis on only a few occasions and deplored *Scrutiny*'s propensity to recruit from the ranks of Downing College. Elsie Duncan-Jones recalled that Margaret Bottrall was delighted when Eliot accepted her essay on Chapman for publication in the *Criterion*. Elsie Duncan-Jones in conversation with Jason Harding, 21 Jan. 1998, Cambridge.

[94] 'Retrospect of a Decade', *Scrutiny* (June 1940), 72. By 1963, Leavis was not sure if the *Criterion* contained a 'single reference' to *Scrutiny* ('A Retrospect', *Scrutiny* (Cambridge, 1963), 21).

[95] Eliot had decided to begin a summary of English periodicals after the increasing difficulty of obtaining foreign periodicals. See T. S. Eliot to Hugh Gordon Porteus, 18 Jan. 1937. Yale. Porteus had previously written reviews of English periodicals for the *New English Weekly*, including favourable notices of the *Criterion*. See 'Reviews' (11 Oct. 1934), 526, and 'Avant Garde' (29 Oct. 1936), 54.

current issue of *Scrutiny* was a 'more than usually lively number' and in the final issue of the *Criterion*, he described *Scrutiny* as 'quite exceptionally good'.[96]

Eliot's personal estimation of *Scrutiny* is harder to fathom. In *Purpose*, he claimed: 'it is impossible not to respect the work that [Leavis] has done with *Scrutiny*, and his rather lonely battle for literacy', a remark coextensive with his approval of *Fiction and the Reading Public* six years earlier.[97] One may speculate to what extent Eliot was irritated by the unfavourable comparisons between his beliefs and those of D. H. Lawrence frequently made in *Scrutiny*.[98] The sources of that trouble predate *Scrutiny*, reaching back to Lawrence's death in 1930:

> it is a suspect wisdom that dismisses him [Lawrence] in fear or revulsion or contempt. That is why some who a good while ago formed the habit of taking the *Criterion* seriously, now, when they compare the obituary attention given to Harold Monro with that given to Lawrence, feel a kind of final depression.[99]

But Leavis overlooked the fact that Monro, one of the founding members of the Criterion group, was a good personal friend of Eliot. He later embellished the grievance by suggesting that the *Criterion* had not printed *any* obituary notice of Lawrence—in fact, the loose-leaf insert 'In Memoriam' (not recorded in E. Alan Baker's 1967 *Criterion* Index) described Lawrence as a 'distinguished' contributor who 'represented something for which *The Criterion* stands'.[100]

Leavis, of course, was quite entitled to dissent from Eliot's withering and patronizing remarks upon Lawrence made in the course of his *Criterion* review of Murry's *Son of Woman*—the strangely insulting remark about the 'frightful consequences' had

---

[96] 'Periodicals', *Criterion* (Apr. 1938), 594, and (Jan. 1939), 402.

[97] 'On a Recent Piece of Criticism', *Purpose* (Apr.–June 1938), 92. Eliot also expressed his respect for Leavis and *Scrutiny* in a letter to Ronald Bottrall, 24 Mar. 1943. Texas.

[98] See F. R. Leavis: '[Lawrence] helps those of us who, respecting intensely Mr. Eliot's mind and personality, have, though conscious of theological incapacity and lack of experience, attempted to follow his religious utterances, to define our attitude towards them' (*Scrutiny* (Dec. 1932), 277).

[99] F. R. Leavis, 'Reminiscences of D. H. Lawrence', *Scrutiny* (Sept. 1932), 190.

[100] 'In Memoriam' also noted the death of two other *Criterion* contributors: Charles Whibley and C. K. Scott-Moncrieff.

Lawrence become a don at Cambridge 'rotten and rotting others' was particularly galling to the Leavises.[101] Eliot developed his religiously based condemnation of Lawrence in *After Strange Gods*.[102] Leavis's extreme dislike of these verdicts was emphasized, however, only *after* the demise of the *Criterion*.[103] The decisive breach appears to date from 1941 when Eliot visited Chesterton Hall Crescent, irritating Queenie by dropping his cigarette ash on the hearth. Leavis believed that Eliot had made a pilgrimage to Cambridge in order to confess and expiate a feeling of guilt towards him—a strange delusion that is testimony to the alarming *folie des grandeurs* that characterized his retrospective valuations of *Scrutiny*; nowhere more voluble in its hyperbole than the claim: 'We were, and knew we were, Cambridge—the essential Cambridge in spite of Cambridge.'[104]

Francis Mulhern's valuable study, *The Moment of 'Scrutiny'* (1979), chose not to approach the periodical 'as the "expression" of a master-subject (Leavis)'. But his overarching narrative of historical materialism failed to engage fully with the Leavis hegemony in *Scrutiny*. If Mulhern was right to listen to the 'play of many voices' as a gauge of the *Scrutiny*'s competing ideological discourses, he was ultimately mistaken to pretend that no voice was heard more frequently or more insistently than any other.[105] Queenie complained that Mulhern incorrectly assumed that 'anyone who (even once) contributed to *Scrutiny*'s position was endorsed by the editors, or at any rate by Leavis'.[106] She confirmed that the co-editors were frequently scolded for soliciting work from undesirables, such as Richards and Spender.[107] Thompson, according to his own testimony, was ostracized in 1935;[108] Knights and Harding offered, on more than one occasion, to resign from the editorial board;

---

[101] See 'Books of the Quarter', *Criterion* (July 1931), 771.

[102] For Leavis's response, see 'Mr. Eliot, Lewis and D. H. Lawrence', *Scrutiny* (Sept. 1934), 184–91.

[103] Leavis's first sustained polemic against Eliot on Lawrence was made in 'Mr. Eliot and Lawrence', *Scrutiny* (June 1951), 66–73.

[104] *Two Cultures? The Significance of C. P. Snow* (London, 1962), 29.

[105] See Francis Mulhern, *The Moment of 'Scrutiny'* (London, 1979).

[106] Cited in Singh, *F. R. Leavis*, 43.

[107] Remarkably, Queenie Leavis claimed that 'we suffered from the fact that other editors could not be prevented from commissioning contributions on their own initiative' (ibid. 189).

[108] See Denys Thompson, 'Teacher and Friend', *The Leavises*, 49–50.

even a later and largely nominal editor, Wilfrid Mellers, was unceremoniously 'shown the door'.[109] Knights described Leavis as the greatest intellectual influence on his early life, but he added tellingly: 'He was a great liberator from received opinion; but like other liberators he did not always leave his followers free.'[110]

Two years after the demise of *Scrutiny*, Laurence Lerner commented upon 'the bickering and pettiness that surrounds the work of F. R. Leavis'.[111] The tiresome succession of squabbles and shibboleths by which the Leavises set the tone and agenda for *Scrutiny* provides an interesting contrast to Eliot's increasingly light-fingered editing of the *Criterion*. It has been vigorously contested to what extent such editorial control qualifies the achievement and legacy of either journal, as witnessed in Spender's meditation upon the subject in his obituary of Eliot.[112] Opinion continues to differ sharply, but perhaps the person in the best position to judge, L. C. Knights, offered the following temperate characterization:

There was no deliberate 'rivalry' between *Scrutiny* and the *Criterion*, though Leavis, who became editor-in-chief of *Scrutiny*...became increasingly critical through the 1930s. Our attitude—the attitude of the original *Scrutiny* group—was as I stated it in the first number: [The *Criterion*] was necessary, but not the one thing necessary. We hoped to have a more clearly defined policy, with a more belligerent attitude towards the cultural evasions we saw around us, and an educating drive that, we hoped would have some influence in schools and universities.[113]

It appears that when pressed to choose, many of the original group of Cambridge educated admirers of Eliot—in particular, Empson and Knights—dissented from the opinions espoused by F. R. Leavis, the nettle amongst the *Scrutiny* bouquet. Some of them found a more sympathetic home in the *Criterion*, as well as greater freedom and encouragement from 'a certain critic and poet'.

[109] Wilfrid Mellers, letter to Jason Harding, 6 Feb. 1999.
[110] 'Remembering *Scrutiny*', 581.
[111] 'The Life and Death of *Scrutiny*', *London Magazine* (Jan. 1955), 69.
[112] See 'Remembering Eliot', in Allen Tate (ed.), *T. S. Eliot: The Man and His Work*, (London, 1967), 56–7.
[113] L. C. Knights to Loretta Johnson, 13 Nov. 1977. New York (Columbia).

4

New Verse
An Oxford Clique

> There is nothing so blinding as trying to see both sides, and
> there is only one way of avoiding cliques—to have your own
> clique. Only you must make sure that your clique is a clique
> of the best and truest and most lively writers of the time.
>
> Geoffrey Grigson, *New Verse* (May 1939), 63

Geoffrey Grigson's *New Verse* stands alongside Wyndham Lewis's
Enemy as the supreme example of a twentieth-century little magazine dominated by a combative and controversial editor. In 1980
Grigson explained: 'There is no excuse for such a magazine unless
it promulgates the strong message of a new clique or group.'[1] The
strength and vigour of *New Verse* has never been in doubt and the
image of Grigson plotting his literary campaigns from the brasserie
of the Café Royal has not dimmed. *New Verse* occupies a central
place in the literary-historical mythology of the 1930s. In the words
of A. T. Tolley: 'Undoubtedly the most important periodical in the
history of poetry in the nineteen-thirties was *New Verse*.'[2] It was a
judgement endorsed by Robin Skelton, whose influential anthology, *Poetry of the Thirties*, drew heavily upon *New Verse*.[3] And
yet, it is a moot point to what extent *New Verse*'s pre-eminence was
due to a demonstrable poetic merit and how much to the vagaries
of what *Scrutiny* called the 'clique-puffery' of the metropolitan
literary world. The success of the magazine certainly owed a lot to
self-advertisement and the politics of the literary market-place.

---

[1] 'Viewpoint', *TLS* (8 Feb. 1980), 141.
[2] *The Poetry of the Thirties* (London, 1975), 203.
[3] See 'Introduction', *Poetry of the Thirties* (Harmondsworth, 1964).

Examination of the files of *New Verse* uncovers a strategically embattled position within the London world of letters—a position that makes plain Grigson's co-operation with Eliot and the *Criterion*.

I

Geoffrey Grigson was 'unhappily born' in 1905, the son of an elderly Anglican clergyman; the youngest of seven sons, three of whom were killed in the First World War. A strong sense of belatedness, of being cheated out of his inheritance, is recorded in Grigson's autobiography *The Crest on the Silver*, which catalogues a long list of perceived privations, from the shabby gentility of the family vicarage in Cornwall, to his minor public school, St John's Leatherhead, and from there (after failing to win a scholarship) to one of the more unfashionable Oxford colleges, St Edmund Hall; all of which appears to have left a lasting scar.[4] After graduating from Oxford with an undistinguished third-class degree in English, Grigson found a more congenial home in the rough-and-tumble of Fleet Street journalism, quickly observing the first rule of the journalistic profession: 'keep your name going, keep it public.' After working at the London office of the *Yorkshire Post*, Grigson secured a position as the feared and waspish literary editor of the *Morning Post*. Controversial reviews make good copy regardless of their inadequacy as fair-minded criticism. It is to be remembered that the recurrent image of the reviewer's practice in Grigson's autobiography was not the scourge and minister, or cauterizing and healing the afflicted, but the gratuitously offensive 'slash of the billhook'. It was Grigson's intention to draw blood.[5]

In October 1932, after a conversation with Hugh Ross Williamson, the young editor of the *Bookman*, Grigson and his American wife, Frances Galt, planned a new periodical devoted to verse and criticism. Grigson wrote to three poets—Auden,

---

[4] See Grigson: 'The Hall at any rate was a substitute for the right thing. It was as much as I could have; and that much had to be charged to my own account, to the dunce tuition of a minor public school, and to that last fling for a daughter by my elderly parents which had produced only a seventh son' (*The Crest on the Silver* (London, 1950), 89).

[5] See Grigson: 'a slash with the billhook, which was far too much my weapon and which I endeavoured to keep sharp, wiping off the blood from time to time—when it happened, that is, to catch someone in whom any blood was flowing' (ibid. 162).

Day Lewis, and MacNeice—whom he had encountered in recent volumes of *Oxford Poetry*. Day Lewis offered encouragement: 'I feel somehow that it is really quite a practical matter, the purveying of our brand of salvation—a matter of distribution and advertisement and business methods.'[6] A week later, in a letter to Herbert Read, Grigson sketched out the magazine's *raison d'être*. He claimed that the idea of a new poetry magazine had come to him after reading Auden's *The Orators* and after reading the literary criticism of Eliot, Richards, and Read himself. Grigson explained that the periodical could offer no payment and would depend upon the good will of contributors. He informed Read in a postscript that Eliot would vouch for his good intentions.[7] In January 1933, Grigson launched *New Verse* from his flat at Keats Grove, Hampstead; a slim, coverless 20-page poetry magazine, scheduled to appear 'every two months' and handsomely set up, although printed on low quality paper, by an old acquaintance from the *Yorkshire Post*. It was affordably priced at sixpence—as Grigson joked, the cost of ten Players cigarettes or a bus ride from Piccadilly Circus to Golders Green. *New Verse* soon discovered an enthusiastic readership of around 1,000 aspiring poets and poetasters.[8]

The funding of *New Verse* remains something of a mystery. Grigson later claimed that 'no papers or accounts remain'.[9] It appears that it was possible to raise enough funds from subscriptions, advertising rates, private donations, and the sale of *Morning Post* review copies to keep the journal going. Grigson chose to accentuate the role of London booksellers, fondly recalling 'the king of the review booksellers' T. J. Gaston in the Strand:

Those of us who were 'poets and hacks' . . . needed to sell books sent to us to review, which we could excuse since for the most part they were books we did not want, so 'review booksellers' came into being, paying each of us reviewers half the published price for books which they in turn sold for 3/4 of the price to public libraries. They took everything in those days good and ridiculous, learned and books which were beginning to be

---

[6] Cited in Sean Day-Lewis, *C. Day-Lewis: An English Literary Life* (London, 1980), 72.   [7] Geoffrey Grigson to Herbert Read, 12 Oct. 1932, Victoria.
[8] Established poet-subscribers included Wallace Stevens and the Poet Laureate, John Masefield.
[9] *Recollections: Mainly of Writers and Artists* (London, 1984), 30.

called 'coffee table'. . . . Sometimes quite late I would take my review books from my basement quarters off Tudor Street down to the Strand, where Thomas J. Gaston would be waiting, after which I would take another cab up to the brasserie of the Café Royal for a late supper of chicken livers and scrambled eggs and a Mont Blanc with whoever was there for literary gossip.[10]

Grigson's romantic evocation of London literary life in the 1930s places an undue emphasis on the financial support of twilight figures like Gaston, diminishing the journal's dependence upon the regular advertising revenue derived from Faber and Oxford University Press. Of *New Verse*'s twenty-two front-page advertisements, twenty of them were for Faber publications: all but two of the thirty-four issues of *New Verse* carried a Faber advertisement. In his autobiography, Grigson remarked that he 'often laughed at the extreme innocence or brazenness of those who exclaim indignantly that advertisements never affect the contents of the editorial columns of a paper'.[11] It could be argued that Eliot's patronage was decisive in allowing *New Verse*, from the third issue onward, to pay for verse contributions—a far from insignificant factor among London's down-at-heel poets.

Grigson's opening editorial for *New Verse* staked out a place for an independent poetry magazine within the jungle of metropolitan literary journalism, described with virulence as a 'poisonous and steaming Gran Chaco of vulgarity, sciolism and literary racketeering'.[12] Although initially respectful of the example set by the *Criterion* and *Scrutiny*, he did not want readers to think of *New Verse* as a 'verse supplement' to these highbrow quarterlies.[13] *New Verse* was quite simply a showcase for the poetry of the younger generation, an aesthetic, or rather the lack of an aesthetic, formulated in terms of a cure for an 'ulcerous' literary establishment:

New Verse, then, has a clear function. When respectable poems (as it believes) are being written and forced to remain in typescript, it can add

---

[10] Ibid. 41–2.   [11] *The Crest on the Silver*, 174–5.

[12] 'Why', *New Verse* (Jan. 1933), 1.

[13] In early 1933, Grigson contributed reviews and exchanged subscription lists with *Scrutiny*. However, their co-operation ceased when Grigson upset Leavis by describing *Scrutiny* as 'too adolescent, too self-righteous, too ready to accept the naiveties of ledger-criticism informed with a little sour yeast of Eliot and Lawrence' ('The Danger of Taste', *New Verse* (July 1933), 2).

itself as a publishing agent to those few publishers who bring out (with conscience money) a few books of verse.[14]

For six years, *New Verse* brought a number of young poets to the attention of a small, highly literate reading public. Several *New Verse* poets were also Faber authors, presumably one of the fellow-travelling 'few publishers' Grigson had in mind. The advertising arrangement with *New Verse* certainly suited Faber, who were assembling an unrivalled stable of young poets.[15] More than that, Grigson's distillation of a Faber *New Verse* anthology from the polyphony of its contributors raises some delicate questions about the effect of Eliot's patronage on the posthumous reputation of this magazine.

Eliot employed Grigson as a *Criterion* reviewer of modern poetry. In a survey of 'Recent Verse' in October 1933, after an initially restrained treatment of Robert Graves and Walter de la Mare (whose son was a Faber director), Grigson broke out into a scathing attack on Sacheverell Sitwell:

His new poems are 'a sliding gentle that is made of nothing'. Using a dead, individual language, full of favourite empty words for bogus images, a language which is relevant to the not very valuable or extensive experience which it carries, they are briefly of that kind which is always produced by the amateur.[16]

The attack on Sacheverell Sitwell owed a lot to the example of Wyndham Lewis who had satirized the Sitwells in *The Apes of God* as 'an ageing group of wealthy romantic amateurs'.[17] It is noteworthy that the resumption of hostilities with the Sitwells should have taken place in the *Criterion*, since Eliot had been happy to solicit work from this socially well-connected triumvirate during the period of Lady Rothermere's financial reign. Edith Sitwell mounted a defence of Sacheverell in *Aspects of Modern Poetry* (1934), together with an attack on 'members of Mr and Mrs Grigson's little circle'.[18] Grigson retaliated with brickbats in

[14] 'Why', 2.
[15] See James Reeves: 'The fashionable poets of that time were published by Faber & Faber; that had an enormous cachet attached to it' ('Interview with James Reeves', *Review* (1964), 69).   [16] 'Books of the Quarter', *Criterion* (Oct. 1933), 140.
[17] *The Apes of God* (London, 1930), 530.
[18] 'It may be said with truth that it would be impossible to find a poet who has been more foolishly underrated than Mr. Sitwell, and for reasons that have no connection with poetry' (*Aspects of Modern Poetry* (London, 1934), 142).

a number of *New Verse* later advertised as 'A Whipping for Sitwells'. He accused Edith Sitwell of plagiarism and performed a variety of Ovidian metamorphoses on 'these three versifying oddmedods'; from bower birds into starlings, before the final *coup de grâce* as 'contemptible elvers, wriggling away in their dull habitat'.[19] Edith Sitwell (or 'The old Jane' as she became known) was regularly exhibited in her own 'private zoo'—a *sottisier* that some readers of *New Verse* professed to find the most entertaining part of the journal.[20] Eliot followed the Sitwell controversy with interest, informing Pound that there was some good in Grigson, even if he had not yet learnt to box properly—presumably a reference to Grigson's proclivity to ignore the Queensberry rules of periodical debate.[21]

In October 1934, Grigson insulted his Hampstead neighbours, Sylvia Lynd (who was married to the *New Statesman* essayist Robert Lynd) and Edwin Muir. The remarks on Muir's *Variations on a Time Theme* were particularly surprising, given that Grigson had already reviewed the volume favourably in the *Morning Post*. MacNeice's *New Verse* review, on the other hand, had been cold and dismissive.[22] A few months later, Grigson followed suit in the *Criterion*:

The 'Variations' make a sequence only by calling them a sequence. There is little form about them individually or together; and there are not many lines which ought not to have been improved. Formal inharmonies and inharmonies line by line must come partly from a defective self-training in verse; and partly they may come from what Yeats has called the great temptation of the artist: creation without toil. Mr. Muir, that is, resembles many other writers of the day in being the Amateur Poet attached to the Professional Man of Letters.[23]

Muir was deeply wounded by the criticism and had nightmares in which he believed Grigson had physically assaulted him.[24]

---

[19] 'New Books on Poetry and Miss Sitwell', *New Verse* (Dec. 1934), 16–17.
[20] Grigson dedicated his first volume of poetry, *Several Observations* (London, 1939) to 'my publicity manager, *Edith Sitwell*, with love and thanks'.
[21] T. S. Eliot to Ezra Pound, 7 Jan. 1934 [1935?]. Yale.
[22] MacNeice described *Variations* as 'a type of Royal Academy picture of a decade or so back—stilted allegorical nudes walking through a grey landscape' (*New Verse* (June 1934), 20).   [23] 'Books of the Quarter', *Criterion* (Oct. 1934), 142.
[24] See *An Autobiography* (London, 1954), 240.

Similarly, Robert Waller, a poet who had come to Eliot's attention as an undergraduate at University College, London, received a blunt rejection from Grigson, 'So far, so bad', and was asked to send the cost of postage before his manuscripts could be returned.[25] John Betjeman cursed Grigson from the White Horse in Oxfordshire after an equally petulant rejection note. Muir, Waller, and Betjeman received encouragement from Eliot: all had work published in the *Criterion*.[26] Nevertheless, Grigson's appearance as a *Criterion* reviewer was an indication that Eliot could find gainful employment for the 'billhook'.

Grigson's *Criterion* review of Day Lewis's *A Hope for Poetry* (1934), an exploration of the relationship between communism and post-war poetry, was the occasion of another damning turnabout. Day Lewis had initially maintained good relations with *New Verse* and published poems from *The Magnetic Mountain* in the opening number. However, Grigson may have been upset when Day Lewis began to contribute regularly to *Left Review* and declined to reply to a *New Verse* questionnaire circulated in the summer of 1934.[27] Day Lewis instructed Blackwell's to send a copy of *A Hope for Poetry* to Grigson, but after a snide editorial remark in *New Verse* he must have been dreading the full-blown review.[28] When it appeared in 1935 it was extremely discourteous by *Criterion* standards:

The name 'A Hope for Poetry' warns one by its slight scent of pragmatism of the nature of this book; and the scent grows quickly into a stench.

[One] begins Mr. Day Lewis's exposition with some dislike, which his manner, his statements, his mis-statements and his conception of poetry do not disperse. . . . All through, the book is written in a snappy outward metaphorical style which is unpleasant.[29]

Grigson's chief complaint that Day Lewis's 'left-handed' didacticism produced sterile political poetry was an opinion shared by

[25]   Robert Waller in conversation with Jason Harding, 24 Nov. 1997, London.
[26]   See Eliot's glowing 1935 testimonial for Edwin Muir in the National Library of Scotland, Edinburgh. For acceptance of work in the *Criterion* see T. S. Eliot to Robert Waller, 22 Apr. 1938. London (British Library); T. S. Eliot to John Betjeman, 3 Aug. 1938. Victoria.   [27]   Eliot, Auden, and Spender also chose not to reply.
[28]   'Mr. Day Lewis has written a bad book', *New Verse* (Dec. 1934), 14.
[29]   'Books of the Quarter', *Criterion* (Jan. 1935), 326, 328, 329.

Eliot.[30] Day Lewis, a Hogarth poet, was the only member of the 'Macspaunday' group who did not appear in the *Criterion*. In fact, Grigson set the keynote for subsequent *Criterion* reviews of Day Lewis, who continued to receive unfavourable notices, even a gruff editorial reprimand in 1937 for his *Left Review* pamphlet on the Spanish Civil War, *We're Not Going to Do Nothing*.[31]

Grigson denounced Day Lewis for his 'failure to see or at least affirm the merits of the poetry of Mr Louis MacNeice (but Mr MacNeice is not half-communist)'. In 1932, MacNeice, a lecturer in Classics at Birmingham University, submitted a portfolio of poetry to Faber. Eliot found the poems 'very interesting' but 'not quite ripe for [book] publication'. John Lehmann attempted to persuade MacNeice to join the Hogarth Press, but Eliot kept him on board by trying out his poetry in the *Criterion*.[32] In 1935, Faber eventually published MacNeice's *Poems*. Eliot passed the volume to Grigson in full knowledge that he admired MacNeice's poetry.[33] Grigson's *Criterion* review stated baldly: 'Of my contemporaries who write verse, those I get most satisfaction from are Mr Louis MacNeice and Mr Auden.'[34] Later that year, MacNeice, who had moved to London University, took up residence at Keats Grove, which, following the collapse of the *Morning Post*, the Grigsons had vacated in search of a less expensive Hampstead flat. There certainly appears to be a strong suspicion of log-rolling in Grigson's promotion of two Faber poets in the pages of the *Criterion*; both personal acquaintances and, more pointedly, the leading lights of *New Verse*. In his essay on contemporary poetry in *The Arts Today* (1935), edited by Grigson, MacNeice commented: 'The eclectic is usually impotent; the alternative to eclecticism is clique-literature. The best poets of today belong to, and write for, cliques.'[35]

---

[30] Grigson claimed that Day Lewis was 'too able to wither himself as a poet by being politically active' ('Faith of Feeling', *New Verse* (Mar. 1933), 17).

[31] Eliot chastised the 'demerit of this kind of pamphleteering warfare' ('A Commentary', *Criterion* (Apr. 1937), 473).

[32] See Jon Stallworthy, *Louis MacNeice* (London, 1995), 162–4.

[33] See T. S. Eliot to Geoffrey Grigson, 16 Aug. 1935. Texas.

[34] 'Books of the Quarter', *Criterion* (Jan. 1936), 320.

[35] 'Poetry Today', in Geoffrey Grigson (ed.), *The Arts Today* (London, 1935), 30.

II

Grigson claimed that *New Verse* had been launched to foster the poetic talent of W. H. Auden.[36] Auden received almost unqualified approval in *New Verse*[37] and was honoured in November 1937 in a special double number—studded with encomiums from the 'group'.[38] His poetry, submitted on almost illegible foolscap notepaper, featured in *New Verse* from beginning to end. However, it would be an oversimplification to describe the poetic house style of *New Verse* as 'Audenesque'. It is not really possible to identify any stylistic commonality between Auden and the neo-romantic poetry of Dylan Thomas and George Barker, the surrealism of David Gascoyne and Philip O'Connor,[39] or the witty juvenilia of Gavin Ewart. Even the most pro-Auden of poets, Stephen Spender, claimed that he had been 'prowled on and barked at and shepherded by Grigson' into remaining in the *New Verse* fold.[40] There were many *New Verse* contributors who cannot be corralled under the 'Audenesque'. Kathleen Raine pursued her own metaphysical inklings. Norman Cameron, a fiercely independent poet, owed little to Auden and his imitators. Andrew Young, a Scottish Presbyterian minister twenty years older than the Auden generation, was by Grigson's own admission a Georgian nature poet, but not excluded on that account. William Empson found a temporary home in *New Verse* before his 'smack' at Auden.[41] There was also room for the epigrams of Geoffrey Taylor, a host of Indian and English folk songs and *disjecta membra* such as that oddity the 'Oxford Collective Poem'.[42]

---

[36] It would be equally true to say that *New Verse* had been founded to nurture the minor poetic talent of Martin Boldero, Grigson's pen-name. Boldero was his mother's maiden name.

[37] The crown slipped slightly when Auden accepted the 1937 King's Medal for Poetry, eliciting a mild rebuke from Grigson. See 'Remarks', *New Verse* (Jan. 1938), 14.

[38] See 'Auden Double Number', *New Verse* (Nov. 1937). Day Lewis's contribution was a magnanimous gesture given the animus displayed towards him in *New Verse*.

[39] Grigson commissioned some 'Honest Doubts' from Auden, published under the initials 'J.B.' to coincide with the opening of the International Surrealist Exhibition in London. Grigson later said of *New Verse*'s support of surrealism: 'I was being fashionable, not critical' ('A Conversation with Geoffrey Grigson', *Review* (June 1970), 21).

[40] Stephen Spender to Herbert Read, 11 Apr. [1934]. Victoria.

[41] See 'Just a Smack at Auden', *Contemporary Poetry and Prose* (Autumn 1937), 24–6.

[42] The brainchild of Charles Madge and Mass-Observation: it comprised pentameters written by twelve Oxford undergraduates. See 'Oxford Collective Poem', *New Verse* (May 1937), 16–19.

There is no need to labour the point further, except to say that when in 1950 Grigson praised *New Verse* for its evasion of 'that dotty inclusiveness, that mental masturbation which has come to be character of "little magazines" '[43] there was an element of self-promotion at work, an attempt to cast order over the miscellaneous and occasionally extempore offerings of a bimonthly poetry magazine. The character of *New Verse* owed as much to tactical manœuvres in the literary market-place as to any privileged insight into the poetic *Zeitgeist*. Grigson's public flapping of scolds sometimes had the appearance of trading shares on the literary stock market. Take his notoriously insulting comments on George Barker's *Poems* (1935): 'Why has anyone published, does anyone praise, does anyone read, the verse of Mr George Barker? . . . I have never attempted, I am certain, to review more nauseating poems, and I have never read more inept juvenilia.'[44] One can only conclude that Grigson's attack on Barker, a poet published in *New Verse* but currently enjoying greater praise from Eliot,[45] signalled a public shift in the networks of sentiment and loyalty that interlaced literary London. Other poets expelled from the *New Verse* fold may similarly have raised the spectre of divided loyalties: A. S. J. Tessimond (Michael Roberts and *New Signatures*); John Pudney (David Archer's Parton Street café poets); Randall Swingler (an editor of *Left Review*); Rayner Heppenstall (freelance contributor to the *Adelphi*, the *Criterion*, and the *New English Weekly*); Ronald Bottrall (Leavis's hope for *Scrutiny*[46]). The role of 'clique-puffery' in the formation of literary reputations should not be discounted. As Spender observed dourly in *New Verse*: 'Literary life is largely a contemporary racket, and if one goes in for it, I suppose one can't be squeamish.'[47]

---

[43] *The Crest on the Silver*, 163.

[44] 'Nertz', *New Verse* (June 1935), 17–18. Grigson later softened his opinion of Barker, claiming that his poetry had emerged from a period of 'psychopathic exhibitionism'. Barker might have replied *tu quoque*.

[45] In July 1934, Eliot praised Barker's 'strange gift' to Virginia Woolf. See *The Diary of Virginia Woolf*, iv. *1931–1935*, ed. Anne Olivier Bell and Andrew McNellie (London, 1982), 231.

[46] Bottrall claimed to have suffered from the poetry cliques of the 1930s and their general hostility to Leavis. See Ronald Bottrall to John Hayward, 10 Jan. 1943, Cambridge (King's).

[47] See 'The Left-wing Orthodoxy', *New Verse* (Autumn 1938), 12–16.

Early appearances by Read, Richards, and Allen Tate had promised a degree of critical sophistication, but Grigson's peremptory and hasty verdicts were symptomatic of the failure of *New Verse* to give careful and sympathetic consideration to many of the poets reviewed in its pages. Too often assertion stood in place of argument, allied to a sort of reviewing practice closer to the sensationalism of daily Fleet Street journalism than the leisurely urbanity of the higher journalism from which the *Criterion* took its cue. In 1937, Empson explained to readers of *Poetry* (Chicago) that Grigson's 'trick of being rude to everybody is, of course, paying journalism of a certain kind'. He commented that Grigson 'does not so much as pretend to give reasons for insulting people' adding 'he has a good journalistic nose for what he can safely be rude to'.[48] Poets like Laura Riding and Roy Campbell, outsiders from the London literary establishment, found themselves sitting targets for caricature. All the same, Grigson did not always lash with total impunity. Riding penned a beautifully poised rebuff to *New Verse* expressing her contempt for him. Some years later, Campbell exacted a more tangible revenge.[49]

There has been an unusual tolerance in academic circles of Grigson's 'trick' of racial, class-bound, and anti-feminist taunts. It would certainly be a mistake to equate *New Verse*'s jeremiads against the snobbism of the literary editors of Sunday newspapers and the intellectual weeklies as commensurate with a Marxist critique of bourgeois cultural production. *New Verse* was first and foremost a poetry magazine, expressing no ideological position. Grigson explained:

It has been the aim of *New Verse* to be tied to no clique or salvation army. It is neither True Blue nor Red, nor Liberal nor white, a dull confusion of all colours, believing that the extent of a political situation is strict and near and mean compared with the immensely far-off limit of every rich individuality that needs to be explored as belief of individuals.[50]

In fact, Grigson's 'natural inclination' towards socialism remained largely unexamined. Following Wyndham Lewis, he claimed there

---

[48] See 'Correspondence', *Poetry* [Chicago] (Jan. 1937), 237.
[49] For Riding's letter see 'Correspondence', *New Verse* (Jan. 1939), 30. In 1948 Roy Campbell told Robert Waller that he had met 'Griggers' outside the BBC and 'slapped his face'. Robert Waller in conversation with Jason Harding, 29 July 1997, London.　　　　　　　　　　　　　　[50] 'Third Year', *New Verse* (Dec. 1934), 2.

was little to choose between a 'reasoned attitude of toryism' and a 'communist attitude',[51] explaining why he could work by day on the staunchly Tory *Morning Post* and yet edit *New Verse* contributions from proto-Communist intellectuals by night. In Christmas 1936, Dmitri Mirsky, the scourge of the English intelligentsia, charged *New Verse* with having become 'a cesspool of all that is rejected by the healthy organism of the revolutionary moment'.[52] It was a complaint Grigson vehemently rejected, since the pages of *New Verse*, though sprinkled with Communists, had never been heard to speak *for* revolution. And although, after the reverberations of Munich, Grigson hastily put together a double number on 'Commitments' it was too little too late. It was only there at all because it had become impossible, with London bracing itself for war, to ignore the contemporary crisis in Europe.

III

In 1939, Derek Savage, a contributor to a rival London poetry magazine, *Twentieth Century Verse*, formulated a hypothesis to account for *New Verse*'s success. Savage was critical of *New Verse*, claiming that the disconcerting fossilization of its leading poets into comfortable establishment careers exposed the basis of the magazine as a clique composed of public school and Oxbridge men.

the truly remarkable phenomenon is this: more than half of the persons who are offered to the people as poets in this country have been educated at either of those two expensive and exclusive universities, Oxford and Cambridge. And about two-thirds, I should think, are public school men. . . . At any rate, New Verse has a distinct Oxford-and-Cambridge flavour. Its three editors were all at one university or the other, and so were most of their contributors. I do not think the significance I attach to this is exaggerated.[53]

Kenneth Allott and Bernard Spencer, *New Verse*'s editorial assistants following Frances Grigson's death from tuberculosis in 1937,

---

[51] 'Politics: and a Request', *New Verse* (Mar. 1933), 1.
[52] 'About Stephen Spender and C. Day Lewis', *International Literature* (Oct. 1936), 86. Mirsky contributed to the *Criterion* during his time as a lecturer on Russian Literature at King's College, London.
[53] 'Poetry Politics in London', *Poetry* [Chicago] (Jan. 1939), 205.

were Oxford men. In point of fact, Auden, Spender, MacNeice, Day Lewis, and Spencer were all former editors of *Oxford Poetry*. It was also true that some contributors to *New Verse* had attended Cambridge. However, Gavin Ewart first appeared in *New Verse* as a Wellington schoolboy and Charles Madge appeared in *New Verse* after he had scandalously left Cambridge with Kathleen Raine, but without a BA degree.[54] Two poets with a following in Cambridge circles, William Empson and Ronald Bottrall, received uncompromisingly harsh treatment in *New Verse*. In truth, *New Verse* represented an Oxford-educated clique attracted to Grigson's Hampstead circle, 'the milieu in which *New Verse* existed'.[55]

Grigson affected to be upset by Savage's 'malicious' and 'quite exceptionally stupid' characterization of literary London. He defended himself by explaining that what united the editors and some of the contributors to *New Verse* was really a detestation of the values represented by public school and Oxbridge. If they happened to have been educated by these venerable institutions that was not prima facie a reason to dismiss their poetry. Besides, Grigson asked Savage: 'tell me what good "non-bourgeois" poet is ringing the door-bell of *New Verse* without getting an answer?'[56] Savage himself, a winner of the Jeanette Sewell Davis Prize from *Poetry* (Chicago), subsisting on £3 per week for his work at the London office of the Transport and General Workers Union, had strong 'non-bourgeois' credentials.[57] So, too, did Idris Davies, a former coalminer from south Wales, who, following unemployment in the aftermath of the 1926 coal strike, had retrained as a schoolteacher and begun to write poetry. The answer Davies received when he rang *New Verse*'s doorbell is further testimony of the limits of Grigson's editorial sympathy.

By 1937, Davies had published verse in *Wales*, a nationalist magazine edited from Carmarthenshire by Keidrich Rhys. The following year, after a recommendation from Eliot, Dent published *Gwalia Deserta*, a series of lyrics documenting the dereliction of the Rhymney mining community. Reviewing the volume in

---

[54] See Kathleen Raine, *The Land Unknown* (London, 1975), 78–81.
[55] Grigson, *Recollections*, 34.
[56] 'Letter', *Poetry* [Chicago] (Apr. 1939), 52–3.
[57] D. S. Savage, letter to Jason Harding, 3 Oct. 1997.

New Verse Grigson informed his readers: 'Nothing to bother about.'[58] What, indeed, was there for *New Verse* to 'bother' about? In a spirited letter, Davies tried to ascertain his offence. He answered the criticism that the collection was 'naive' and the product of a 'simple and superficial mind' by pointing out that Grigson had misunderstood the implied readership of *Gwalia Deserta*, which was not '*New Verse* and literary cliques' from London WC1 (Bloomsbury) or NW3 (Hampstead). Davies concluded: 'permit me to express the opinion that *New Verse* has gradually, but certainly, degenerated into a magazine of a clique. The same names appear and reappear in its pages. Auden, Allott, MacNeice, and Spender—it is like a refrain.'[59] It is not necessary to make large claims for Davies's poetry, although Herbert Palmer defended *Gwalia Deserta* in the correspondence columns of *New Verse*.[60] All the same, there is something wretchedly narrow-minded about Grigson's mockery of Davies's portrayal of industrial south Wales during the Depression, especially in a special issue on 'Commitments'.[61]

Like it or not, many poets who found the *Criterion* receptive and open-minded also found *New Verse* to be a narrow clique magazine. It is not fanciful to link the contributors to *New Verse* to a shared experience of an English upper-middle-class education, exemplified in Auden's 'To a Writer on his Birthday' with its chummy apostrophe to 'Christopher' Isherwood, and the plummy reference to 'The stuccoed suburb and expensive school'.[62] To draw attention to (what George Barker called) the 'snobbery of clique' that pervaded *New Verse* is not necessarily to impugn the success of this minority magazine. It does, however, help to account for some of the machinations evident in its pages. For example, one could see how the pronouncements of *New Verse*'s 'yellow twicers'

---

[58] *New Verse* (Autumn 1938), 26.

[59] 'Letter', *New Verse* (Jan. 1939), 30. Grigson invalidated any magnanimity in publishing Davies's letter by appending the caption 'Simple Simon' underneath.

[60] See 'Correspondence', *New Verse* (May 1939), 56. Eliot wrote of Davies's *Selected Poems*: 'they are the best poetic document I know about a particular epoch in a particular place, and I think that they really have a claim to permanence.' Cited in Islwyn Jenkins, *Idris Davies* (Cardiff, 1972).

[61] By contrast, Eliot published James Hanley's stories of working-class life. See, for example, 'From Five Till Six', *Criterion* (Apr. 1938), 432–42.

[62] 'To a Writer on his Birthday', *New Verse* (Oct.–Nov. 1935), 7.

might grate upon the ears of a vehement Anglophobe like Hugh MacDiarmid.[63] MacDiarmid's *Second Hymn to Lenin,* first published in the *Criterion,* was dismissed by Grigson with condescending inattention as 'these 77 pages of unvarying twitter. . . . only a little better than the ballads hawked around by the unemployed'.[64] Eliot, on the other hand, actively courted MacDiarmid. Discussing MacDiarmid's *Criterion* article 'English Ascendancy in British Literature' over lunch, Eliot expressed 'agreement with some of its contentions'.[65] MacDiarmid left London in the early 1930s, but the contact was resumed in 1938 when he wrote from Shetland to offer work for consideration. The final number of the *Criterion* contained no less than three separate contributions from him.[66] He wrote a letter of condolence, expressing his sincere regret at the demise of Eliot's broad-minded quarterly review. Although a Communist and a Scottish Nationalist, MacDiarmid had been proud to appear in the *Criterion.*[67]

Given the small constituency of modern poetry, it was inevitable that there should be significant areas of overlap between *New Verse* and the *Criterion.* The Auden special number of *New Verse* provides a glimpse of the nebulous subterranean workings of literary London. It carried a full double-page Faber advertisement: one page listed poetry by Barker, Bottrall, Campbell, Eliot, Wyndham Lewis, MacNeice, Marianne Moore, Pound, Read, Siegfried Sassoon, Sacheverell Sitwell, and Spender; the second was devoted to 'Vin Audenaire'.[68] The advertisement also gives an indication of the changing connections/disconnections between *New Verse* and the *Criterion.* While *New Verse* had been a fledgling magazine, it was natural and prudent that Grigson should view the *Criterion* with courtesy and restraint. However, as *New Verse* grew in

---

[63] See Hugh MacDiarmid, 'An Enquiry', *New Verse* (Oct. 1934), 18.

[64] *New Verse* (Feb.–Mar. 1936), 17.

[65] See Alan Bold, *MacDiarmid* (London, 1988), 258–9. Eliot presumably agreed with MacDiarmid's contention that 'Confinement to the English central stream is like refusing to hear all but one side of a complicated case' ('English Ascendancy in British Literature', *Criterion* (July 1931), 600).

[66] See 'Cornish Heroic Song for Valda Trevelyan', 'Correspondence', and 'Books of the Quarter', *Criterion* (Jan. 1939), 195–203, 312, and 379–84.

[67] See Hugh MacDiarmid to T. S. Eliot, 20 Jan. 1939. *The Letters of Hugh MacDiarmid,* ed. Alan Bold (London, 1984), 450–1.

[68] 'Auden Double Number', 38–9.

confidence and prestige, in tandem with the ascent of Auden, it was equally politic that Grigson should eventually take a side-swipe at Eliot, the radical modernist poet turned churchman and elder statesman of letters. Polite criticism of Eliot's 'traditionalism' in Spender's *The Destructive Element* (1935) was evidence of an uneasy *détente* between the *Criterion* and the Auden generation. In May 1935, Eliot advised Spender not to take his critical standards from Grigson.[69]

Eliot made his only contribution to *New Verse*, in a special number on poets and the theatre, in December 1935.[70] The following year, Grigson was openly hostile:

And there is still Mr. Eliot, I mean there is Mr. Eliot the Politician, Mr. Eliot the Publisher, Mr. Eliot politically ringing himself with new nobodies, picked out for him by the lamentable Ezra [Pound] or by his now somewhat seditious Eye, Mr. Herbert Read. There are still *Criterion* parties. But what do you find there? Do you find the first writers? You find the old relics of imagism with moths in their feathers, you find parsons from Oxford, you find adventurer-journalists from the weeklies, crooked excursionists into a good thing, lisping surrealists, experts in Persian on leave from Rapallo, museum officials, and oozings from the undrained cess-pit of the Orage mythomania. . . . Eliot even, the poet shrinking inside him, has recognised his falling price and tries to jack it up with grass stems. A cynical ex-associate of his watches the Birthday and New Year Honours, waiting for Eliot to win his Order of Merit, or his knighthood.[71]

Explaining the rationale behind the Auden double number, Grigson noted, in passing, that: 'There are angles from which Mr Eliot seems a ghost.'[72] Eliot declined to contribute to the Auden volume on the curious grounds that he was Auden's publisher.[73] In the summer of 1938, *New Verse* published William Nettleford's satirical 'Fan Mail for a Poet' poking fun at Eliot's eminence in literary London.[74]

---

[69] T. S. Eliot to Stephen Spender, 9 May 1935. Northwestern.
[70] See 'Audience, Producers, Plays, Poets', *New Verse* (Dec. 1935), 3–4.
[71] 'A Letter from England', *Poetry* [Chicago] (Nov. 1936), 101, 102.
[72] 'Auden Double Number', 1.
[73] T. S. Eliot to Geoffrey Grigson, 19 Mar. 1937, Texas.
[74] A parody of 'How Nice to Meet T. S. Eliot' with the refrain:

> How nice for a man to be clever
> So famous, so true;
> So sound an investment; how EVER
> So nice to be YOU.

This was only topped by the consummate bad taste of Charles Madge's mock-obituary of Eliot, commissioned by Grigson for the 'Commitments' issue.[75] *New Verse*, it appears, was as anxious to read Eliot his funeral rites as to assist at the coronation of Auden.

However, given Madge's close ties to Eliot, the obituary has some of the markings of an artificially manufactured provocation. Eliot described Madge to his secretary, Anne Bradby, as a very 'enterprising young man' and offered him regular reviewing work for the *Criterion*.[76] Furthermore, he personally intervened to help Madge secure a job as a reporter on the *Daily Mirror*. In 1937, Faber published Madge's first volume of poetry, *The Disappearing Castle*, containing several poems that had first appeared in the *Criterion*. If the usually diffident Madge repaid Eliot's generosity with a tongue-in-cheek *New Verse* obituary, that did not prevent the *Criterion* from publishing his leading review on the anthropologist Bronislaw Malinowski a few months later.[77] In point of fact, *New Verse* received extremely favourable coverage in the *Criterion*.[78] Presumably the editor of the *Criterion* could appreciate *New Verse*'s publicity stunts (he had, after all, not been above employing Grigson's journalistic 'billhook'). Moreover, the Faber director and sponsor of diverse young poetic talents might have looked with Christian charity, not to say mild amusement, at his own premature canonization. An obituary notice is, at the very least, a mark of respect.

In January 1939 Grigson went to Russell Square to discuss the publication of an anthology of poetry from the first thirty numbers of *New Verse*.[79] Grigson had recently relaunched *New Verse*, illustrated and enlarged to 32 pages and priced one shilling. Its future was precarious: the demise of the *Criterion* and the

---

[75] Printed complete with the Gothic header, 'In Memoriam T.S.E.—Jujus Anima Propitietur Deus', *New Verse* (Autumn 1938), 18–21.

[76] Anne Ridler in conversation with Jason Harding, 9 Dec. 1997, Oxford.

[77] See 'Books of the Quarter', *Criterion* (Oct. 1938), 99–103.

[78] See Hugh Gordon Porteus: 'Mr. Grigson makes some observations which confirm our conviction that few periodicals, even among those larger and wider in nominal scope than *New Verse*, are so fortunate in an intelligent and responsible editorship' ('Periodicals', *Criterion* (Apr. 1938), 593). Porteus had earlier referred to *New Verse* as 'the best contemporary verse racket' ('Books of the Quarter', *Criterion* (Jan. 1936), 354).

[79] Grigson had tried for some years to interest Eliot in a new Faber anthology. See T. S. Eliot to Geoffrey Grigson, 27 Mar. 1936. Texas.

prospect of war raised questions about the difficulty of securing paper, advertising, and copy. At the end of January, Auden sailed into self-imposed exile in New York and Grigson had quarrelled with MacNeice. Both Auden and MacNeice now contributed to John Lehmann's *New Writing*. *New Verse* was obliged to fill the New Series with unknown poets (quite a number have sunk without trace). A Faber anthology of *New Verse* poetry, then, would allow Grigson to define in retrospect (what he tellingly called) the 'criterion' of *New Verse*—Auden, MacNeice, and poetic objectivism[80]—whilst simultaneously recording and preserving *his* selection of the best verse from its pages. Eliot encouraged Grigson to write a trenchant preface surveying the contemporary poetry scene, suggesting it was spiced up with some provocation and knocking of Edith Sitwell.[81] Grigson could be charming when the occasion demanded and, whatever their private reservations, there is nothing unusual in the collaboration of a Faber director with the most influential young poetry editor in London.[82] When the *Criterion* folded Grigson offered a judicious public tribute:

Efforts were made . . . to keep *The Criterion* what such a periodical should be. It disappointed all those who wished it to be better than its best numbers, but now it has come to an end, we can think that from *The Criterion* next to no English writer of value was ever excluded. We can be grateful indeed to Mr. Eliot. He was catholic and serious. His *Criterion* has died a natural death. Its job was really over, and it has faded away like a biennial after its seeds have matured and been dispersed.[83]

Grigson wrote these words in the final issue of *New Verse* in the knowledge that his own seeds would be dispersed. Eliot duly obliged in August 1939 by preserving *New Verse* in Faber amber.

Looking back at various influential inter-war periodicals, Grigson emphasized the necessity for the little magazine to be fresh, lively, and immediate: 'there must be a confrontation of proposition and opposition, there must be impatience with an

---

[80] See Grigson: 'I always judge every poem written now, by poets under forty, by the degree to which it takes notice, for ends not purely individual, of the universe of objects and events' ('Preface', *New Verse: An Anthology* (London, 1939), 24).

[81] See T. S. Eliot to Geoffrey Grigson, 26 Sept. 1938 and 16 Nov. 1938, Texas.

[82] Grigson recalled his feelings towards Eliot as 'a blend of reverence and antipathy—a personal antipathy which I suspected was mutual' ('A Conversation with Geoffrey Grigson', 19).

[83] '*Criterion* and *London Mercury*', *New Verse* (May 1939), 62.

old mode.'[84] Not surprisingly, he recalled the *Criterion* as too austere and solemn, taking away with one hand what he gave with the other:

Eliot's *Criterion* should have been this century's influencer. I held it in awe, as an undergraduate. Eliot could entice contributions which looked over the confines of Russell Square into other countries of Europe. But Eliot niggled, and Eliot was not Tolstoy's little finger. Thought, in the well designed pages of the *Criterion*, was not always disturbing in the better way; covert politics slightly defiled its superiority. Wonderful as it was to be asked to write in the *Criterion*, even at the back end, I can't say that Eliot's review, since he was not that kind of editor or that kind of complete man or complete mind, ever glowed with an infectious healthiness of art.[85]

The implication was that Grigson, not the cautious mandarin Eliot, was that 'kind of editor' and *New Verse* that sort of magazine. But its success, such as it was, was not simply a case of presenting the best poets of a generation: it required other talents, of which Grigson's self-promotion as the co-ordinator of an Oxford educated clique ensured that whatever merit *New Verse* had would be bequeathed, along with the billhook, to posterity.

[84] *Recollections*, 37.   [85] 'Viewpoint', 141.

PART II

The Politics of Book Reviewing

5

Herbert Read
Anarchist Aide-de-Camp

> When [Eliot] announced in the preface to *For Lancelot Andrewes* (1928) that he was a classicist in literature, a royalist in politics, and an anglo-catholic in religion, I could only retort that I was a romanticist in literature, an anarchist in politics, and an agnostic in religion. But such a statement of differences he could respect; what he could not tolerate was any false interpretation of the position he himself held.
>
> Herbert Read, *Sewanee Review* (January–March 1966), 46–7

The contents of a literary magazine are heterogeneous and not every contribution has the same level of editorial approval. The chapters in this section concentrate on the individual biographies of leading contributors to the *Criterion* in an attempt to explore the internal dynamics that shaped the character of the periodical. The case of Herbert Read's changing role on the *Criterion* is highly illustrative in this regard. Eliot chose his metaphor carefully when he described Read as a 'rock': the most frequent book reviewer in the files of the *Criterion*, a contributor of numerous essays, poems, published correspondence, and up to 1929 regular reviews of American periodicals.[1] Read provided essential support in the form of copy throughout the run of Eliot's quarterly magazine. In his memoir of Eliot, he described their friendship as a matter of 'deep personal devotion'. He had been Eliot's 'aide-de-camp' in the struggles and campaigns of inter-war London literary journalism.[2]

---

[1] Read contributed 68 book reviews, 4 articles, and 5 poems to the *Criterion*.
[2] See 'T.S.E.—A Memoir', in Allen Tate (ed.), *T. S. Eliot: The Man and His Work* (London, 1967), 17.

And yet, the generous acknowledgement is apt too readily to smooth over tangible and deeply held differences. The subversive energies of Read's championing of psychoanalysis, romanticism, surrealism, and anarchism in the pages of the *Criterion* inescapably raises questions about the surface improbability of a close collaboration between two men, who were as Read phrased it, 'so fundamentally different in background and temperament'.[3] In fact, the *Criterion* was a broad enough church to encompass dissenters, even if Eliot's editorial strategy in the *Criterion* often worked to neutralize a variety of positions expounded and defended by Read.

I

The first meeting between Read and Eliot highlighted characteristics that were to remain evident throughout their long relationship. They met in a Piccadilly restaurant in 1917, where Frank Rutter had invited Eliot in order to solicit a contribution to *Art and Letters*.[4] During their lunch Eliot exhibited a certain defensiveness regarding Read's exemplary war record (Read had come from Buckingham Palace where he had been decorated for gallantry); on Read's part there was a feeling of intellectual inferiority towards Eliot's philosophical education at Harvard, the Sorbonne, Marburg, and Oxford (Read's formal education at a Halifax orphanage and at Leeds University had been cut short by the war). It appears that Eliot was initially cautious about the company he would keep in *Art and Letters*. However, from the spring of 1919, after the quarterly had gathered momentum, he contributed regular articles and some poetry to *Art and Letters* until the journal's demise, owing to financial difficulties, in the summer of 1920. By that time, Eliot, buoyed by the completion of the manuscript of *The Sacred Wood*, told his mother that Read, five years his junior, seemed almost childlike.[5] It was a measure of Eliot's growing reputation and self-confidence in literary London. By 1922, the roles were reversed: Eliot wrote

---

[3] Ibid. 18.
[4] Subtitled 'An Illustrated Quarterly' in homage to its *fin-de-siècle* forebears, the *Yellow Book* and the *Savoy*, *Art and Letters* was launched in the summer of 1917 after Rutter had lost his position as director of the Leeds City Art Gallery.
[5] *Letters*, 391.

to Read to ask for a contribution to his quarterly review. He explained:

The review will differ from *Art and Letters* in that it will not be illustrated and that it will contain a much smaller proportion of verse and fiction. There will also be room for longer articles than was possible in *Art and Letters* . . . It will be mainly critical and reflective.[6]

Read's literary enthusiasms and choice of subject-matter close to Eliot's heart soon earmarked him as a valued and trusted collaborator. For example, Read's article on metaphysical poetry, published in the *Criterion* in April 1923, owed a great deal to Eliot's review of Grierson's anthology; hardly surprising given that Eliot had corrected the article in typescript. Eliot praised the essay, an opinion seconded by Richard Aldington, at that time the *Criterion*'s assistant editor.[7] Eliot also took a keen interest in Read's edition of T. E. Hulme's miscellaneous notebooks and manuscript notes. The papers had been passed to Read, following Hulme's death in the First World War, on the recommendation of Alfred Orage—Read's mentor at the *New Age* where he cut his teeth as a literary journalist.[8] In 1924, Read presented Eliot with an advance copy of his selective and idiosyncratically arranged volume, *Speculations*. The publication was timely for Eliot who cited the work in support of the *Criterion*'s 'classical tendency'. Read later edited further unpublished papers which appeared in the *Criterion* as 'Notes on Language and Style' in July 1925. It was clear that at this time Eliot considered Read essential to the success of the *Criterion*.

In October 1924 Read felt emboldened to question the direction in which Eliot, as the leader of a group of critics, was taking the *Criterion*. Somewhat defensively, Eliot pointed to the constraints imposed by Lady Rothermere who desired a society magazine, 'a more chic and brilliant *Art and Letters*, which might have a fashionable vogue among a wealthy few'. Eliot defined his editorial role as primarily a 'necessary organ' facilitating 'others to do their

---

[6] Ibid. 547.

[7] T. S. Eliot to Herbert Read, 14 May 1923. Victoria. See also David Thatcher, 'Richard Aldington's Letters to Herbert Read', *Malahat Review* (1970), 6.

[8] Read contributed a regular 'Readers and Writers' column to the *New Age* during the latter half of 1921. See Wallace Martin, *'The New Age' Under Orage* (Manchester, 1967), 52–5 and 279–82.

best work' and he spelt out the difficulties attendant upon setting out a too dogmatic programme for the *Criterion*:

If I say generally that I wish to form a 'phalanx', a hundred voices will forthwith declare that I wish to be a leader, and that my vanity will not allow me to serve, or even to exist on terms of equality with others. . . . I wish, certainly, to get as homogeneous a group as possible: but I find that homogeneity is in the end indefinable: for the purpose of the Criterion, it cannot be reduced to a creed of numbered capitals. . . . What is essential is to find those persons who have an impersonal loyalty to some faith not antagonistic to my own.[9]

During the summer of 1925, when the *Criterion* was thrown into turmoil by Lady Rothermere's threat to withdraw her financial backing, Aldington was certainly antagonistic. He grumbled to Read: 'Yes, we do entirely lack co-ordination and organisation', adding uncharitably 'Eliot has funked his responsibilities to us since 1921'.[10]

Read suggested, convincingly, that the cooling in the relationship between Eliot and Aldington was evidence of an 'intense jealousy' on Aldington's part.[11] The problem was not simply that Aldington could earn considerably more money for his freelance contributions to wide-circulation London magazines, it was a deeper feeling that he had been left trailing in the wake of Eliot's ascendency as a poet and critic. In November 1925, Aldington explained: '[Eliot] has never asked me to contribute any poems to the Criterion, nor did he ask for a full-length article. I'm hanged if I'll be a mere camp-follower.'[12] Matters were not eased by Eliot's aggressive policy in building up the literary section of Faber & Gwyer. In particular, Faber's joint sponsorship of Routledge's Republic of Letters series of critical biographies cost Aldington an editorial role on the project. Similarly, Eliot's success in persuading Read to transfer to Faber was a coup that upset Virginia Woolf at the Hogarth Press.[13]

---

[9]   Cited in Tate (ed.), *T. S. Eliot: The Man and His Work*, 20–1.
[10]   Thatcher, 'Richard Aldington's Letters to Herbert Read', 17.
[11]   Cited in Alister Kershaw and Frédéric-Jacques Temple (eds.) *Richard Aldington: An Intimate Portrait* (Carbondale, Ill., 1965), 125.
[12]   See 'Richard Aldington's Letters to Herbert Read', 9 and 20–1.
[13]   See *The Diary of Virginia Woolf*, iii. *1925–1930*, ed. Anne Olivier Bell and Andrew McNellie (London, 1980), 45. In 1925, the Hogarth Press had published *In Retreat*, Read's documentary account of the Mar. 1918 retreat from St Quentin. Aldington, shell-shocked during the First World War, described the pamphlet as the

Aldington rationalized his growing hostility toward the *Criterion* by claiming that Thomas MacGreevy's unfavourable review of George Moore's latest novel, *Héloïse and Abelard*, was ample reason to sever his connection with the journal.[14] By this time, Read had already replaced Aldington as the unofficial assistant editor of the *Criterion*.

By the launch of the *New Criterion* in 1926, Read was justified in hailing Eliot as 'our undisputed leader'.[15] Eliot's new position at Faber allowed the scope for extended business lunches and their editorial collaboration was strengthened by the introduction of a series of weekly meetings in a downstairs room at the Grove Tavern, walking distance from the Victoria and Albert Museum where Read worked.[16] The *Criterion* lunches were marked by their informality, at times gaiety, although visiting American guests noted that Read was extremely shy and self-effacing in company.[17] It is hard to avoid the suspicion that Read went to the Grove Tavern during the mid-1920s to sit at the feet of the editor of the *Criterion*.[18] There was, however, a certain amount of tolerant give-and-take between Eliot and Read although latent tensions underlying their collaboration would eventually surface and require editorial countermeasures. The first source of editorial discontent can be seen in the *Criterion*'s reception and mediation of psychology and psychoanalysis.

Looking back on English literary criticism in the 1920s, Eliot recalled that the 'psychological subtleties' of I. A. Richards and the 'more general and increasingly political aesthetics' favoured by Read had been the dominant forces.[19] It was certainly through

only English work that had been able to 'record the reality' of the war ('Books of the Quarter', *Criterion* (Apr. 1926), 363–7).

[14] Richard Aldington to Bonamy Dobrée, 25 Apr. 1926. Leeds.

[15] Tate (ed.), *T. S. Eliot: The Man and His Work*, 15.

[16] Read was an Assistant-Keeper in the Victoria and Albert Museum from 1922 until 1931.

[17] John Gould Fletcher commented upon Read's 'taciturn habits of speech' (*Life Is My Song* (New York, 1937), 309); Read was 'farouche' according to Conrad Aiken (*Ushant* (Boston, 1952), 232–3); Allen Tate noted Read's native 'Yorkshire shyness' (*Selected Writings of Herbert Read* (London, 1963), 7).

[18] It is possible to see Eliot's tutelary influence at work in Read's sudden interest in Dante and scholastic philosophy, as well as in the dramatic monologue 'The Lament of Saint Denis', *Criterion* (Oct. 1926), 673–9.

[19] 'A Commentary', *Criterion* (July 1937), 668.

Read and Richards that the belated application of modern psychological research to literary texts began to gather force. In January 1925, the *Criterion* published Read's expository 'Psycho-analysis and the Critic' in which he asserted:

Traditional criticism, therefore, in so far as it can claim to be fundamental, is a structure whose very foundations have perished, and if we are to save it from becoming the province of emotional dictators, we must hasten to relate it to those systems of knowledge which have to a great extent replaced transcendental philosophy.[20]

Read was referring to the psychoanalytic theories of Freud, Jung, and Adler. At the same time, Eliot had written a flattering letter to Richards, a rising star in the English School at Cambridge. Richards replied:

Certainly I can do something for the *Criterion*. Very glad to. I'm just getting together some ideas on current changes in the world picture due to penetrations into general awareness from Psychology (including Psycho Analysis), physics, biology, anthropology, etc. etc.; with a view to considering how they may be affecting poetry.[21]

Richards added that he was pleased that *Principles of Literary Criticism*, published in C. K. Ogden's International Library of Psychology, Philosophy, and Scientific Method, was going to be reviewed in the *Criterion*. Although Read and Richards shared many of the same goals and opinions—the mission to set literary criticism on a scientific footing, a belief in the essential psychological health of the artist, an opposition to psychological Behaviourism—their relationship was an uneasy one.[22]

It was significant that Eliot did not disclose that Read would review *Principles* in the *Criterion*. When the review appeared, Read praised the book's 'sustained scientific nature' as the most 'important contribution to the rehabilitation of English criticism', but he was critical of a perceived lack of 'moral consciousness': 'It is not enough to believe that art is a mechanical and unrelated harmony

---

[20] 'Psycho-analysis and the Critic', *Criterion* (Jan. 1925), 214.
[21] I. A. Richards to T. S. Eliot, 26 Nov. 1924. *Selected Letters of I. A. Richards*, ed. John Constable (Oxford, 1990), 31–2.
[22] They had propounded rival aesthetics in *Arts and Letters*. See Read, 'Definitions Towards a Modern Theory of Poetry' (Jan. 1918), 73–8, and Richards, 'Four Fermented Aesthetics' (Autumn 1919), 186–93.

of impulses or balance of appetencies.'[23] Always a touchy recipient of reviews, Richards wrote immediately to Read. He opened bluntly: 'You've gone wrong at various points in reading *Principles*.' Waving aside alleged shortcomings, Richards affirmed: 'In fact I'm all *for* the existence of the moral consciousness, recognised for what it is—a matter of the progressive organisation of impulses.'[24] In a brief exchange of letters, Read and Richards continued to cavil over psychological concepts and the nature of Richards's utilitarian theory of value. Richards directed Read to his forthcoming *Criterion* article, 'A Background for Contemporary Poetry', in which he introduced his formulation of the emotive 'pseudo-statement' described as 'a form of words which is justified entirely by its effect in releasing or organising our impulses or attitudes'. In that article, Richards made the celebrated pronouncement that *The Waste Land* had enacted a 'complete severance between poetry and *all* beliefs'.[25] Read remained unconvinced countering: 'The mind must make a leap into the dark: it must construct ideals, hypotheses. Of these the moral consciousness is mainly constituted.'[26]

Eliot chose not to intervene in the quarrel between Read and Richards. He did, however, publicly criticize during this time the psychological approach to literary criticism. In the *Criterion* in October 1926, Eliot gave a less than enthusiastic review of Read's Faber collection, *Reason and Romanticism*, incorporating several *Criterion* articles. In brief, Eliot located a contradiction between Read's interest in a Thomist conception of intelligence and in his interest in psychoanalysis and 'unconscious symbols'. He concluded: 'the great weakness of Mr Read's book (if I have read these essays correctly) is that it represents a period of transition from psychology to metaphysics.' Bracketing the work with Ramon Fernandez's *Messages*, Eliot commented: 'both are encumbered by the wipings of psychology.'[27] The image was hardly complimentary and it is difficult to ignore a tone of barely muted distaste informing the review. Eliot's preoccupation with metaphysics was undoubtedly coloured by his imminent entry into the Church of

[23] 'Books of the Quarter', *Criterion* (Apr. 1925), 449.
[24] *Selected Letters of I. A. Richards*, 37.
[25] 'A Background for Contemporary Poetry', *Criterion* (July 1925), 518, 520 n.
[26] Herbert Read to I. A. Richards, 18 Apr. 1925. Victoria.
[27] 'Books of the Quarter', *Criterion* (Oct. 1926), 756.

England. Read, however, would have seen only a disappointing refusal to endorse publicly his synthesis between 'reason' (a formulation that owed a great deal to Eliot[28]) and his own 'romanticism'. He later explained to a correspondent:

[Eliot's] influence is responsible for my early attempt to reconcile reason and romanticism—not entirely, because the contradiction exists in my own personality. It exists in Eliot, too, in an even more complicated form; but whereas he has sought to reconcile the contradiction by accepting what I would regard as historical crystallizations of the romantic spirit (in particular, Anglo-Catholicism), I on the contrary have tried to relate my synthesis to my immediate sense of reality in particular, the reality of the aesthetic experience.[29]

Read had Eliot's review of *Reason and Romanticism* on his mind when he complained to Wyndham Lewis about the manner in which he had been treated by the *Criterion*: 'Perhaps [Eliot] has not got the "party spirit", in which case he should not lead a party.'[30] However, Read would shortly be served even worse. There was certainly a strange concatenation of appetencies at work when Eliot invited Richards, an infrequent *Criterion* reviewer, to notice Read's handbook of rhetoric *English Prose Style*.[31] Oddly, Eliot claimed that Read would rather have Richards do the review than anyone else.[32] After Richards read the book, he revealed that certain sections had made him 'very angry' and that he should have 'cooled off' before writing the review.[33] Eliot received the proof copy in October 1928 and his response was highly interesting. He confided that he found

---

[28] Read defined 'reason' as 'the sum total of awareness, ordained and ordered to some specific end or object of attention' (*Reason and Romanticism* (London, 1926), 27).

[29] Herbert Read to Hans Häusermann, 6 Aug. 1937. Victoria. In an obituary notice, the Swiss critic, Häusermann described the *Criterion* as the best inter-war English literary quarterly. See 'Das Ende einer europäischen Zeitschrift: the *Criterion*', *Der Kleine Bund* (1939), 44–6. Häusermann, a friend of Read, corresponded with Eliot during the Second World War.

[30] Cited in James King, *The Last Modern: A Life of Herbert Read* (London, 1990), 85.

[31] Richards had reviewed only one book to date: J. B. Watson's *Behaviourism* in Apr. 1926 (372). Richards declined to review a translation of Leone Vivante's *Note Sopra l'Originalità Del Pensiero*, an extract from which had appeared in the *Criterion* (June 1926), 436–53. The book was passed to Read, whose review was praised as 'beautiful' by an effusive Vivante. See Leone Vivante to Herbert Read, 6 Oct. 1927. Victoria.   [32] T. S. Eliot to I. A. Richards, 28 June 1928. Cambridge (Magdalene).

[33] *Selected Letters of I. A. Richards*, 45.

Richards's censorial tone persuasive; in particular, he liked the criticism of Read's paraphrase of a passage discussing the effects of the Oxford Movement on the Church of England.[34] Eliot went so far as to say that the review would be good, not only for Read who had lacked telling criticism, but that it would help to dispel recent complaints that the *Criterion* represented a monolithic 'school' of criticism.[35] Richards repaid Read in kind: praising the 'psychological basis' of *English Prose Style* as 'very satisfactory', he went on to catalogue a series of 'slips' and simplifications in Read's textual analysis.[36]

The episode is particularly illuminating in demonstrating how Eliot's editorial diplomacy might use the review pages of the *Criterion* to deal with a fashionable mode of criticism he found uncongenial. Eliot could exploit the differences between Read and Richards, although remaining on friendly terms with both authors, as a sort of self-cancelling comment upon the application of psychology to literary criticism. As early as 1923, Eliot had warned Read: 'Psychology is worse than anything, because it is a young science (if it be a science) and hardly born before jargonising was well advanced.'[37] Eliot remained sceptical of the value of psychology and psychoanalysis and maintained that the observations they furnished were merely of the order of ordinary common sense and required no special warrant.[38] Interestingly, in the final issue of the *Criterion*, Middleton Murry attacked Read's use of psychoanalysis to elucidate literary texts. Sounding remarkably like Eliot, Murry now believed that Christian theology offered the only reliable insight into human psychology.[39]

---

[34] See Herbert Read, *English Prose Style* (London, 1928), 29–30.

[35] T. S. Eliot to I. A. Richards, 30 Oct. 1928. Cambridge (Magdalene). Eliot was presumably referring to Edwin Muir's remark about the *Criterion* 'school' in the *Nation and Athenaeum*.

[36] 'Books of the Quarter', *Criterion* (Dec. 1928), 315–24. Read forewarned friends about the tone of Richards's review. See Bonamy Dobrée to Herbert Read, 2 Dec. 1928. Victoria.

[37] Cited in *The Varieties of Metaphysical Poetry*, ed. Ronald Schuchard (London, 1993), 130 n.

[38] See 'A Commentary', *Criterion* (Apr. 1932). A. A. W. Ramsay argued, with reference to Read's application of psychology in literary criticism: 'A psychological study of the poet's mind has nothing to do with literary criticism.' See 'Psychology and Literary Criticism', *Criterion* (July 1936), 629.

[39] See 'Books of the Quarter', *Criterion* (Jan. 1939), 333–9.

II

John Gould Fletcher claimed to have seen enough of Read at the Grove Tavern to discern that he 'remained an unbeliever, despite his association with Eliot, in the official dogmas of Christianity, and that he had leanings towards political and economic radicalism'. According to Fletcher, Read was a 'disguised romantic'.[40] The disguise looked pretty threadbare when Read chose to deliver the Clark Lectures in 1929 (Eliot had supplied his nomination) on Wordsworth; the choice of subject occasioned some surprise in an undergraduate Cambridge under the sway of influential apologists for Eliot's anti-romantic theory. When the lectures were collected and published in book form Eliot told Bonamy Dobrée:

The book is excellent, the views just; but I did not feel that he was deeply enough moved by the subject to justify it. His remark that criticism should be written like philosophy does not worry me, because it does not seem to me to mean much; there are many ways in which *good* philosophical works have been written. The danger is chiefly in writing criticism like second rate philosophy.[41]

It is clear that Eliot believed that Read's criticism courted these dangers.

Read's preoccupation with delineating the contours of the creative 'personality' of the poet, using the tools of a rather *ad hoc* psychoanalytical kitbag, was developed in a critical manifesto, *Form in Modern Poetry* (1932); published by the Catholic firm, Sheed & Ward, in their programmatic Essays in Order series. The book was recognized by Arthur Wheen as a definite break with Eliot.[42] In the course of an impassioned defence of the romantic 'tradition' in modern poetry, in itself a notable redaction of Eliot's formulation, Read replaced the impersonal theory of art sketched out in 'Tradition and the Individual Talent' with his own homespun psychology of poetic personality. Read's diffidently dropped gauntlet sufficiently annoyed Eliot for him to take Read to task on his lecture tour of the United States. In November 1933, Eliot

---

[40] *Life Is My Song*, 309.

[41] See Dobrée, 'A Personal Reminiscence', in Tate (ed.), *T. S. Eliot: The Man and His Work*, 80.

[42] Arthur Wheen to Herbert Read [*c*.1933]. Victoria. Orlo Williams found the book 'disappointing' ('Books of the Quarter', *Criterion* (Apr. 1933), 513–17).

explained to Paul Elmer More that his lectures were fundamentally a criticism of the lack of moral criteria in modern literary
criticism. He added tellingly: 'on a fundamental matter like this I
seem to take up an isolated position, and dissociate myself from
most of my contemporaries, including Yeats, Richards, Read.'[43]

In the course of the lectures that Eliot delivered at Harvard he
cited Read and Richards as the only two contemporary critics
with whom he did not like to disagree. That said, Eliot used the
publication of these lectures, entitled *The Use of Poetry and the
Use of Criticism*, publicly to dissociate himself from both Read
and Richards.[44] Eliot added a note to the published version of his
lecture, 'Wordsworth and Coleridge', extremely critical of Read's
tradition of English poetry.[45] He even went so far as to cite Read's
quibbling and somewhat dubious distinction between character
and personality in the 'heresy' appendix to *After Strange Gods*.[46]
At this time, Eliot told Richards that he thought that Read was a
philosophical amateur.[47] Only a few months earlier, he had
informed Read that he objected to Richards's recourse to what he
strikingly characterized as pseudo-religious nonsense.[48] The frosty
reception of Read's work in the *Criterion*, as well Eliot's public
strictures, marked a turning-point in their relationship. Read's
involvement with the *Criterion* gradually diminished to writing
short notices on books about the English romantics, a role that
could hardly be construed as at the heart of the journal's mission.
From now on, Read would be less guarded about expressing his
own convictions: one might even argue that the growing split
allowed him the necessary freedom in which to articulate them.[49]

Read and Eliot's collaboration reflected in essence certain complex patterns evident in the pages of the *Criterion*: namely, the
manner in which Eliot's fastidious editorial control was tempered

---

[43] T. S. Eliot to Paul Elmer More, 7 Nov. 1933. Cited in Ronald Schuchard, *Eliot's
Dark Angel* (Oxford, 1999), 145–6.

[44] Cf. T. S. Eliot to Paul Elmer More, 8 Dec. 1933. Princeton.

[45] See *The Use of Poetry and the Use of Criticism* (London, 1933), 81–5.

[46] See *After Strange Gods* (London, 1934), 67.

[47] T. S. Eliot to I. A. Richards, 24 Feb. 1934. Cambridge (Magdalene).

[48] T. S. Eliot to Herbert Read, 31 Oct. 1933. Victoria. Eliot particularly disliked the
five 'spiritual' exercises that Richards appended to *Practical Criticism* (1929).

[49] Cf. Herbert Read to Glenn Hughes, July 1930: 'In a sense I am too closely
associated with him [Eliot] for me to want to objectify him.' Cited in King, *The Last
Modern*, 89.

by a willingness to air opposing views. Eliot later characterized his editorial openness: 'The ideas with which you did not agree, the opinions which you could not accept, were as important to you as those which you found immediately acceptable.'[50] However, during the 1930s, as Read developed an interest in avant-garde art movements, the rift between them deepened. Partly due to a shortage of English art critics, Read had been commissioned by Ben Nicolls, Controller of Publications at the BBC, to contribute regular weekly 'Notes on Art' to the *Listener*, at extremely handsome financial terms.[51] These contributions helped to persuade Herbert Grierson that Read would be suitable for the Watson Gordon Chair of Fine Art at Edinburgh University. Unfortunately, due to personal difficulties, Read relinquished his position after less than two years.[52] He returned to London in 1933, settling in Hampstead where he formed close friendships with several resident artists, including Henry Moore, Ben Nicholson, and Barbara Hepworth. Read took on the role of an impresario of contemporary art, helping Paul Nash to launch Unit One to publicize the cause of abstract and surrealist art. Over the following years, the eminently respectable Read became an unlikely *agent provocateur* on behalf of surrealism.

An exotic Parisian import, surrealism initially made few inroads in Britain, except for some nascent interest in the Cambridge student periodical *Experiment*.[53] Hugh Sykes Davies, one of the founders of *Experiment*, supplied Read—a distant relative—with copies of the magazine. Sykes Davies graduated to the book reviewing section of the *Criterion*, although it was some years later, in the post-prandial atmosphere of one of Read's dinner parties, before Eliot asked to see samples of his poetry. In 1934, Eliot published a section from Sykes Davies's surrealist prose-poem, *Petron*, in the *Criterion*, although not without misgivings.[54] A year later, Read's incendiary 'Why

[50] *Notes Towards the Definition of Culture* (London, 1948), 117.

[51] Eliot encouraged Read to accept the *Listener's* attractive financial terms. See T. S. Eliot to Herbert Read, 28 Dec. 1929. Victoria.

[52] Although Read initially saw his move to Edinburgh as a great liberation he believed that his affair with Margaret Ludwig and the break-up of his marriage made his position untenable.

[53] See my '*Experiment* in Cambridge: A Manifesto of Young England', *Cambridge Quarterly* (Dec. 1998), 287–309.

[54] Sykes Davies claimed to have purchased his first bottle of brandy with his *Criterion* payment. See Hugh Sykes Davies, unpublished memoir. Cambridge (St. John's).

the English Have No Taste' detonated in the Parisian art magazine *Minotaure*.[55] In November 1935, David Gascoyne's *A Short Survey of Surrealism* strengthened the attack on the English public's resistance to foreign artistic currents.[56] By 1936 surrealism had attracted enough attention for Roland Penrose and E. L. T. Mesens to organize an International Surrealist Exhibition in London. Supported by the luminaries of the Continental surrealist movement—including Breton, Eluard, and Dali—Read's organizing committee managed to co-opt a remarkable number of English 'sympathizers'; eager no doubt for free public exposure, not to mention a place in which to promote their work.[57] In anticipation of the exhibition, Eliot published the teenage surrealist poet, Roger Roughton, in the *Criterion*.[58] Moreover, David Gascoyne's translation of Breton's pamphlet *Qu'est-ce que le Surréalisme?* was published in the Criterion Miscellany series. Eliot's decision was amply rewarded when the International Surrealist Exhibition, which he toured with Read, proved 'more than a *succès de scandale*' in the summer of 1936.[59]

Attempting to capitalize upon the notoriety of the exhibition, Faber sponsored another manifesto volume, *Surrealism*, edited by Read. Eliot may have felt uncomfortable reading Read's lengthy introduction to *Surrealism* (Read insisted on calling the English phenomenon 'superrealism' but no matter) which openly attacked the 'classicist-capitalist tradition' as the 'intellectual counterpart of political tyranny'.[60] Michael Roberts noted the appearance of *Surrealism* in the *Criterion* with polite scepticism.[61] It was the last

Rayner Heppenstall, reviewing *Petron*, observed: 'Mr. Davies furnishes us, in fact, with several good showings of the unsatisfactoriness of Surréalisme as a very broad whole' ('Books of the Quarter', *Criterion* (Jan. 1936), 334).

[55] Read's essay was reprinted in *Poetry and Anarchism* (London, 1938).

[56] Noticed briefly by Brian Coffey, 'Books of the Quarter', *Criterion* (Apr. 1936), 507.

[57] See Hugh Sykes Davies, 'Sympathies with Surrealism', *New Verse* (Apr.–May 1936), 15–21. Among the British artists and poets associated with the International Surrealist Exhibition in London were Read, Sykes Davies, Gascoyne, Humphrey Jennings, Henry Moore, Paul Nash, Roland Penrose, George Reavey, Roger Roughton, Dylan Thomas, Ruthven Todd, and Julian Trevelyan.

[58] See 'Poems', and 'Books of the Quarter', *Criterion* (Apr. 1936), 455–7 and 575.

[59] See Roger Hinks, 'Art Chronicle', *Criterion* (Oct. 1936), 70.

[60] 'Introduction', *Surrealism* (London, 1936), 23.

[61] 'Books of the Quarter', *Criterion* (Apr. 1937), 551–3.

exposure the movement was to receive in the *Criterion*. By then, Roughton had used a family inheritance to found the short-lived sixpenny monthly, later a quarterly, *Contemporary Poetry and Prose* (May 1936–Autumn 1937), an outlet for many of the English sympathizers with surrealism: a forum where surrealism could breathe in a less rarefied atmosphere than the *Criterion*.

Read's continued defence of romanticism and surrealism uncovered dormant tensions with Eliot. Read believed that Eliot's condescension towards English romantic poetry was based on 'moral or religious scruples', a standpoint he later characterized as 'the criterion of *The Criterion*'. He could have added that it was also based on Eliot's hostility to the political Jacobinism of some of the English romantics.[62] Read stressed surrealism's affinities with romanticism, suggesting certain continuities in his thought. The real underlying consistency, however, was a belief in radical political change. Read was fond of quoting the slogan: 'the cause of the arts is the cause of revolution.'[63] In November 1936, the English Surrealist Group, who took an active part in anti-fascist demonstrations, issued a 'Declaration on Spain' in *Contemporary Poetry and Prose* urging arms for the Spanish government.[64] Read, however, did not follow Sykes Davies and join the Communist Party. Instead, he pledged his allegiance to anarchism. The term requires some clarification, for it would be wrong to associate him with the violent, bomb-throwing anarchism of nineteenth-century Europe.[65] In point of fact, Read's anarchism grew out of his traumatic experience of trench warfare.

III

In the course of a *Criterion* batch review of First World War novels, Read delivered a bitter denunciation of the political structures that had fuelled the war:

The whole war was fought for rhetoric—fought for historical phrases and actual misery, fought *by* politicians and generals and *with* human

---

[62] Tate (ed.), *T. S. Eliot: The Man and His Work*, 29. Read believed that Eliot's 'disdain' for Shelley was not 'a critical judgement, but some moral asceticism'. See *In Defence of Shelley and Other Essays* (London, 1936), 142.

[63] *Poetry and Anarchism*, 40.

[64] Read was expelled from the British Surrealist Group in 1939.

[65] For a discussion of Read's anarchism, see David Goodman, 'The Politics of Herbert Read', *Herbert Read Reassessed* (Liverpool, 1998), 177–95.

flesh and blood, fanned by false and artificially created mob passions . . .
I can conceive of no values, least of all the political ideals conceived by
the men of poor character and intelligence who mostly prevail in the
political counsels of the caucus-ridden democracies of modern Europe,
for which human life indiscriminately and in the mass should be forcibly
sacrificed.[66]

Read's war experience had led him to a deep commitment to
pacifism, in conscious defiance of Freud's postulation of humanity's
aggressive and self-destructive 'death instinct'.[67] Read abandoned his Guild Socialism for a form of anarcho-syndicalism modelled on the small anarchist co-operatives and local communities
that flourished in Spain.[68] In the *Criterion*, Read suggested that
anarchism and pacifism were compatible: 'a radical alteration of the
state of the world . . . organised in territorial and economic units,
instead of national units, would remove the fundamental causes of
war.'[69] Eliot, on the other hand, attempted in his *Criterion*
Commentaries to view the pacifist debate within the framework of
Christian doctrine.[70] There is little doubt that Read's social and
political opinions during the 1930s were anathema to Eliot, and vice
versa. In October 1937, Read and Eliot clashed in the pages of
the *Criterion* over the decision by a party of Oxford dons to boycott
the bicentennial celebrations of Göttingen University, 'a question of
professional and cultural solidarity', according to Read, but really
a measure of his hatred of fascism and Hitler.[71] On this point, Eliot
favoured appeasement.[72]

---

[66] 'Books of the Quarter', *Criterion* (July 1930). The review drew a warm letter of
approval from F. R. Leavis, who had served as a medical orderly on the Western Front.
See F. R. Leavis to Herbert Read, 6 July 1930. Victoria.

[67] See Read's review of the League of Nations pamphlet *Why War?* in which
Einstein and Freud exchanged letters discussing the basis of modern war ('Books of
the Quarter', *Criterion* (Jan. 1934), 323–5).

[68] There were over two million members of anarchist collectives in Spain until
Franco's victory in the Spanish Civil War.

[69] 'Books of the Quarter', *Criterion* (Oct. 1933), 151.

[70] 'It has now become almost obligatory for every intellectual to issue some public
statement of opinion on the subject of peace' ('A Commentary', *Criterion* (Apr. 1937),
472). See also Eliot's reflections on the launch of Canon Dick Sheppard's populist Peace
Pledge Union ('A Commentary', *Criterion* (July 1936), 663–5, and (Oct. 1936), 68).

[71] Read described Hitler as 'a vulgar and pretentious demagogue' in 'The Necessity
of Anarchism', *Adelphi* (Oct. 1937), 14.

[72] See 'Correspondence', *Criterion* (Oct. 1937), 123–4.

Eliot recommended, without enthusiasm, Read's *Poetry and Anarchism* to the Faber book committee, securing publication in June 1938. The following month, Read reviewed Rudolf Rocker's *Anarcho-Syndicalism* in the *Criterion*. Finding it an important statement of the anarchist position, Read argued that Rocker was more tolerant and persuasive than ideologues for authoritarian government, such as Marx and Spengler. His explanation was couched in apologetic terms:

Anarchism is best conceived as an extreme form of liberalism; it regards the freedom of the individual as a necessity at every stage of social evolution. . . . That many young people in England, including the reviewer, should during the last 20 years have allowed their instinctive liberalism to become entangled with a doctrine so utterly opposed to their essential principles can only be explained by the ambiguity which characterises the whole terminology of socialism.[73]

Read conceded that anarcho-syndicalism in Britain lacked a practical programme: the vagueness of his own formulations indicate not so much a blueprint for political action as a gesture of protest at the forms of rationalized madness he saw prevalent in contemporary parliamentary politics. At any rate, Read's defence of Rocker did not seem to ruffle the conservative readership of the *Criterion*. In the closing issue, Hugh Gordon Porteus remarked: 'There is something to be said for pacific anarchy, and Mr Herbert Read has said it with courageous honesty.'[74]

The *Criterion* was never likely to become a platform for anarchism. Eliot published Read's review of Rocker because he believed that Read was really more of a social-democrat than an anarchist. He told Stephen Spender, who had complained in *New Verse* that the left-wing intelligentsia ignored *Poetry and Anarchism*: 'Sometimes when I read Herbert's inflammatory anarchist pamphlets, I have the impression that I am reading the pronouncements of an old-fashioned nineteenth-century liberal.'[75] Be that as it may, the fact that Eliot permitted Read to defend anarcho-syndicalism in the *Criterion* at all was arguably an index of the crisis besetting British parliamentary democracy. It was, at the same time, Read's

---

[73] 'Books of the Quarter', *Criterion* (July 1938), 767–8.
[74] 'Periodicals', *Criterion* (Jan. 1939), 395.
[75] See Stephen Spender, *The Thirties and After* (London, 1978), 251.

final contribution to the *Criterion*. When, in January 1939, Ronald Duncan and Ezra Pound discussed the possibility of Read reviving the *Criterion*, they were unaware of the gulf that now separated him from Eliot.[76] Shortly after the outbreak of the Second World War, Eliot warned John Betjeman against the intellectual nonentities that Read was assembling at Routledge.[77]

On the surface at least, relations between Eliot and Read remained cordial. In August 1938, Read lamented the demise of the polite essay perfected by the great nineteenth-century quarterlies and monthlies, an extended essay-review form that he claimed the *Criterion* had upheld in the twentieth century.[78] But for all the public professions of gratitude, Read privately confided his frustration with Eliot.[79] In 1943, he told Richard Church that although his intellectual debt to Eliot was immense: 'he has been rather like a gloomy priest presiding over my affections and spontaneity.'[80] Read was more tactful when he came to evaluate the nature of his relationship with Eliot in an obituary address delivered at the Center for Advanced Studies at Wesleyan University. He suspected that 'as time passed and our opinions continued to diverge', Eliot maintained a personal affection for him but ceased to respect his judgements as a critic.[81] Wyndham Lewis was more explicit, albeit malicious, in reporting Eliot's alleged characterization of their relationship:

Not long ago Tom [Eliot] expressed to me his misgivings for having, in effect, given Herbert Read his start, encouraging him to contribute to *The Criterion* and publishing some of his books, saying that there was no one whose ideas he considered more pernicious, and I agree with Tom.[82]

In *Men Without Art* (1934), Lewis satirized the *Criterion* as a vessel where the skipper would not entrust navigation to the

---

[76] See Ronald Duncan to Ezra Pound, 30 Jan. 1939. Yale.

[77] T. S. Eliot to John Betjeman, 18 Sept. 1939. Victoria.

[78] See 'Introduction', *Collected Essays in Literary Criticism* (London, 1938), 11.

[79] E. W. F. Tomlin described Read as a 'firm' rather than a 'close' friend of Eliot during the 1930s. See *T. S. Eliot: A Friendship* (London, 1988), 187.

[80] Cited in King, *The Last Modern*, 76.

[81] See Tate (ed.), *T. S. Eliot: The Man and His Work*, 26.

[82] Cited in Jeffrey Meyers, *A Biography of Wyndham Lewis* (London, 1980), 312. It should be noted that Lewis's remark was made shortly after a bitter quarrel with Read.

first-mate: presumably for fear that with Read at the helm the boat would drift with every current of intellectual fashion.[83]

Critics of the *Criterion* have been quick to capitalize upon demonstrable disjunctions and contradictions of tone and content. One does not have to endorse Geoffrey Grigson's arresting critical epitome of Read as Eliot's 'seditious Eye': 'quoter, taster, and politico-aesthetic chameleon.'[84] However, it is difficult to ignore the flagrant contradictions in Read's stated convictions: the champion of avant-garde art who simultaneously edited the establishment *Burlington Magazine*; the political anarchist who accepted a knighthood; not least, the repressed romantic who initially did much to sustain the 'classical' tendency espoused by the *Criterion*. Read, a keen student of Hegelian dialectic and the irrational interconnections of the Freudian psyche, was untroubled by accusations of inconsistency, countering rather coyly: 'if they come as a natural consequence of a natural disposition I leave them to be reconciled in that synthetic judgement which is the Last Judgement.'[85] A 'natural disposition', it is implied, is willing to moderate the expression of pronounced differences to a thinking, educated audience. Montaigne, who pondered the inconsistency of our actions, understood that paradox is an integral part of human nature. One might add that such inconsistency is also an inevitable constituent of the nexus of the literary periodical.

[83] See *Men Without Art* (London, 1934), 95.
[84] 'A Letter from England', *Poetry* [Chicago] (Nov. 1936), 102.
[85] *Surrealism*, 88.

6

Bonamy Dobrée
Agreeable Sceptic

You need not agree with Mr. Eliot on some points, I mean in his view of the contemporary scene: I, personally do not share his love of the Church; but you have to admit that his views are important views that matter at the present day.

Bonamy Dobrée, *New English Weekly* (8 November 1934), 92

Bonamy Dobrée was a close friend of Eliot and a frequent and prolific contributor to the *Criterion*. His style of reviewing was colloquial and familiar, notable for its geniality and touches of flippancy, balanced with the urbane tones of the cultivated dilettante. In some respects, he exemplifies the *Criterion*'s links to the world of the gentlemanly Edwardian 'man of letters'; a figure at some remove from the academic professionalism and specialization that increasingly came to influence literary journalism in the 1930s. Dobrée's dislike of scholarly pedantry or solemnity, 'pribbles and prabbles' as he called them, gave his reviewing a spirit (to adapt his words on eighteenth-century literary society) 'so gay, so graceful, so agreeably sceptical'.[1] Douglas Jefferson, a colleague at Leeds University, remarked of him: 'he was always a little afraid of the deadening effect of academic attitudes.'[2] He certainly wrote scornfully in the *Criterion* of the 'academic racket' and the 'academic gangsters'.[3] Although F. R. Leavis was perhaps closer to the truth when he suggested that Dobrée had one foot in university circles and one in the fashionable world of

[1] 'Whig Satire', *Nation and Athenaeum* (26 June 1926), 358.
[2] *University of Leeds Review* (1975), 178.
[3] 'Books of the Quarter', *Criterion* (July 1938), 743.

metropolitan literary journalism.[4] Even so, he was occasionally shot from both sides. An examination of Dobrée's role on the *Criterion* reveals tension and friction, especially when it came to matters of theological doctrine. It is worth bearing in mind that Richard Hoggart, a promising undergraduate at the University of Leeds during the late 1930s, was struck by Dobrée's public-school code of manners and his military briskness in dealing with practical affairs; in short, by his 'style'.[5] In fact, there was a great deal in Dobrée's independent-minded character that tempered his affection for Eliot and tested his loyalty to the *Criterion*.

I

Bonamy Dobrée was born in London in 1891, the only son of a family of wealthy Guernsey bankers. He was educated at Haileybury, a boys' boarding school founded in 1862, ostensibly to prepare the boys for their future careers as soldiers and administrators in the far-flung regions of the British Empire. After the school OTC, Dobrée graduated to the Royal Military Academy at Woolwich. He was commissioned to the Royal Field Artillery in 1910, resigned as a subaltern in 1913 following his marriage to Valentine, the daughter of Lt.-Col. Sir Alexander Brooke-Pechell, but he rejoined for the duration of the First World War. During active service he was stationed in France, Egypt, and Palestine and was mentioned in dispatches. After the war, Dobrée went up to Christ's College, Cambridge, and captained the university fencing team against Oxford. He also distinguished himself academically at Cambridge, winning the respect of several teachers of the recently established English tripos. In August 1920, his long essay on 'Elizabethan Drama on the Modern Stage' appeared in the *London Mercury*. The article acknowledged a debt to Eliot's 'Some Notes on the Blank Verse of Christopher Marlowe' published in *Art and Letters* the previous autumn; it was clear that he was also familiar with the poetry that Eliot had published in *Art and Letters* and other little magazines. When John Rodker presented

---

[4] Leavis included Dobrée in a negative survey of contemporary literary criticism. See 'What's Wrong with Criticism?', *Scrutiny* (Sept. 1932), 132–46.
[5] See Richard Hoggart, 'Teaching with Style', in *Speaking to Each Other* (Harmondsworth, 1973), ii. 189–204.

Dobrée with a copy of *Ara Vos Prec* (1920) it confirmed his opinion that Eliot had a particular relevance to contemporary society: 'Here, I felt, was a poet who meant something in terms of today.'[6]

After graduating from Cambridge in 1921, the Dobrées travelled through Continental Europe, eventually settling in the village of Larrau in the French Pyrenees. It was here that Dobrée pursued his research into the dramatic wits of the English Restoration stage. He was drawn to the risqué badinage, cultivated upper-class refinement, and worldly scepticism of the drama of the period: his pioneering study *Restoration Comedy* was published in 1924. Meanwhile, the Dobrées maintained cordial connections with Francophile London groups. Valentine became embroiled in the louche sexual relations of the Bloomsbury set and had an affair with Ralph Partridge. Perhaps it was not surprising that Dobrée, who had written that the approach of Restoration comedy to marriage represented 'not licentiousness, but a deep curiosity, and a desire to try new ways of living' amiably tolerated his wife's infidelities.[7] At any rate, he benefited from the Bloomsbury connection when Leonard Woolf invited him to contribute to the *Nation and Athenaeum*. It was at a party at the Woolfs' Richmond House in 1924 that Dobrée and Eliot met for the first time. A subscriber to the *Criterion*, Dobrée daringly reversed the editor's question: 'Do you read *all* the *Criterion*?' with the teasing reply: 'Not *all*: do you?'—Eliot apparently confessed he did not.[8] Later that year, Dobrée submitted an essay on Laforgue to the *Criterion*. Eliot's encouraging and carefully worded rejection of the article was a token of his generous response to Dobrée's display of wit at their first encounter.[9] It was the beginning of a long and friendly correspondence.

In September 1925, Dobrée was appointed a lecturer in dramatic history at Queen Mary College, East London. A frequent visitor to the London theatres he became, at the instigation of Francis Birrell,

---

[6] See 'T. S. Eliot: A Personal Reminiscence', in Allen Tate (ed.), *T. S. Eliot: The Man and his Work* (London, 1967), 66.

[7] For Dobrée's position see *Restoration Comedy* (Oxford, 1924).

[8] See Tate (ed.), *T. S. Eliot: The Man and His Work*, 67.

[9] Eliot encouraged Dobrée to 'go thoroughly into the philosophical basis of Laforgue's thought'. Cited in Ronald Schuchard, *Eliot's Dark Angel* (Oxford, 1999), 231 n. 27.

the drama critic of the *Nation*, writing under the pseudonym of 'Omicron' (it is likely that Eliot was aware of the provenance of these reviews). In January 1926, Richard Aldington wrote to Dobrée to inform him that he had received the *Criterion* review copy of *Restoration Comedy* from Eliot, together with four other of his recent volumes of criticism, including a dialogue on stage speech, *Histriophone*, published by the Hogarth Press.[10] Aldington's *Criterion* review concluded in the manner of an enthusiastic head-master's report: 'His work has already procured him a distinct place as biographer and critic, and he may look forward to the future with confidence.'[11] In February 1926, Aldington wrote again to convey Eliot's agreement with his magisterial judgement in the *Criterion*[12]— an estimation confirmed by Eliot's decision to nominate Dobrée as his successor as the Clark Lecturer at Cambridge.[13] During the year he taught at London University, Dobrée could often be found down-stairs at the Grove Tavern with a faithful band of *Criterion* contribu-tors: the regular lunches cemented his friendship with Eliot. In fact, from the mid-1920s onward Dobrée was one of Eliot's closest associates on the *Criterion*. He published several of his imaginary conversations—a rather dated genre, derived principally from Landor, albeit a form admired and practised by Eliot—in its pages. Not only was Dobrée recruited as a regular *Criterion* reviewer, but Eliot entrusted him with leading reviews of important contempor-ary figures, some of them Faber authors.

The issue of how far Eliot dictated an editorial line for the review section of the *Criterion* raises some delicate questions that are best approached through example. In June 1926, Eliot solicited a review of several works by Jean Cocteau, whom he numbered among the 'significant figures of the twenties'[14] by virtue of his versatile work as an avant-garde poet, novelist, dramatist, and film director. Cocteau's 'Scandales' was published

---

[10] See Richard Aldington to Bonamy Dobrée, 8 Jan. 1926. Leeds. Eliot had origi-nally wanted to review *Restoration Comedy* personally in the *Criterion*. See T. S. Eliot to Bonamy Dobrée, Mar. 1925. Leeds.

[11] 'Books of the Quarter', *Criterion* (Apr. 1926), 381.

[12] See Richard Aldington to Bonamy Dobrée, 11 Feb. 1926. Leeds.

[13] In fact, Eliot was succeeded by E. M. Forster. Dobrée eventually delivered the Clark Lectures in 1952, later collected as *The Broken Cistern* (1954).

[14] See 'Foreword' to Joseph Chiari, *Contemporary French Poets* (London, 1952), p. ix.

(in French) in the *Criterion* in 1926 and an English translation of his eclectic series of essays, *Le Rappel à l'ordre*, seen through the press by Eliot, appeared in Faber's first spring catalogue. Eliot was particularly interested in Cocteau's collaboration with the Ballet Russe; for one thing he was searching for hints on how to write a modernist drama. He informed Dobrée: 'the one side of Cocteau's work which so far has shown itself to be of incontestable value and interest is his theatrical side.'[15] There are a number of points about Eliot's letter to Dobrée that are worth mentioning: firstly, the invitation to review a volume, *A Call to Order*, from Faber's current publishing list; secondly, Eliot's blandly persuasive flattery of Dobrée's suitability for the task. Most importantly, Eliot's letter offered gentle suggestions—signposted by recourse to the auxiliary verbs 'could', 'should', 'would'—leading the reviewer towards the path preferred by the editor. Dobrée's *Criterion* review followed Eliot in locating Cocteau's central interest in his dramatic work and mixed admiration for his dazzling creativity with a sense of the limitations of his experimentalism. Dobrée described *Orphée*—he saw the play at the Théâtre des Arts in Paris—as 'a delicious toy, an exquisite trifle, which has hardly anything in it to spoil a fugitive enjoyment'.[16] The review drew an indignant letter from Cocteau, who complained in a postscript: 'C'est 12 ans de drame jetés/cachés la.' Significantly, the message was conveyed to Dobrée with some reassuring editorial words: 'There is no pleasing people like that.' Eliot added rather pertly: 'I shall write and rebuke him and point out the English view of such matters.'[17]

In September 1926, Eliot instructed Irene Fassett to send copies of books by William Ralph Inge, the 'gloomy' Dean of St Paul's, to the Royal University of Egypt in Cairo where Dobrée had succeeded Robert Graves as Professor of English. Inge enjoyed a popular reputation as a public moralist, voicing his pessimistic and often provocative views on contemporary society in a weekly column for the *Evening Standard*. Eliot felt that Inge's influence

---

[15] T. S. Eliot to Bonamy Dobrée, 23 June 1926. Cited in Schuchard, *Eliot's Dark Angel*, 237 n. 29.

[16] 'Books of the Quarter', *Criterion* (Oct. 1926), 766. Eliot and Dobrée travelled together to Paris in the summer of 1926.

[17] Cited in Tate (ed.), *T. S. Eliot: The Man and His Work*, 68–9.

was inimical and made him the subject of a withering attack in his *Criterion* Commentary for April 1924. He wrote to Dobrée to inform him that Inge was a heretic—Inge stressed the primacy of personal, even mystical, religious intimations in opposition to the dogmatic assertions of the Catholic Church—and in Inge's pronouncements as a social critic Eliot detected an intellectual dishonesty in his failure to argue at the level demanded by his own intellect. In his *Criterion* Commentary Eliot laid out the matter with tough-minded insistence:

It is possible that the Dean [Inge] feels it necessary to write down to the level of newspaper readers: if so, he is wholly mistaken; for nothing is ever gained by writing *down* to any level; writing *down* is itself an assertion of superiority which no one is entitled to make.[18]

Eliot advised Dobrée to read this Commentary on Inge before writing his review.[19]

If *writing* down to readers (as opposed to *talking* down to opponents) was an indefensible token of superiority, Eliot's condescension towards Inge was presumably excusable on the grounds that it emanated from a 'higher' form of print life, circulated among a discerning and disinterested few. Whatever the truth, it is highly revealing that Dobrée ascribed Inge's popularity, in his dulcetly destructive leading review for the *Criterion*, as a case of flattering the opinions of the 'average, uninformed reader'. He concluded: 'In short, Dr Inge is a most efficient journalist.'[20] The terms in which he chose to couch his critique are intriguing since Dobrée was, in Eliot's editorial eyes, a notably 'efficient' reviewer. In 1927, his utility could be gauged from the fact that he had succeeded in negotiating the most tricky and troublesome of all *Criterion* undertakings; namely, pleasing Wyndham Lewis (and by extension Eliot) with a very perceptive review of Lewis's characteristically idiosyncratic but penetrating study of Shakespeare, *The Lion and the Fox*.[21] In fact, Dobrée's contributions from Cairo do not so much reveal the impress of Eliot's fastidious control of the *Criterion* as

---

[18] 'A Commentary', *Criterion* (Apr. 1924), 233.
[19] T. S. Eliot to Bonamy Dobrée, 1 Oct. 1926. Leeds.
[20] 'Books of the Quarter', *Criterion* (Jan. 1927), 109.
[21] See 'Recent Books', *Criterion* (June 1927), 339–43. For Lewis's positive response to the review, see Wyndham Lewis to Bonamy Dobrée, 11 July 1927. Leeds.

a deep understanding and sympathy, on aesthetic and cultural matters, between the two men. In February 1927, Eliot wrote to Dobrée to say that his continued support was crucial to the success of the *Criterion*.[22] This was the period, it might be recalled, of the Bolovian high jinks that passed among an intimate circle of friends: Dobrée remembered it as the time when Eliot was at his 'most encouraging to myself' and to his wife.[23]

II

Approached from a different direction, Dobrée's contributions highlight an important constitutive feature of the *Criterion*: namely, the journal's measured, even ambivalent response to the Victorian inheritance. In point of fact, surprisingly few of the authors from the syllabus and reading list of Eliot's wartime Extension lectures on Victorian literature received coverage in the *Criterion*, although there were appreciative essays, from a number of hands, on Cardinal Newman, Thackeray, Arnold, George Eliot, Dante Gabriel, and Christina Rossetti.[24] Dobrée's contributions on Victorian subjects, however, are particularly valuable in constructing the overall profile of the *Criterion*: their mixture of nostalgia for the serious-ness and disinterestedness of the Victorian sage, combined with an attack on the putative philistinism, hypocrisy, and coercive moral-ity of the Victorian age takes on a kind of representative status.

Dobrée's review of the two-volume *Early Victorian England*, edited by G. M. Young, spoke with an equal measure of fascination and repulsion on the subject of the 'roseate confidence which gave something godlike, or at least heroic to their [i.e. the Victorians'] countenances',[25] just as his *Criterion* essay on his boyhood hero, Macaulay, praised the energetic, narrative momentum of his his-tory of England, while at the same time adding that the myth of progress that structurally underpinned it had been exploded by the

[22] See T. S. Eliot to Bonamy Dobrée, 28 Feb. 1928. Leeds.
[23] See Tate (ed.), *T. S. Eliot: The Man and His Work*, 70. Valentine Dobrée con-tributed a short story, 'Nearer God', to the *Criterion* (Oct. 1929), 61–9. She had ear-lier received a favourable *Criterion* review of her novel, *Your Cuckoo Sings by Kind*.
[24] For details of Eliot's wartime Extension lectures on Victorian literature, see Schuchard, *Eliot's Dark Angel*, 32–44.
[25] 'Books of the Quarter', *Criterion* (July 1935), 638.

subsequent course of world history.[26] It was natural, given his Bloomsbury connections, that Dobrée should have been influenced by the vogue for Lytton Strachey's debunkings of various prominent Victorian public figures; and yet, he noted in the *Criterion* that the suave felicities of Strachey's prose style were often tendentiously impressionistic and failed to mask a wayward attention to precise, historical documentation.[27] Moreover, his lukewarm review of *Elizabeth and Essex*, written in full knowledge of Eliot's strained relations with Strachey,[28] prepared the ground for a subsequent bitter denunciation of Stracheyan historiography by the irascible Tory historian, the Revd Charles Smyth, Fellow of Corpus Christi College, Cambridge.[29]

Rudyard Kipling was the Victorian writer who received the most extensive, as well as the most favourable, coverage in the *Criterion*. In his Commentary for October 1926, Eliot had taken the occasion of Kipling's award of the Gold Medal of the Royal Society of Literature to praise him as the 'greatest master of the short story in English'.[30] Shortly after this date, Eliot commissioned a lengthy essay on Kipling from Dobrée.[31] Dobrée's admiration for the 'Kiplingesque' ideals of duty, moral action, and 'masculine' strength of character are a distinctive feature of his contribution to the *Criterion*. Richard Hoggart recalled vividly Dobrée's contempt for calculating 'intellectuals' who sought to remain above the fray; on the other hand, in the *Criterion* Dobrée praised Kipling's discovery of the 'philosophy of action' founded upon 'devotion to something each man must conceive of as bigger than himself'.[32] In Kipling's case, of course, this higher court of appeal was not the rather tepid Christian pieties espoused by many late Victorians, but the paternalistic attitudes of the British Empire. Having said that, Dobrée was careful to appraise the idea and

[26] See 'Macaulay', *Criterion* (July 1933), 593–604.
[27] See 'Books of the Quarter', *Criterion* (Apr. 1929), 524–9.
[28] See T. S. Eliot to Bonamy Dobrée, 11 Dec. 1928 and 1 Feb. 1929. Leeds. Eliot reviewed *Elizabeth and Essex* anonymously in the *TLS* (6 Dec. 1928).
[29] 'A Note on Historical Biography and Mr Strachey', *Criterion* (July 1929), 647–60. Revd Charles Smyth (1903–87) contributed 46 book reviews to the *Criterion*. For a discussion of Smyth as an Anglican reactionary, see Maurice Cowling, *Religion and Public Doctrine in Modern England* (Cambridge, 1980), 72–95.
[30] 'A Commentary', *Criterion* (Oct. 1926), 627.
[31] T. S. Eliot to Bonamy Dobrée, 13 Nov. 1926. Leeds.
[32] See 'Rudyard Kipling', *Criterion* (Dec. 1927), 499–515.

rhetoric of imperialism, not only with his customary vigour, but also with some delicacy. One can only speculate upon the complex emotions with which the schoolboy Dobrée contemplated the recently completed South African War Memorial when he arrived at Haileybury in 1903.

Dobrée's vision of British imperialism was certainly not without a strong element of Edwardian liberal-dissident scorn for any Kiplingesque cant about the White Man's burden. He sought with great scrupulousness to avoid falling into the trap of reinforcing a crude, binary opposition between an English 'us' and a colonial, racially distinct 'other':

> Mr. Kipling's love of the Empire and his admiration for those virtues it brings out in men, makes him apt to find qualities in Englishmen only, which really exist in all races, and this part of the deformation Mr. Kipling the artist has at times undergone at the hands of Mr. Kipling the man of action, who found his weapon in the press and his altar on the British Empire.[33]

Not that Dobrée's own opinions were always entirely free of the chauvinistic hypocrisy that looked at the British Empire and saw a high-minded 'civilizing' mission, but not the heavy-handed political, military, and economic bullying that invariably accompanied it. In his review of books dealing with the Napoleonic invasion of Egypt[34] and with British rule in Egypt—a rare treatment of African issues in the Euro-centred *Criterion*—one cannot fail to detect a whiff of pride in the idea of Empire that he had encountered at Haileybury.[35] However, Dobrée's *Criterion* contributions on Kipling professed to despise the aggressive patriotism of his popular newspaper journalism. At the same time, they defended Kipling as a consummate artist.

The approach exercised a marked influence on Eliot when he came to write an introduction to *A Choice of Kipling's Verse* in 1941. In the course of his introduction, Eliot referred to Dobrée's article as a 'valuable essay'. He even followed the structure of the earlier *Criterion* piece: Eliot posed Dobrée's question whether

---

[33] Ibid. 508.
[34] Eliot had studied *L'Expédition de Bonaparte en Egypt* at Smith Academy, which may account for the unusually high number of *Criterion* book reviews on Napoleon.
[35] See 'Books of the Quarter', *Criterion* (Oct. 1934), 128–30.

there was more to Kipling than Max Beerbohm's caricature of
him as a one-dimensional jingoist, then he proceeded to answer
emphatically in the affirmative.[36] Eliot's reflections on the subject
are worth reproducing:

For too many people, an Empire has become something to apologize
for . . . and patriotism itself is expected to be inarticulate. But we must
accustom ourselves to recognizing that for Kipling the Empire was not
merely an idea, a good idea or a bad one; it was something the reality of
which he felt. And in his expression of his feeling he was certainly not
aiming at flattery of national, racial or imperial vanity, or attempting to
propagate a political programme: he was aiming to communicate the
awareness of something in existence of which he felt that most people
were very imperfectly aware. It was an awareness of grandeur, certainly,
but it was much more an awareness of responsibility.[37]

Eliot spoke of 'responsibility' and Dobrée of 'devotion' in relation to the burden of Empire; both were ultimately concerned with
highlighting a sense of duty to a code of conduct transcending the
individual. In his *Criterion* essay, Dobrée linked Kipling's worship
of the British Empire with 'old Rome' and described it as his
Catholic Church.[38] Eliot went further by suggesting that behind
Kipling's idea of Empire there was something more permanent—
namely, the Roman Empire and the Holy Roman Empire. In the
introduction to his choice of Kipling's verse, Eliot commented
tellingly: 'The vision is almost that of an idea of empire laid up in
heaven.'[39] Frank Kermode, in the course of a fascinating discussion
of Eliot's conception of Empire, pointed out that the full meaning
of this remark could only be appreciated when read as the culmi-
nation of a series of editorial statements in the *Criterion*, perhaps
the most germane being his citation, in ancient Greek, of Plato's
reference to a 'pattern laid up in heaven' in April 1935.[40] Eliot's
idea of an empire of the mind, an empire laid up in heaven, was
the guiding principle behind the *Criterion*'s spiritualized cultural
imperialism: a defence of the Christian West in general.

---

[36] See 'Rudyard Kipling', *On Poetry and Poets* (London, 1957), 228–51. Eliot
praised the essay more highly in private. See T. S. Eliot to Bonamy Dobrée, 24 Jan. 1928.
Leeds. Beerbohm's caricature 'Mr Rudyard Kipling takes a bloomin' Day aht, on the
blasted 'Eath, along with Britannia, 'is Gurl' appeared in *The Poet's Corner* (1904).
[37] *On Poetry and Poets*, 243.   [38] 'Rudyard Kipling', 505.
[39] *On Poetry and Poets*, 245.
[40] For a full discussion, see ch. 1 of *The Classic* (London, 1975).

III

In his obituary 'personal reminiscence' Dobrée fondly recalled Eliot's editorial generosity and integrity: 'You felt all the time that he respected your personality, and that any person was entitled to his views so long as they were honestly held, and not produced for the sake of controversy.'[41] In private, however, he could be more forthright about the expression of differences. In 1929, Dobrée told Herbert Read that he was concerned about Eliot's editorial management of the *Criterion*, complaining that: 'We are asked to condemn the Revolution [the Revolution of 1688] because it was not Anglo-Catholic! I am beginning to feel a little uncomfortable in that galley.'[42] In his preface to a collection of essays on modern literature, *The Lamp and the Lute* (1929), reprinting his essay on Kipling and introducing a new one on Eliot, Dobrée acknowledged that the three greatest influences on his criticism were Eliot, Read, and Richards. Nevertheless, after reading *For Lancelot Andrewes* he was sceptical of the value of Eliot's 'eternal search for assurance' in religious doctrine. The general terms of the indictment went further: 'The tendency of criticism today is away from one of pure aesthetic towards one of values. It is even stated that the critic of literature, however much he may desire to stick to art, is bound sooner or later to find himself stepping over his fence into the domain of ethics.'[43] Dobrée was extremely reluctant to enter the public arena as a moralist, noting in passing that although Eliot used Christian belief to elucidate literary texts it was unclear if other critics would be well advised to follow his example. *The Lamp and the Lute* was dedicated to Herbert Read who doubtless shared Dobrée's anxiety that the *Criterion* was becoming weighed down with eschatological baggage.[44]

In January 1930, Dobrée complained to another *Criterion* contributor, John Hayward, that literary criticism was too often subordinated to ethical or theological values.[45] The following month, he issued a critical credo in the *Spectator*, entitled 'The Future of Criticism'. Dobrée argued that literary criticism had

---

[41] See Tate (ed.), *T. S. Eliot: The Man and His Work*, 71–2.
[42] Bonamy Dobrée to Herbert Read, 9 Apr. 1929. Cited in James King, *The Last Modern* (London, 1990), 89.   [43] *The Lamp and the Lute* (Oxford, 1929), p. xi.
[44] In 1931, Read and Dobrée co-edited *The London Book of English Prose*.
[45] Bonamy Dobrée to John Hayward, 11 Jan. 1930. Cambridge (King's).

once usefully policed the passage of literary movements. In recent years, however, he believed that it had become something different, in fact it had ceased to be literary criticism at all and was now a department of moral philosophy, amateur psychology, or, worst of all, a 'high priest'. After some remarks on Eliot, Dobrée observed dryly: 'I for one wish that he would return to literary criticism.'[46] After 1930, Dobrée's influence and role on the *Criterion* began to diminish in importance and lose its centrality. A strongly icono-clastic critic, at times a little wilful, he published articles express-ing disagreement with Eliot's religious and political position in the *Spectator*, the *Listener*, and the *New English Weekly*, peri-odicals where he did not feel any obligation to stroke to an Anglo-Catholic drum and where he might flaunt his witty and elegant prose style—to cut a dash, as it were. In the *Listener* Dobrée confessed: 'I always feel slightly uneasy when I'm told what I ought to feel: as Keats remarked, we hate a work that has a palpable design upon us.'[47] In 1934 in the *New English Weekly*—a journal expressly founded to provide an open forum for dissenting voices[48]—Dobrée summed up his ambivalence towards Eliot's post-conversion criticism: 'We see Mr Eliot veer-ing from a technical interest to a moral one.' Veering, of course, suggests a less than careful change of direction, and yet Dobrée could still endorse the belief that Eliot's opinions were extremely relevant to the current politico-economic crisis.[49]

Dobrée's role on the *Criterion* during the 1930s was complicated by a number of factors. Although he, in common with several other regular contributors to the *Criterion*, did not share Eliot's religious belief or conservative political position, his support of Major Douglas's 'Social Credit' theories did something to alleviate or simply paper over the deeper disquietudes at work. For example, in the *New English Weekly*, Dobrée made his own brisk about-turn: offering a public recantation of the high aesthetic line of 'pure' literary criticism:

Everybody will agree that the business of literature is with the quality of human life, and that the writer tries to improve this quality. . . . There are periods when the immediate physical problem is so pressing, so

[46] 'The Future of Criticism', *Spectator* (Feb. 1930), 189.
[47] 'Seas and Sails', *Listener* (May 1933), 800.
[48] See Philip Mairet to Maurice Reckitt, 18 Oct. 1936. Sussex.
[49] See 'Views and Reviews', *New English Weekly* (8 Nov. 1934), 92.

urgent, when the whole quality of human life is so bound up with what we shall do now, at this moment, in the practical field, that the Ivory Tower seems blasphemy.[50]

In April 1934, Dobrée and Eliot were signatories of a letter to *The Times* advocating a government study of a 'scheme of national credit'.[51] In the *Criterion* that month, Dobrée voiced his extreme impatience with the theories of Evan Durbin, a lecturer at the London School of Economics. In a world of overproduction and unemployment, of poverty amid plenty, Dobrée attacked the degree of mathematical abstraction in the remedies proposed by many professional economists: 'One wonders if the average economist', he remarked bitterly, 'even begins to realise what the intelligent public really thinks about his singularly sterile gymnastics.'[52] Writing from his country retreat at Mendham Priory in Norfolk, Dobrée, the son of a family of affluent Victorian bankers, laid the blame for the current economic crisis firmly at the doorstep of unregulated nineteenth-century capitalism. More than that, his anti-industrialism and support for Social Credit theories had some affinities with Eliot's Anglican critique of the modern acquisitive society.

If Eliot found some solace and a glimmer of hope in the Anglican assemblies and discussion groups that he increasingly turned towards during the 1930s, Dobrée was never shy about expressing his profound scepticism regarding all religious solutions to worldly ills. This fundamental difference could bring them close to outright polemical exchange. In 1936, Dobrée wrote to Eliot to say that he was appalled by the asceticism of the epigraph Eliot had taken from St John of the Cross: 'Hence the soul cannot be possessed of the divine union, until it divests itself of the love of created beings.'[53] Later that year, Eliot sent a letter to Leeds University, where Dobrée had accepted the chair of English Literature, informing him in a facetious jotting that he now edited the *Criterion* 'without any help from my friends'.[54] It was certainly

---

[50] 'Views and Reviews', *New English Weekly* (27 June 1935), 211–12.

[51] See 'Letters', *The Times* (4 Apr. 1934). Other signatories included Lascelles Abercrombie, Aldous Huxley, the Revd Hewlett Johnson, Edwin Muir, Hamish Miles, Herbert Read, and I. A. Richards.

[52] 'Books of the Quarter', *Criterion* (Apr. 1934), 488.

[53] For Eliot's response, see T. S. Eliot to Bonamy Dobrée, 17 Apr. 1936. Leeds.

[54] See Tate (ed.), *T. S. Eliot: The Man and His Work*, 78.

true that Dobrée's input no longer appreciably determined the character of the quarterly, although his association with the journal remained benign and supportive; a manifestation of the well-brushed *noblesse oblige* that determined their social relations.[55] Hardly surprisingly, they shared an antipathy to Chamberlain's 'ungentlemanly' part in the dismemberment of Czechoslovakia; a betrayal of principles that they believed rendered war highly likely. Dobrée described 1938 in the *Criterion* as a year of 'humiliation and disgrace'—a sentiment subsequently echoed by Eliot.[56] They discussed the gloomy European situation during the final months of the *Criterion*: the sobering tone of their correspondence makes the high spirits of their initial collaboration seem a rather forlorn memory.[57] Their solidarity at this difficult time was publicly reinforced when Dobrée presented Eliot for an honorary degree at Leeds University in the summer of 1939.

In the difficult task of attempting to reconstruct the nature of Dobrée's role on the *Criterion* or to discern a pattern to his contributions, it is hard not to turn to Richard Aldington's initial estimation of his work. Aldington introduced him to readers of the *Criterion* as an 'attractive personality'—a writer of some wit and panache.[58] A connoisseur of prose styles, Dobrée had a pet theory that the reader can hear the spoken voice of a good writer. If one is to recapture the distinctive quality of the printed voice of Bonamy Dobrée it is to savour the conversational inflections of his highly digressive style: a winning vivacity, unpretentious if at times a touch snobbish, usually courteous notwithstanding an occasional flash of bluff, no-nonsense honesty. Surprisingly, in 1935, Dobrée asserted that he did not admire the conventional public-school code of manners.[59] The admission might seem odd because the strengths and limitations of his *Criterion* contributions appear to be inextricably bound up with a patrician 'public-school' tone: an assumption of authority and superiority that contemporary critics might judge as a form of intellectual imperialism, but a

---

[55] The well-mannered expression of differences broke down only once, briefly in 1951, when they quarrelled about the internal politics at Leeds University. See T. S. Eliot to Bonamy Dobrée, 22 June and 26 June 1951. Cambridge (King's).

[56] See 'Books of the Quarter', *Criterion* (July 1938), 741.

[57] See T. S. Eliot to Bonamy Dobrée, 2 Nov. 1938. Leeds.

[58] 'Books of the Quarter', *Criterion* (Apr. 1926), 381.

[59] 'Views and Reviews', *New English Weekly* (27 June 1935), 212.

rhetorical gesture which was presumably received with sympathy and understanding by readers of the *Criterion*.

In his affectionate tribute to a formative teacher, almost a surrogate father, Richard Hoggart recounted Dobrée's self-depreciating admission to a student at Leeds that he lacked a really 'first-rate' mind.[60] The self-doubt carries some force: Dobrée is a critic we more readily respect than admire. The pub-lic-school accent is there, too, on 'first-rate' as it was in his espousal in the *Criterion* of the virtues of duty, manliness, and practical action, a corrective to what he ultimately saw as the hot-house aestheticism of Bloomsbury, the academic dogmas of Leavis and his epigones, and Eliot's search for Anglican panaceas. To tease out such distinctions is to enquire into the differences that constitute the overall profile of various English inter-war lit-erary periodicals; to discern the subtle and not so subtle differ-ences between, say, the *Criterion, Scrutiny*, or Desmond Mac-Carthy's *Life and Letters*. It is important, however, that Dobrée's adherence to Kiplingesque or public-school codes and customs should not be confused with a conservative political position or a blind defence of tradition. He was a consistently independent writer, neither progressive nor reactionary, a critic who believed passionately in liberty in the political as well as in the artistic sphere.[61] Perhaps the really distinctive timbre of his critical voice, overheard above the polyphony of the *Criterion*, is a genial, worldly, and dissenting note of 'agreeable scepticism'.

In a roll call of great prose essayists, Dobrée celebrated some of the highest achievements of the genre and, with a delicate sense of discrimination, his own intellectual ancestry: Montaigne, Bacon, Addison, Lamb, and Beerbohm.[62] The inclusion of Max Beerbohm on the list would today be viewed as an idiosyncratic choice, at the very least a cause of raised eyebrows. On closer examina-tion, the characteristics of the best Beerbohm essays—whimsy, charm, a sort of worldly and amused poise—are precisely those elements that have been ruthlessly excised from the critical essay since the triumph of the post-Eliot New Critical revolution. It is important not to forget that Dobrée exemplifies the vanished

---

[60] 'Teaching with Style', *Speaking to Each Other*, 201.
[61] See 'Omicron', *Nation and Athenaeum* (3 Oct. 1925), 17.
[62] See the *Nation and Athenaeum* (24 Oct. 1925), 154.

ethos of the Edwardian man of letters, the free play of the non-specialist intellect over the domain of texts we loosely call 'literary'.[63] He admitted as much when discussing, and partly defending, Lytton Strachey to the readers of the *Criterion*. Dobrée remarked that neither he nor Strachey 'could escape the influence of that decade [the Edwardian] in our experience'.[64] The 'Edwardian' element should certainly not be excised from a fully textured account of the *Criterion*: it was still operative in the 1930s, even though the lamps did flicker and ultimately fade in the long shadows cast by Sarajevo and the Somme.

Analysis of Dobrée's role on the *Criterion*, then, highlights the richness and diversity of the milieu of inter-war London literary journalism, with its incipient tensions between aestheticism, academicism, and religious dogma, not to mention the highly complicated networks of personal loyalty and sentiment which academic literary histories tend to overlook. There is some distortion here, for today's hyper-professionalized world of learned monographs and doctoral dissertations too readily dismiss, as uncongenial, amateur, or mere dilettantism, approaches to literature which do not conform to the current codes of academic discourse. One problem faced in reconstructing the pattern of Dobrée's miscellaneous contributions to the *Criterion* is to counter charges of frivolity, but it must be understood that a stylistic lightness of touch is not incompatible with an intensely serious appraisal of literature for a readership whose seriousness could be taken for granted. There are still those who mourn the passing of the cultivated and expansive taste of the 'man of letters', Eliot's self-description of his role as editor of the *Criterion*, just as there are those who would happily exchange today's specialist academic publications for the breadth and urbanity of the *Criterion*.[65]

---

[63] See Hoggart: 'Bonamy Dobrée had a dream of "the man of letters"—a widely read man, a good scholar who yet wore his scholarship easily' (*Speaking to Each Other*, 200). [64] 'Books of the Quarter', *Criterion* (Jan. 1931), 135.

[65] Eliot described the unity of European culture from 'the point of view of a man of letters' in his 1946 broadcast to Germany (*Notes Towards the Definition of Culture* (London, 1948), 110).

7

Montgomery Belgion

Useful Irritant

[Eliot's] willingness to publish this ugly review suggests that
he was blind to the martyrdom of German Jewry. Certainly,
in the whole period from the Nazi seizure of power to the
closure of the *Criterion*, he did not publish a single article or
review correcting the false impression given by Belgion of
life (and death) for Jews under Nazism.

Anthony Julius, *T. S. Eliot, Anti-Semitism and Literary
Form* (Cambridge, 1996), 170–1

In May 1996, Tom Paulin 'turned' on T. S. Eliot. The occasion was
a review-article championing Anthony Julius's controversial study
T. S. Eliot, Anti-Semitism, and Literary Form; a work that sought
to demonstrate that anti-Semitism was inseparable from, indeed
constitutive of, Eliot's art. The centrepiece of Paulin's attack, published in the *London Review of Books*, was an apparently anonym-
ous review of *The Yellow Spot: The Outlawing of Half a Million
Human Beings*, a book publicizing the persecution of German
Jews, which appeared among the *Criterion*'s 'Shorter Notices' in
July 1936. In a lengthy discussion of the notice, Julius commented:
'The review crawls with impatient distaste, wilfully refusing to do
its subject justice.'[1] This remark, however, might well be turned on
Julius, who had impatiently and unjustly attributed the review to
Eliot. Similarly, Paulin had no hesitation in finding the 'sinister
dismissiveness' of the review indicative of Eliot's tone, and he
embellished Julius's fanciful inference that Eliot had altered the
typographical style of the *Criterion* in order to 'mock' Jewish

[1] *T. S. Eliot, Anti-Semitism and Literary Form* (Cambridge, 1996), 168.

suffering.[2] Although both the attribution of the review and the strange insinuation regarding the *Criterion*'s typography were totally without foundation, the cumulative effect of Julius's charges, it appears, has been to associate the *Criterion* in some minds with fascism and anti-Semitism.[3]

After inspection of the financial files of the *Criterion*, Valerie Eliot disclosed to readers of the *Times Literary Supplement* that the review had, in point of fact, been written by Montgomery Belgion,[4] although it might have been evident to anyone who consulted the index to volume 15 of the *Criterion* that Belgion had been the author—batch reviews were conventionally signed with initials at the bottom of the last entry, in this case 'M.B.'[5] This, however, does not diminish an editor's responsibility to assess what is being printed in his magazine, or the rightful indignation surrounding this *Criterion* review. The wider question is, what does *The Yellow Spot* review tell us about the nature of Eliot's relations with Belgion, who was the most frequent contributor of essays and book reviews to the *Criterion* during the 1930s,[6] and who was considered by some observers a possible future editor of the quarterly? One searches the vast secondary literature on Eliot in vain for clues about Belgion, beyond E. W. F. Tomlin's tendentious claim that Eliot disliked Belgion.[7] In 1976, A. L. Rowse recalled the 'mystery man' Montgomery Belgion: 'who on earth was he? Though I met him several times over years, I never succeeded in making him out.'[8] It is possible, however, to piece together, from unpublished sources, some details of the close relationship between Eliot and Belgion. Their collaboration has far-reaching implications for our understanding of the *Criterion*'s ideological character in the 1930s and of Eliot's policy as editor.

[2] See 'Undesirable', *London Review of Books* (9 May 1996), 13–15.
[3] See Christopher Hitchens: '[Eliot's] magazine of high culture, *The Criterion*, was at best loftily indifferent to the rise of fascism' (*Nation* (12 Aug. 1996)).
[4] 'Letters to the Editor', *TLS* (31 May 1996), 17.
[5] For an object lesson on how to identify authorship in inter-war literary periodicals, see Daniel Adamski, 'Letters', *London Review of Books* (20 June 1996), 4.
[6] E. Alan Baker's 1967 *Criterion* Index lists 38 book reviews by Belgion. A further 24 short notices should be added.
[7] 'Eliot of whom [Belgion] made some absurd insinuations, imputing plagiarism, told me later on that he found Belgion an exceedingly tiresome man to deal with' (*T. S. Eliot: A Friendship* (London, 1988), 116). Belgion and Tomlin had quarrelled in 1945.   [8] *A Cornishman Abroad* (London, 1976), 280.

I

Harold Montgomery Belgion or 'Monty', as he was known, was born in Paris on 28 September 1892. Although a British citizen he was educated privately in France, thereafter launching a career as a journalist in Paris, as the editor in charge of the European edition of the *New York Herald*. In 1916, Belgion was called up and served with the British Expeditionary Force in France as a private in the Honourable Artillery Company up until July 1918 when he was commissioned to the Dorsetshire Regiment. After demobilization, he returned to journalism as a peripatetic editor and writer on the staff of various London and New York newspapers, among them the *Daily Mail*, the *New York World*, and the *Westminster Gazette*; and, in 1925, he took a position with the New York publisher Harcourt Brace & Company. At the same time, Belgion was anxious to broaden his professional horizons and establish a reputation as a public intellectual commentating on literary and cultural matters.

During his stint at Harcourt Brace, Belgion translated Ramon Fernandez's *Messages* into English, including an article from the *Nouvelle Revue française* discussing Eliot's prose writings, entitled 'Le Classicisme de T. S. Eliot'. In 1927, Belgion wrote to the *Nation and Athenaeum* to defend himself against Richard Hughes's complaint that the translator's preface to *Messages* was 'foolish' and that the style of translation resembled an American Ph.D. thesis. Belgion's letter is notable for its characteristic tone of touchy disagreeableness. He explained:

Although I write to you from New York, I, the translator, happen to be English, and I have had no opportunity of copying the manner in which Americans write their theses. Hence it is as an Englishman's work that my translation should be judged. If to Mr. Hughes it seems poor, let him call it poor.[9]

The letter was published in the same edition of the *Nation* as Eliot's essay on 'The Mysticism of Blake'. It is highly unlikely that Eliot missed Belgion's letter and even had it escaped his notice, it appears that Fernandez brought Belgion to his attention.[10]

---

[9] 'Letter', *Nation and Athenaeum* (17 Sept. 1927), 773.
[10] In a letter to the editor of the *Hound and Horn*, Eliot mentioned Belgion as a friend of Fernandez. T. S. Eliot to Lincoln Kirstein, 16 Nov. 1928. Yale.

In 1929, Belgion met with Eliot to discuss Faber's imminent publication of *Our Present Philosophy of Life*. Belgion's *causerie*, an attack upon four 'representative fathers of our present philosophy of life'—Bernard Shaw, André Gide, Freud, and Bertrand Russell—a quartet of 'irresponsible propagandists' propounding what he believed to be muddled and pernicious theories pertaining to education, art, ethics, sexuality, and religion, would certainly have met with Eliot's approval. Indeed, Belgion's critique of modern acquisitive materialism from the perspective of Anglican conservatism, or what he called 'the Christian philosophy of life', bore many points of resemblance to recent comments made by Eliot in the editorial and review pages of the *Criterion*.[11] The tell-tale difference was Belgion's dictatorial mode of argument and his awkward and unidiomatic syntax. Reviewing *Our Present Philosophy of Life* in the *Cambridge Review*, George Rylands commented:

His short summary of aesthetics bristles with assumptions which, though of very dubious validity, he confidently sets down as proved. . . . One could wish also that Mr. Belgion had a more attractive style. Too many remarks are interpolated into his arguments, making the text jerky and broken, and so unpleasant to read. Moreover there is an irritating tendency to nag and to be sarcastic about petty inconsistencies and modes of expression. A little good humour would have been of advantage in more ways than one.[12]

By the summer of 1929, Belgion had gained an entrée to the *Criterion* circle. Eliot informed Dobrée, teaching in Cairo, that Belgion was livening up the Grove Tavern lunches.[13] Dobrée, like several regular contributors to the *Criterion*, did not care for Belgion. On his return to England, he consulted Eliot on how best to avoid Belgion at the Athenaeum. Eliot, however, frequently met Belgion for lunch at various London clubs, often in the company of T. O. Beachcroft, a short story writer and a contributor to

[11] See Eliot's sarcastic comments on Shaw: 'No one can grasp more firmly an idea which he does not maintain, or expound it with more cogency, than Mr. Shaw' ('A Commentary', *Criterion* (Oct. 1924), 41). Eliot described Freud's *The Future of an Illusion* as 'shrewd but stupid' ('Books of the Quarter', *Criterion* (Dec. 1928), 350–3). See also Eliot's hostile review of Russell's *Why I am not a Christian* ('Books of the Quarter', *Criterion* (Aug. 1927), 177–9).

[12] *Cambridge Review* (31 Jan. 1930). By contrast, Ramon Fernandez praised *Our Present Philosophy of Life* as 'a brilliant specimen' of philosophical criticism ('Books of the Quarter', *Criterion* (July 1930), 760).

[13] T. S. Eliot to Bonamy Dobrée, 4 July 1929. Leeds.

the *Criterion* on seventeenth-century literature.[14] Eliot described Beachcroft to I. A. Richards as a 'very charming young amateur, a contemporary of David Cecil's at Oxford, who is now in the advertising business in London'.[15] Beachcroft, educated at Clifton and Balliol (he first met Eliot as an Oxford undergraduate[16]), was an advertising manager for Unilever, resident in fashionable Kensington. Eliot's description of Beachcroft conjures up in the gestures of its studied decorum the language of the urbane clubman. It is also indicative of the milieu in which *Criterion* business was conducted, a male, upper-middle-class, metropolitan circle—an intellectual élite that tended to infuriate those writers, like Pound and Wyndham Lewis, who perceived themselves as outsiders.

Certainly, Belgion's first contribution to the *Criterion*, 'Meaning in Art' (January 1930), an article dealing with the self-descriptions of their art by Jacob Epstein and the French Surrealist Group, provoked a reply from Pound in the *Criterion*.[17] Although Pound aimed at a 'possible rectification of Mr Belgion' he was ultimately disappointed. Belgion reiterated his differences from Pound in a long essay-review of Richards's *Practical Criticism* (1929) entitled 'What is Criticism?' in which he argued that Pound, unlike Richards, did not place enough emphasis on reader response. Pound responded in the *Hound and Horn* in October 1930. Coining the term 'Criterionism' to describe a highbrow English tone of 'dead and moribund writing', he saddled Belgion with a large measure of the blame for the *Criterion*'s current 'diet of dead crow'.[18] In his correspondence with Eliot, Pound often referred to Belgion in a derogatory manner. In fact, throughout the 1930s he warned Eliot that his association with Belgion was having a harmful effect on his intellectual acumen. In December 1937, Pound told Ronald Duncan: 'We respect the Eliot of the Agon / Most of contributors to Criterion for past 17 years have been petrified shit (publishable terms to define Belgions, I leave to you). . . .'[19]

---

[14] Details of Belgion's dining arrangements can be found in his private notebooks at Churchill College, Cambridge.

[15] T. S. Eliot to I. A. Richards, 4 Apr. 1934. Cited in *Selected Letters of I. A. Richards*, ed. John Constable (Oxford, 1990), 78 n. 5.

[16] See Robert Sencourt, *T. S. Eliot: A Memoir*, ed. Donald Adamson (London, 1971), 92.   [17] See 'Epstein, Belgion and Meaning', *Criterion* (Apr. 1930), 470–5.

[18] 'Criterionism', *Hound and Horn* (Oct.–Dec. 1930), 113–16.

[19] Ezra Pound to Ronald Duncan, 12 Dec. 1937. Yale.

Richards also had good reason to dislike Belgion after 'What is Criticism?' appeared in the *Criterion*.[20] Belgion's chief disagreement with Richards concerned the issue of whether 'the reading of poetry can be a substitute for the holding of religious or other fundamental beliefs'.[21] Eliot and Richards were currently locked in an entrenched debate about the nature of what a poet believes, and whether the reader need share the poet's belief in order to fully appreciate the work.[22] Interestingly, when Eliot outlined his theory of the relations between poetry and belief, in an article for the *Bookman* in February 1930, he used Richards and Belgion as the horns of the dilemma. According to Eliot, Belgion's *Our Present Philosophy of Life* advanced a 'Platonic' point of view asserting that if a work of art is to succeed, the reader must be convinced or emotionally hoodwinked into accepting the beliefs of the artist. If Eliot's own embryonic theory was a little too underdeveloped to carry full conviction,[23] perhaps more enlightening was his readiness to use Belgion and Richards to pursue an apparently equable middle way between factitiously polarized alternatives—a familiar argumentative strategy in his rhetorical armoury:

The one extreme [Belgion] is to like poetry merely for what it has to say: that is, to like it merely because it voices our own beliefs or prejudices— which is of course to be quite indifferent to the *poetry* of the poetry. The other extreme [Richards] is to like the poetry because the poet has manipulated his material into perfect art, which is to be indifferent to the material, and to isolate our enjoyment of poetry from life. The one extreme is no enjoyment of poetry at all, the other is enjoyment of an abstraction which is merely *called* poetry. But between these extremes occurs a continuous range of appreciations, each of which has its limited validity.[24]

Richards, a visiting professor at Tsing Hua University in Peking, had not read *Our Present Philosophy of Life*, but when

---

[20] One wonders at Eliot's reasons for commissioning Belgion's article, since John Gould Fletcher had already reviewed *Practical Criticism* favourably in the *Criterion*. See 'Books of the Quarter', *Criterion* (Oct. 1929), 162–4.

[21] 'What is Criticism?', *Criterion* (Oct. 1930), 118–39.

[22] For a thorough discussion of the belief debate, see John Constable, 'Introduction', *I. A. Richards and his Critics* (London, 2001), pp. ix–xviii.

[23] Eliot suggested that when reading Dante's *Commedia* the question of belief is held in abeyance: 'you suspend both belief and disbelief.' See *Dante* (London, 1929), 42.

[24] 'Poetry and Propaganda', *Bookman* (Feb. 1930), 595–602.

Eliot sent him a copy of the *Criterion* containing 'What is Criticism?' he wrote to say that he had been incensed by Belgion's remarks.[25] In 'Notes on the Practice of Interpretation', published in the *Criterion*, Richards claimed that Belgion had grossly misinterpreted his position, ascribing to him positions that were 'rubbish', 'queer', or 'nonsense': 'Whether Mr Belgion's reasons—in view of his condition—for disliking my remarks are excellent or not I am unable to judge. The important thing is to make clear that the opinions he attributes to me are all of his own concoction—not of my expression.'[26] Following his usual editorial practice in *Criterion* controversies, Eliot circulated the proof of Richards's article in advance of formal publication, so that the April 1931 issue also carried a 'brief rejoinder' from Belgion. In it, Belgion repeated the complaint that Richards's theories were unduly obscure. He added, with typical petulance, that Richards's 'pseudo-correction' (a swipe at the theory of the emotive 'pseudo-statement') would take up 'valuable space' in the *Criterion* 'to no purpose'. Perhaps Belgion was secretly hopeful that Richards's reply would not be published. In any case, deliberately or otherwise, the exchange brought into the open a disagreement between Eliot and his friend Richards. Belgion, after all, tartly reiterated Eliot's main bone of contention. Belgion wrote:

Now the main point at issue between Mr. Richards and myself is that he would have the world accept the theory that the reading or 'interpretation' of poetry can be made a substitute for the holding of religious and other fundamental beliefs, and that I think the theory is nonsense.[27]

'What is Criticism?', slightly modified in the light of Richards's defence, together with Belgion's other *Criterion* essays and reviews appeared in *The Human Parrot* (1931). Eliot sent the *Criterion*'s review copy to Jacob Bronowski, lately the chief editor of *Experiment*, an avant-garde Cambridge student magazine. Bronowski's private correspondence makes it clear that he was considerably more sympathetic to Richards than he was to Belgion.[28]

[25] I. A. Richards to T. S. Eliot, 30 Nov. 1930. Cambridge (Magdalene).
[26] 'Notes on the Practice of Interpretation', *Criterion* (Apr. 1931), 420.
[27] 'Correspondence', *Criterion* (Apr. 1931), 508.
[28] 'Talking of critics, I observe that [Edward] Titus has acquired the inimitable Montgomery Belgion for his magazine [*This Quarter*]. . . . Well, well, Mr. Belgion "continues not to surprise me" ' (Jacob Bronowski to Julian Trevelyan, 5 Mar. 1931. Cambridge (Trinity)).

Bronowski had previously discussed the problem of poetry and belief in the pages of *Experiment*.[29] Not surprisingly, he singled out 'What is Criticism?' for extended treatment in his *Criterion* review. Finding a great deal of misunderstanding in the recent enquiry into the relation of poetry and belief, Bronowski commented: 'So far, so much confusion, and the confusion is mainly Mr Belgion's.'[30] The youthful assurance, bordering upon arrogance, exhibited in Bronowski's review would certainly have angered Belgion. He wrote to Eliot, rather after the manner of Richards, to complain that as a 'steady contributor' to the *Criterion* he had hardly expected this kind of 'misrepresentation'.[31]

In fact, it is clear that Eliot was anxious to use Belgion to prolong this *Criterion* controversy during his lecture tour of the United States. In February 1932, a letter sounding out Richards gives a fascinating insight into the behind-the-scenes editorial manœuvres underpinning the dignified exterior of the *Criterion*. Belgion had sent Eliot an essay on belief which discussed the viewpoints of Richards and Martin D'Arcy. Eliot told Richards: 'I do not think that it is a very good essay but I should like to use it if there is any prospect of it starting you and D'Arcy off on a further exposition of your views, and if possible arguing with each other rather than with Belgion.' Eliot intended to circulate the proof copy of Belgion's article to both Richards and D'Arcy, thereby hoping to generate a *Criterion* symposium on the subject of poetry and belief, to be staged during his absence in the United States. By way of conclusion, Eliot commented that Belgion 'is extremely useful as an irritant and for provoking other people to develop their own theories on important subjects'.[32] The letter is an unusually candid account of the manner in which Eliot occasionally stage-managed debate in the *Criterion*. Richards, doubtless suspicious after the treatment meted out to both *Principles* and *Practical Criticism*, had good reason to be wary of entering into further controversy with Eliot's *Criterion* subalterns. Bearing in mind that the Oxford Jesuit, Martin D'Arcy, advocated a Thomist approach to literature,

---

[29] See 'Postscript', *Experiment* (Feb. 1930), 34–5.

[30] 'Books of the Quarter', *Criterion* (Jan. 1932), 324.

[31] See 'Correspondence', *Criterion* (Apr. 1932), 510–11. Interestingly, Belgion's pocketbooks record a meeting with Bronowski in July 1932.

[32] T. S. Eliot to I. A. Richards, 24 Feb. 1932. Cambridge (Magdalene).

Richards sensibly refused to be drawn.[33] Eliot reluctantly conceded that Belgion's pyrotechnics were an improper catalyst for intellectual debate and his article, although excellent copy, was not published.[34]

II

Belgion continued to be a mainstay of the *Criterion*: an *agent provocateur* who could be relied upon to stoke up the coals of controversy on carefully selected topics. He contributed more than sixty book reviews and short notices during the 1930s. Furthermore, from October 1932, he began to contribute a regular 'French Chronicle' to the *Criterion*. Resident for part of each year in Paris, Belgion's bulletins on French literary and intellectual life were lively and well informed, albeit animated by a predilection for very right-wing French authors. The *Criterion*'s treatment of André Gide, a leading intellectual *de gauche* and founder of the monthly *Nouvelle Revue française*, often regarded as the hub of Parisian literary life in the inter-war period, is symptomatic.[35] Gide recruited Eliot as the London correspondent of *Nouvelle Revue française*, but, unlike a number of contemporary French writers, and in spite of Eliot's overtures, Gide did not reciprocate by contributing to the *Criterion*: he was conspicuous by his absence.[36] In July 1927, Eliot wrote to the Irish poet and critic, Thomas MacGreevy, a lecturer at the Ecole Normale Supérieure, to suggest that he review Gide's *Les Faux-Monnayeurs* and the accompanying *Journal des Faux-Monnayeurs* for the *Criterion*.[37] In August, Eliot recommended that MacGreevy read an indictment of Gide by Henri Massis in the second volume of *Jugements*

[33] D'Arcy was politely sceptical of the value of the 'goddess' of modern psychology in his review of Richards's *Mencius on the Mind* ('Books of the Quarter', *Criterion* (Jan. 1933), 282).

[34] T. S. Eliot to I. A. Richards, 2 Mar. 1932. Cambridge (Magdalene).

[35] For details, see Alan Sheridan, *André Gide: A Life in the Present* (London, 1998).

[36] See André Gide to T. S. Eliot, 7 Dec. 1921. *Letters*, 490–1. T. S. Eliot to André Gide, 16 May 1922. Ibid. 516. Robert Sencourt claimed that Gide's patron, Lady Rothermere, put pressure on Eliot to publish extracts from *Les Nourritures terrestres* in the *Criterion*. They did not appear. See Sencourt, *T. S. Eliot: A Memoir*, 96 n. 25.

[37] T. S. Eliot to Thomas MacGreevy, 22 July 1927. Dublin.

(1924); a position that Eliot claimed to be similar to his own.[38] He applauded MacGreevy's judicious review, although even its mild criticism upset Gide's Parisian *cénacle*.[39] In short, it was clear that by the time of the appearance of F. S. Flint's censorious 1928 notice of *Nouvelle Revue française*[40] (Eliot had made his last *NRF* contribution in May 1927), the *Criterion* was on better terms with Massis's rival right-wing and pro-Catholic monthly the *Revue universelle*.[41]

Eliot was receptive to any critique that might call into question the vogue for Gide. Belgion's attack on Gide in *Our Present Philosophy of Life* had occasioned an open letter from Gide, 'À Montgomery Belgion', in the *Nouvelle Revue française*. In January 1933, the year in which Gide embraced the Communist Party, Eliot referred to him in the course of his Turnbull Lectures at Baltimore as a sophisticated 'voluptuary of thought'.[42] Eliot pressed home the criticism by citing Gide as an example of 'arrested development' in his April 1933 Commentary.[43] In the same issue, Eliot permitted Belgion a 'Postscript' to Gide's letter. It appears that what upset Belgion was Gide's irresponsible advocacy of the *crime isolé*: a position described by Gide in *Nouvelle Revue française* in the following terms:

Je crois que souvent, ce que la société et vous-même appelez *le mal* . . . est d'une plus grande vertu éducatrice et initiatrice, que ce que vous appelez *le bien*; et donc susceptible d'entraîner indirectement l'humanité vers le progrès.[44]

In particular, Belgion objected to Gide's advocacy of homosexuality as a natural aspect of human behaviour; an objection ostensibly justified on the grounds of Christian morality. The opposition was tacitly maintained in the 'French Chronicles', where Belgion informed readers of the *Criterion* that they would be better advised

---

[38] T. S. Eliot to Thomas MacGreevy, 11 Aug. 1927. Dublin.
[39] See 'Recent Books', *Criterion* (Jan. 1928), 65–9.
[40] See 'French Periodicals', *Criterion* (Dec. 1928), 375.
[41] cf. the obituary notices of the *Criterion* in both journals. The *Revue universelle* concurred with Eliot that 'une bonne politique implique une bonne théologie'. See André Rousseaux, 'La Vie Littérataire', *Revue universelle* (15 Mar. 1939), 747–51. See also Jean Guérin, 'Mort du *Criterion*', *Nouvelle Revue française* (Mar. 1939), 539.
[42] See *The Varieties of Metaphysical Poetry*, ed. Ronald Schuchard (London, 1993), 276.   [43] 'A Commentary', *Criterion* (Apr. 1933), 470.
[44] 'Lettres', *Nouvelle Revue française* (Feb. 1930), 196.

to read the Marseilles monthly review the *Cahiers du Sud* than the by now 'moribund' *Nouvelle Revue française*.[45] While Gide was all but ignored in Belgion's chronicles, they habitually discussed works by writers, like Massis, the novelist Georges Bernanos, and the philosopher Maurice Blondel,[46] writers with links to Charles Maurras's Action française movement. This sympathy for elements of the French political Right chimed with Belgion's Anglican conservatism and, indeed, to a certain extent, the reactionary Toryism sometimes advocated in the *Criterion*. In 'Last Words', Eliot pointed approvingly to the coverage of French political and theological thinkers in Belgion's chronicles.[47]

In his 1933 article on Gide, Belgion had written:

Scarcely anybody truly disapproves of people like Hatry and De Valera, Kreuger and Hitler. Our admiration of them would be unbounded if only they 'brought it off', and most of us are only restrained from emulating them by lack of self-confidence and fear of the consequences.[48]

In July 1935, reviewing an English translation of Albert Einstein's *Mein Weltbild*, Belgion described the sections on 'Politics and Pacifism', 'Germany 1933', and 'The Jews' as 'rather trivial'—an inattention to the dire consequences of events brewing in totalitarian Europe that appears callous and myopic today.[49] But that is as nothing to Belgion's deplorable treatment of *The Yellow Spot* in the *Criterion*. It is strange that scholars could have mistaken Belgion's execrable syntax here for Eliot's measured prose style. For instance, consider the following extracts culled from the dozen adjacent 'anonymous' short notices:

In arguing that it is open to prose to become the better medium for the expression of poetry, Mr. Smith has the opportunity of being reasonable enough, although as the result of a slightly perverted literary taste he is in fact no more than entertaining and plausible.

---

[45] 'French Chronicle', *Criterion* (Oct. 1935), 83.
[46] Belgion translated an extract from Massis's *Le Cas Marcel Proust* for the *Criterion* (Jan. 1937), 269–86. Interestingly Henry Miller's works were discussed in Belgion's chronicles prior to his appearance in the *Criterion*.
[47] See 'Last Words', *Criterion* (Jan. 1939), 272.
[48] 'A Postscript on Mr. André Gide', *Criterion* (Apr. 1933), 411.
[49] 'Books of the Quarter', *Criterion* (July 1935), 711.

He finds that More in *Utopia* first shook the principle of personal sovereignty and then that Suarez ultimately placed sovereignty in the whole community.

One more instance of how misplaced is the contemporary confidence in the ability of scientists *ipso facto* that they are scientists to dispense philosophy.

Jonathan Edwards (1704–1758) was a New England Calvinist who engaged in much controversy in his lifetime and whose fame in the United States remains green.

And in *The Yellow Spot* review:

There should be somebody to point out that this book, although enjoying a cathedratic blessing, is an attempt to rouse moral indignation by means of sensationalism.[50]

Anne Bradby, copy-editor on the *Criterion* during 1936, recalled persistent difficulties with Belgion over his awkward syntax and clumsy phraseology.[51] But if the 'Short Notices' show signs of unusual haste, more pointedly, they betray certain continuities in Belgion's thought; in particular, a shameful insensibility to the suffering of German Jews, especially shocking to modern readers given that *The Yellow Spot*, far from promoting sensationalism, should have led to some chastening reflection.

III

In so far as Eliot had commissioned a notice on a book highlighting the persecution of German Jews and had failed to exercise his editorial prerogative over its contents, the review (in the words of Christopher Ricks) bore 'the stamp of his approval'.[52] On the basis of this, critics like Anthony Julius have been eager to unmask a latent 'hostility' to Jews in the *Criterion*. But this means taking a single short book notice, occupying less than half a page, as representative of the contents of a periodical whose bound volumes run to over 12,000 pages. Eliot, of course, was ultimately responsible for all the contents of his journal, but one is still entitled to wonder

---

[50] M.B. [Montgomery Belgion], 'Shorter Notices', *Criterion* (July 1936), 756–9.
[51] Anne Ridler in conversation with Jason Harding, 9 Dec. 1997, Oxford.
[52] *T. S. Eliot and Prejudice* (London, 1988), 57.

whether Belgion's review is at least partly offset by Louis MacNeice's review of a work by a Jewish theologian, R. V. Feldman, described as 'very valuable as a corrective to those who find in the Jews a perfect subject for crude generalisation'[53] or by the Revd Edward Quinn's passionate observation, published in the *Criterion* in July 1938, that: 'The racial theories of National Socialism are opposed to the universal claims of Christianity, and leading to immoral legislation, are ultimately in contradiction with Divine law.'[54] The *Criterion*, it should be remembered, was nominally a literary review and any editorial reluctance to speak out clearly in denunciation of the Nazi regime is not necessarily a sign of complicity or an undeclared policy of appeasement.

The charge of anti-Semitism in the *Criterion* invites close attention to Belgion's subsequent contributions. The first point to note is that Belgion was not a principled apologist for National Socialism or anti-Semitism, although one can detect sympathies for both in his writings. In January 1938, Belgion observed: 'There is some reason for supposing that both political systems [the dictatorships of Italy and Germany] have merits, and that each is the system best adapted at the moment to the country in which it has been set up.'[55] In his final 'French Chronicle', written amid an intensifying anti-Semitism in France, fuelled by a large influx of Austrian refugees, Belgion remarked: 'So pronounced is M. Bernanos's antisemitism that the firm which publishes him in England deserves to be congratulated on the breadth of mind of which it gives evidence in striving to further his reputation.'[56] Congratulations do not seem to be the order of the day for this sort of open-mindedness, although it should be pointed out that Belgion praised Louis-Ferdinand Céline for his caricature of the 'prejudices' and 'delusions' that animated Bernanos's febrile anti-Semitism and that his study of contemporary French affairs, *News of the French* (1938), published by Faber, studiously refused to be drawn into an anti-Semitic line on the contentious issue of Dreyfus.[57]

---

[53] 'Books of the Quarter', *Criterion* (Oct. 1934), 163.
[54] 'Christian Politics', *Criterion* (July 1938), 627.
[55] 'French Chronicle', *Criterion* (Jan. 1938), 283–4.
[56] 'French Chronicle', *Criterion* (Jan. 1939), 299.
[57] John Hayward described *News of the French* as 'timely and desirable' ('Books of the Quarter', *Criterion* (Jan. 1939), 342).

It remains difficult to judge the extent to which Eliot endorsed or simply tolerated Belgion's proto-fascism. In January 1939, Ronald Duncan, editor of the rival quarterly, *Townsman*, mentioned to Pound that he thought that Belgion and Read would restart the *Criterion*.[58] A few days later, Pound replied: 'I don't see that Belgion can start Criterion, nor Read, esp. in view of Possum's express remark to contrary.'[59] In fact, Eliot did not consider Belgion as his *Criterion* heir apparent and did not even inform him of the journal's closure in advance.[60] The nature of the few extant letters from Eliot to Belgion written in the 1930s, addressed to 'My dear Belgion', suggest a professional relationship rather than intimacy. However, the fuller correspondence from the 1940s, held at Victoria University, addressed to 'Monty', point to closer personal relations after the Second World War.[61] With a grotesque irony, Belgion's experiences at a German prisoner of war camp in Greece, where as a Captain in the Royal Engineers he delivered a series of lectures on English literature to fellow officers, later collected as the Penguin bestseller *Reading for Profit* (1945), merely confirmed his indifference to the suffering of German Jews.[62] In September 1944, Eliot told Dobrée that Belgion had returned unchanged by his tribulations as a prisoner of war.[63] As news of the German concentration camps became public knowledge, Belgion consistently failed to recognize the scope and inhumanity of the Holocaust. In a letter published in December 1945 in the monthly *Theology* (a periodical read by Eliot),

[58] Ronald Duncan to Ezra Pound, 13 Jan. 1939. Yale. Duncan contributed a book review to the *Criterion* in July 1938. See also Duncan's reminiscences in *All Men Are Islands* (London, 1964), 168–9.

[59] Ezra Pound to Ronald Duncan, 17 Jan. 1939. Cited in *Selected Letters of Ezra Pound*, ed. D. D. Paige (London, 1951), 320–1.

[60] Eliot worried that Belgion would be upset about losing a regular source of income. See T. S. Eliot to John Hayward, 27 Dec. 1938. Cambridge (King's). In fact, Belgion transferred his latest 'French Chronicle' to *Horizon*.

[61] Some 32 letters from Eliot to Montgomery Belgion dating from Feb. 1940 to Sept. 1963 were sold by Churchill College, Cambridge, to the University of Victoria.

[62] In the Preface to *Reading for Profit*, Belgion thanked 'the courtesy of the German military authorities in enabling me to typewrite a portion of my MS. and in allowing me to send the whole of it home'. Eliot read the typescript of *Reading for Profit*, which sold over 100,000 copies in England.

[63] T. S. Eliot to Bonamy Dobrée, 24 Sept. 1944. Leeds. Eliot encouraged Read, Dobrée, Beachcroft, and Hayward to write to Belgion during the period of his confinement. Eliot sent books and cigarettes via the Red Cross.

Belgion wrote with an appalling lack of sensitivity to the evidence of genocide at Belsen:

Was the alleged gas chamber any less humane than are the reported mass expulsions of Germans from Polish-annexed Germany or from the Sudetenland? . . . Why confine the spotlight to the German? Torture? . . . Starvation? At Belsen some internees, it appears, died from lack of food as soon as ten days after admission. Their agony was short.[64]

Belgion's objections were elaborated at length in his indictment of the trial of Nazi war criminals, *Epitaph on Nuremberg*, a work that Eliot praised to Belgion; although he cagily reserved the right to disagree after further reflection.[65]

Further reflection, it seems clear, will hardly sustain the estimation offered by the archivist at Churchill College, Cambridge, who, following Belgion's death on 29 October 1973, catalogued his private papers:

In conclusion it can confidently be stated that Montgomery Belgion merits a place, albeit a modest one, in the gallery of distinguished literary critics of the twentieth century; and in all his work one can detect the integrity and moral courage which gave him the strength to propagate unpopular views and ideas—regardless of the cost and inconvenience to himself.[66]

Compare that with F. R. Leavis's summary judgement made in the inaugural issue of *Scrutiny*:

Then there is Mr. Montgomery Belgion, who is not amiable, but as 'a steady contributor' to *The Criterion* . . . insists on some notice. His function in the commonwealth, he feels, is to expose current confusions and fallacies by rigorous intellectual analysis; and it would not be difficult to expose Mr. Belgion's confusions and fallacies by the method he affects. But few sensitive readers . . . will bother to do that; it is so plain that Mr. Belgion's is not a sensitive intelligence. He does not hazard himself much in the field of literary judgement, but he leaves no room for doubt about the quality of his critical sensibility. For all his aim of nice precision his books are soft and blunt.[67]

---

[64] 'Correspondence', *Theology* (Dec. 1945), 274. Belgion's letter was a response to Canon Hawkins's article 'The Punishment of War Criminals: A Christian Approach', *Theology* (Oct. 1945).
[65] See T. S. Eliot to Montgomery Belgion, 7 Feb. 1947. Cambridge (Churchill).
[66] Anonymous introduction to the Belgion Archive at Churchill College, Cambridge.   [67] 'The Literary Mind', *Scrutiny* (May 1932), 29.

Perhaps most interesting of all, in the autumn of 1939, Delmore Schwartz, a Jewish New York intellectual, noted that Belgion had 'much in common' with Eliot. He concluded that in Belgion's criticism:

what we get is, on the one hand, the standpoint of one who is both a Christian moralist and a tough mind; on the other hand, the infinite hair-splitting of one who, in the attempt to be wholly critical, permitted himself to be as insensitive as the Philistine. He is perhaps not too theological, but rather not theological enough.[68]

Belgion's 'unpopular' response to the persecution, ill treatment, imprisonment, and murder of German Jews does not make for pleasant reading. However, the animus cannot be so easily displaced on to Eliot, still less to a journal as heterogeneous and multivocal as the *Criterion*. Both Julius's book-length portrait and Paulin's polemical review too readily display a zeal to convict Eliot and are ultimately vitiated by a cavalier attitude towards scholarly practice— witnessed, among a significant amount of legerdemain, in the over-hasty misattribution of *The Yellow Spot* review.[69] Ironically enough, Paulin's forensic impatience bears some similarity to the kind of controversy-seeking that encouraged Eliot to employ Belgion as a useful irritant.[70] Eliot's habitual caution and prudence, or more charitably his Christian belief, make it impossible to characterize the *Criterion* as anti-Semitic. This is not a case of special pleading. It is quite simply to observe that what Eliot and Belgion had in common was a strain of reactionary, occasionally intolerant, orthodox Tory Anglican morality; a defining trait of the *Criterion* from the late 1920s onward. Unfortunately, Montgomery Belgion's outbursts of bigotry were a caricature of the *Criterion*'s founding and highly cherished desire to fight a rearguard action on behalf of a tradition of Latin-Christian civilization.

[68] 'The Criterion', *Purpose* (Oct. 1939), 232.

[69] In his 1996 selected essays, *Writing to the Moment*, Paulin added a footnote correctly identifying the authorship of *The Yellow Spot* review. However, in the 1996 paperback edition of *T. S. Eliot, Anti-Semitism and Literary Form*, Julius was less gracious. Claiming that the review was written 'in circumstances which remain obscure' (168), he permitted Eliot's name to stand in the text as the author of the review.

[70] Paulin's professed intention in the *London Review of Books* was to publicize Julius's 'adversarial' reading of Eliot. Tom Paulin in conversation with Jason Harding, 26 Nov. 1998, Cambridge.

8

Michael Roberts and Janet Adam Smith

New Signatures

I hope that his biographers and critics will, in their summing-up
of his achievement, do no less than justice to his editorship of
The Criterion . . . Eliot should certainly be remembered not
only as one of the first great poets of the twentieth century, but
also as the last great periodical editor of the nineteenth. None
of his predecessors could have shown more diligence, courtesy,
and personal concern for the recruiting of young writers, for
exploring the temper of their generation, and encouraging
them to put as good a face as possible on being themselves.

Hugh Sykes Davies, *Eagle* (6 May 1965), 268

Michael Roberts's significance as an anthologist who provided a
platform for a younger generation of poets in his anthologies *New
Signatures* (1932), *New Country* (1933), and, most importantly of
all, *The Faber Book of Modern Verse* (1936), has long been recognized. However, Eliot's collaboration with Michael Roberts and his
wife, Janet Adam Smith, on the *Criterion* has not received due attention. In fact, the extensive reviewing of Roberts and Adam Smith is
particularly helpful in ascertaining the *Criterion*'s relative standing
among the literary periodicals of the 1930s. It sheds some light on
the silent rapprochement between the 'Public School Communists'
(F. R. Leavis's dismissive description of the Auden group of writers)
and the Tory Anglican stalwarts who appeared in the *Criterion*. The
appearance under the same covers of these seemingly dissimilar
groups was perhaps not as unlikely as it may appear and is best
understood in relation to the shaping influences of publishing and
reviewing. The importance of the *Criterion* as a clearing house for

aspiring poets within a London literary milieu of writers, critics, and intellectuals—interlinked by a complex series of periodical networks—was intimately related to Eliot's pre-eminence as a publisher of serious poetry in the 1930s. Examination of the role of Michael Roberts and Janet Adam Smith on the *Criterion* enables one to get away from misleading grand-narratives regarding the 'classicism' of the *Criterion* or the 'Marxism' of the Auden group and to consider instead how a shared sense of the urgent need for social reconstruction could uncover continuities, or at least a partial congruence, between those with affiliations to the Church of England or to the Communist Party.

I

In September 1931, Michael Roberts, a 29-year-old mathematics teacher at the Mercers' School in London, wrote to John Lehmann at the Hogarth Press to praise his recent poetry volume, *A Garden Revisited*, and to suggest a meeting.[1] A few days later, Roberts informed Lehmann that his work belonged with other contemporaries in a manifesto anthology of new poets. Flattered by the interest in his work, Lehmann, who thought that his admirer resembled 'a giraffe that had taken to the serious life of learning', persuaded the Woolfs to sponsor an anthology of modern poetry selected by Roberts.[2] As it turned out, Roberts culled nearly half of the poems from periodicals: the *Criterion*, the *Adelphi, Experiment*, the *Listener*, and *This Quarter*. The slim volume, entitled *New Signatures: Poems by Several Hands*, was published in February 1932. The contributors were four recent Cambridge graduates—Julian Bell, Richard Eberhart, Empson, and Lehmann—three from Oxford—Auden, Day Lewis, and Spender—and two poets Lehmann had met recently in London—William Plomer and A. S. J. Tessimond.

Roberts's programmatic preface to *New Signatures* asserted that the modern poet could no longer write like Keats, rather he must take his imagery from urban and industrial civilization and be 'abreast of his own times'.[3] Searching for a principle of unity,

---

[1] Roberts had reviewed *A Garden Revisited* in the *Adelphi* (Nov. 1931), 127–9.
[2] See *The Whispering Gallery* (London, 1955), 172–4.
[3] 'Preface', *New Signatures* (London, 1932), 8.

Roberts lumped together the several hands under the provocative banner of 'the communist attitude'. Roberts had been vice-president of the Cambridge University Socialist Society and, although christened William Edward, had adopted the name 'Michael' in homage to the eighteenth-century Russian scientist and poet, Mikhail Lomonosov.[4] Nevertheless, the alleged homogeneity of radical politics among the *New Signatures* poets was factitious; especially given the entrenched schism of the Cambridge poets, appearing in two rival undergraduate magazines, the *Venture* and *Experiment*, which were (according to James Reeves, a contributor to both magazines) 'pure of all politics'.[5] In truth, the Cambridge poets shared little in common apart from their lack of regard for the Oxford poets. In December 1931, Julian Bell wrote to Lehmann, à propos *New Signatures*, expressing grave reservations about 'the danger of condoning the heresies of Spender and Auden'.[6] Roberts himself, it should be added, was never an orthodox communist.[7]

Eliot recalled *New Signatures* as 'a book which seemed to promise him [Roberts] the place of expositor and interpreter of the poetry of his generation'.[8] Roberts's public role as a champion of a new generation of poets was timely. In early 1932, Eliot had written to Dobrée to seek some reassurance regarding F. S. Flint's effectiveness as a reviewer of poetry for the *Criterion*.[9] Flint's lack of sympathy with young experimental poets, together with the death of Harold Monro, had left Eliot looking for a new reviewer of contemporary poetry.[10] In 1932, Eliot accepted Roberts's article on T. E. Hulme for publication in the *Criterion*.[11] It seems

---

[4] Curiously, his chosen name was a near homonym of W. B. Yeats's fictional magician, Michael Robartes.

[5] 'Cambridge Twenty Years Ago', in Richard March and Tambimuttu (eds.), *T. S. Eliot: A Symposium* from Conrad Aiken and others (London, 1948), 39.

[6] Cited in *The Whispering Gallery*, 174.

[7] Roberts had been a member of the Communist Party in the mid-1920s, but was expelled within a year.

[8] 'Introduction', in T. W. Eason and R. Hamilton (eds.), *A Portrait of Michael Roberts* (London, 1949), p. x.

[9] See T. S. Eliot to Bonamy Dobrée, 7 Jan. 1932. Leeds.

[10] By 1932, Eliot had ceased to use the poets, Peter Quennell (a *New Statesman* reviewer) and Sherard Vines (Professor of English at Hull University) as *Criterion* reviewers of modern poetry.

[11] In 1936 Eliot commissioned Roberts, on behalf of Faber, to write a critical book on Hulme. Eliot made it clear that although he admired Hulme as a cultural and aesthetic critic, he felt that his ideas were sometimes inconsistent. T. S. Eliot to Michael Roberts, 11 June 1936. Keele.

that Roberts's credentials as the editor of *New Signatures* and the more assertively political sequel, *New Country* (1933), were difficult to overlook.[12] With a portfolio of poetry reviews for the *Adelphi* and the *Poetry Review* under his belt (including appreciative reviews of Eliot, Auden, and Day Lewis), Eliot recruited Roberts to the *Criterion*.

Roberts used the *Criterion* to survey the topography of modern English poetry. A review of Alida Monro's *Recent Poetry 1923–1933*, an anthology liberally sprinkled with Georgian poets, 'these delineators of charming experience and decorators of unemotionally apprehended legends' as Roberts described them, became a platform to promote the new poetic and socialist convictions of the Oxford poets: 'The crowd today can only be approached through the few, and the poetry of W. H. Auden, Stephen Spender, C. Day Lewis is remarkable in that it contains elements which might commend it both to the few and to the many.'[13] However, Roberts became increasingly mistrustful of what he characterized as a 'fundamentalist attitude' towards poetry. There was a noticeable cooling in his *Criterion* reviews of the more politically engaged offerings of the young left-wing poets. By the mid-1930s, Roberts was even prepared to speak out publicly in favour of Eliot's sermonizing choruses from *The Rock* and against the dismissive judgements of so-called 'atheist-communist readers'; a pronouncement that alarmed many left-wing intellectuals.[14]

It is worth examining the nature of this sea-change in the tides of modern poetry. In February 1935, Eliot had invited Roberts to edit a Faber anthology of modern verse. It was agreed that the volume should 'define the modern movement in a way that was not just chronological but a question of sensibility and technique'.[15] The anthology, published in February 1936, displayed a

---

[12] On Eliot's instructions, *New Country* was sent to Ezra Pound for review. Pound, however, passed the volume to the 21-year-old American poet, T. C. Wilson, who observed dryly: 'The disparity between the intention and the accomplished work is substantial' ('Books of the Quarter', *Criterion* (Apr. 1934), 485). Bonamy Dobrée was more enthusiastic in his review for the *Listener* (14 June 1933), 958.

[13] 'Books of the Quarter', *Criterion* (Apr. 1934), 507, 508.

[14] See 'Books of the Quarter', *Criterion* (Apr. 1936), 499, and 'The Poetry of T. S. Eliot', *London Mercury* (May 1936), 38–44. Eliot expressed his gratitude to Roberts for the *London Mercury* article.

[15] Janet Adam Smith, 'Mr. Eliot's Proposals', *TLS* (18 June 1978), 728.

broader catholicity of taste than had been evident in either *New Signatures* or *New Country*. Beginning with Hopkins and Yeats, excluding the Georgians, Roberts's selection followed two main developments: the 'European sensibility', exemplified by the international modernism of Eliot and Pound, and a homespun 'English element', represented by talents as diverse as Graves and Auden.[16] *The Faber Book of Modern Verse* was notable for the inclusion of several American poets who were barely known in England—Wallace Stevens, John Crowe Ransom, Allen Tate, and Hart Crane—Roberts had picked up their work at the Poetry Bookshop in London or at Sylvia Beach's bookshop in Paris.[17] *The Faber Book of Modern Verse* also gave an institutional seal of approval to precocious young British poets, like Dylan Thomas and David Gascoyne, who were scarcely out of their teens.[18] Eliot kept a watchful eye on the composition of the Faber anthology.[19] He informed Roberts that he thought the introduction was 'very interesting indeed' and justly represented 'a newer point of view than my own'.[20] It was not surprising that Richard Church, head of poetry publications at Dent, praised Roberts's introduction in the *Criterion* in unmistakably Eliotic terms: 'It is cool and impersonal, and concentrates on finding a principle of criticism founded on tradition.'[21]

In 1937, Eliot hailed Roberts as 'the most authoritative critic of contemporary poetry'.[22] He had not always been so complimentary. In fact, he had rejected Roberts's *Critique of Poetry* when the typescript was originally sent to Faber. Perusal of that work, however, reinforces various lines of thought expressed in Roberts's *Criterion* reviews. For one thing, *Critique of Poetry* made explicit

---

[16] Roberts secured a significant coup by persuading Robert Graves and Laura Riding to appear in his anthology, bearing in mind the opinions expressed in their *A Pamphlet Against Anthologies* (London, 1928).

[17] See Michael Roberts, 'American Poetry', *Listener* (22 Aug. 1934), 335–6.

[18] Roberts praised Thomas's *18 Poems* as the work of 'the most striking of the new poets who have appeared in the last twelve months' ('Books of the Quarter', *Criterion* (Apr. 1935), 496). Roberts first met David Gascoyne at David Archer's Parton Street bookshop.

[19] Eliot told Pound that Roberts would not be allowed to leave out anyone of importance. (4 Apr. 1935). Yale.   [20] 'Mr. Eliot's Proposals', 728.

[21] 'Books of the Quarter', *Criterion* (July 1936), 738.

[22] Cited by John Haffenden in *Auden: The Critical Heritage* (London, 1983), 84.

Roberts's belief that Hulme's *Speculations* and Richards's *Principles of Literary Criticism*, both published in 1924, had performed the necessary groundwork for a stricter and sharper use of critical terminology. Furthermore, following Empson's distinction between 'analytic' and 'appreciative' criticism in *Seven Types of Ambiguity* (1930), Roberts, in his *Criterion* reviews, was quick to praise the rigorous 'analytic' criticism of the American New Critics, implying a favourable comparison with the work of an earlier generation of 'appreciators'.[23] That said, Roberts's interest in the close verbal analysis of poetry did not obscure what he called the 'sociological implications' of literature: he was highly sensitive to the ways in which a reductive formalism could mask ideological bias. Roberts wrote in the introduction to *The Faber Book of Modern Verse*: 'It is not possible to compile an anthology of serious poetry without reflecting the social and moral problems of our time.'[24] After the publication of the Faber volume, his contributions to the *Criterion* explicitly tackled those social and ethical problems.

II

It comes as a surprise to realize how much reviewing Janet Adam Smith did for the *Criterion*. During the last three years of the journal she reviewed forty-one volumes of poetry and verse drama, making her the most prolific female contributor. Born in 1905, the daughter of the Very Revd Sir George Adam Smith, Principal of Aberdeen University, Janet Adam Smith was educated at Cheltenham Ladies' College and Somerville College, Oxford, where she read English. Her first job after university was as the assistant editor of the *Listener*, a threepenny weekly journal of general culture launched by the BBC in 1929. Eliot and Read were among a distinguished group of writers happy to accept the *Listener*'s shilling. In time, the weekly also began to function as a useful nursery-slope for young poets. By virtue of its circulation of around 28,000, the *Listener* promoted new poetry to a much wider audience than was possible in the specialist little magazines.[25]

---

[23] See 'Books of the Quarter', *The Criterion* (July 1936), 702–5.

[24] 'Introduction', *The Faber Book of Modern Verse* (London, 1936), 3.

[25] See Q. D. Leavis: 'most of those who read at the *Criterion* level are likely to be subscribers, whereas the *Listener*, *Everyman*, *John o'London*'s . . . pass through innumerable hands in the reading-rooms of public libraries, and even then have in

At first the *Listener* did not have a literary editor, but the role soon devolved upon Adam Smith. In July 1933, she rushed through a 4-page poetry supplement that was subsequently brought to the attention of Sir John Reith, the high-minded Director-General of the BBC. Reith complained that he was puzzled by the poetry published in the *Listener*. In particular, he had found Auden's 'The Witnesses' both 'odd' and 'uncouth'.[26]

Read suggested to Adam Smith that she appeal to Eliot for support, and he was duly sent all the poetry printed in the *Listener* between February 1931 and July 1933. However, the captious tone of Eliot's report to the BBC disappointed Adam Smith by its unwillingness to come more wholeheartedly to the defence of modern poetry. She recalled: 'There was no glow of enthusiasm in his grave and measured sentences.'[27] Instead, in his rather *de haut en bas Criterion* manner, Eliot considered the principles upon which a weekly journal should print contemporary verse. He concluded: 'On both moral and practical grounds therefore a weekly, if it publishes poetry at all, should look to the younger writers.' Drawing upon his editorial practice in the *Criterion*, Eliot explained that the periodical should 'take up the young poets who seem to have any *promise*, and give each of them a number of chances, over a period of several years, until we are forced to the conclusion that his promise has not been fulfilled'. He pointed out:

A few of the writers have appeared in the *Criterion*: two of them, W. H. Auden and Stephen Spender, have had volumes published on my recommendation by Faber and Faber. Of all the younger poets, Auden is the one who has interested me most deeply, though I feel that it is impossible to predict whether he will manifest the austerity and concentration necessary for poetry of the first rank, or whether he will dissipate his talents in wit and verbal brilliance.[28]

Eliot assured Reith that the *Listener* was publishing the best poets of the younger generation and that Adam Smith's selection was, with some minor reservations, very creditable. Her anthology of

---

addition a vast body of inert support in the public which buys the large-circulation dailies' (*Fiction and the Reading Public* (London, 1932), 21).

[26] See Janet Adam Smith, 'T. S. Eliot and "The Listener"', *Listener* (21 Jan. 1965), 105.   [27] Ibid.

[28] Cited in Haffenden (ed.), *Auden: The Critical Heritage*, 139.

poems from the *Listener*, entitled *Poems of Tomorrow* (1935), was reviewed favourably in the *Criterion*.[29]

Janet Adam Smith left the staff of the *Listener* in 1935 when she married Michael Roberts, who was then teaching at the Royal Grammar School in Newcastle.[30] The following year, she was pleasantly surprised when Eliot invited her to succeed her husband as the *Criterion*'s chief reviewer of contemporary poetry. Naturally, she felt that her successful literary editorship of the *Listener* encouraged Eliot to think of her as 'a suitable person to sift and review the books of poetry coming in to *The Criterion*'.[31] The domestic background to her time as a *Criterion* reviewer— 'a tale of poems, children, books, anthologies, reviews, climbing, ski-ing, school camps'—provides an engaging contrast to the London poetry cliques of the 1930s:

The batch of poetry books for review in the *Criterion* came to me in Newcastle without any prior selection by me or, as far as I know, by TSE. It was left to me to decide which to review. I was no doubt given an approximate length; otherwise no suggestions as to how or what I should write. I don't remember any significant sub-editing. I was paid about £2 for each review. My general impression was of complete freedom to choose, and to write, all for a paper one so much respected that one forgave them for the meagre fee.[32]

Adam Smith's freedom extended to judicious reviews of *Criterion* poets. William Plomer,[33] George Rostrevor Hamilton,[34] Rayner Heppenstall, and George Barker[35] were chastised in fairly rough reviews. Similarly, after reading F. T. Prince's *Poems* (1938), a Faber volume, Adam Smith posed the question: 'to what extent can an accomplished writer become a poet if he adds nothing to the vision of his carefully chosen models?'[36] Although these poets

[29] George Every described *Poems of Tomorrow* as 'certainly the best introduction so far to the works of the younger writers' ('Books of the Quarter', *Criterion* (Oct. 1935), 145).
[30] During his time at RGS Newcastle, Roberts encouraged members of the sixth form to subscribe to the *Criterion*, *Scrutiny*, and the *New Statesman*.
[31] Janet Adam Smith, letter to Jason Harding, 17 Sept. 1997.
[32] Janet Adam Smith, letter to Jason Harding, 13 Oct. 1997.
[33] See 'Books of the Quarter', *Criterion* (Jan. 1937), 333.
[34] 'Books of the Quarter', *Criterion* (July 1938), 734.
[35] 'Books of the Quarter', *Criterion* (July 1937), 703, 701.
[36] 'Books of the Quarter', *Criterion* (Jan. 1939), 318. Prince recalled his 'gratitude and admiration for Eliot personally', although it had seemed to him 'doubtful whether *The Criterion* could ever have succeeded, as a European-minded, more or less

had only a limited association with the *Criterion*—Heppenstall and Barker were offered occasional reviewing to supplement their incomes—it was refreshing that Adam Smith should come to a tough-minded estimation of poets who had benefited from the *Criterion*'s imprimatur. Only Barker, a Faber poet admired and supported—financially and otherwise—by Eliot, appeared in *The Faber Book of Modern Verse*.[37] In general, Adam Smith gave favourable reviews to authors who had appeared in the Faber anthology. Her praise of the originality of Laura Riding's *Collected Poems* (1938), for example, was almost a lone voice in the hostile male-world of poetry reviewing, and in sharp contradistinction to John Gould Fletcher's dismissive *Criterion* review of *The Close Chaplet* in 1927.[38] Moreover, James Reeves, one of Riding's poetic disciples and a *Criterion* reviewer, received warm praise for his first book of poetry, *The Natural Need*.[39]

In contrast to the exaggerated censure and praise of *Scrutiny* and *New Verse*, who had their own axes to grind, Adam Smith allowed the *Criterion* to come to a discriminating estimation of the Auden group. Eliot had published Auden's charade 'Paid on Both Sides' in January 1930 describing it as 'quite a brilliant piece of work'.[40] However, he quickly began to express reservations about Auden's development. In December 1930, he confided to Read:

I chiefly worry about Auden's ethical principles and convictions, not about his technical ability; or rather, I think that if a man's ethical and

conservative periodical, in the crisis-ridden Europe of the 1930s' (F. T. Prince, letter to Jason Harding, 15 Nov. 1997).

[37] Eliot organized an anonymous subscription fund to help Barker financially. For details see T.S. Eliot to John Hayward, 23 Feb. 1937. Cambridge (King's).

[38] 'By her practice and influence, Miss Riding has helped several poets to write simply about abstractions, to avoid trivial decoration and irrelevant music, and to preserve the integrity of their words' ('Books of the Quarter', *Criterion* (Oct. 1938), 115). Since Fletcher's 1927 review, the *Criterion* had ignored no fewer than nine volumes of Riding's work.

[39] See 'Books of the Quarter', *Criterion* (July 1936), 731. Roberts included Reeves in *The Faber Book of Modern Verse* at Riding's insistence. Gareth Reeves recalled his father's relationship with Eliot: 'As far as I know he only met Eliot once, in the latter's Faber office, when he went to see him about contributions to the *Criterion*. He found Eliot charming, putting the younger man at his ease, interested in his likes and dislikes . . . However, my father never really acknowledged, even to himself I feel, this Eliotic influence; and in later years his remarks, to me at any rate, about Eliot were invariably negative, even hostile.' Gareth Reeves, letter to Jason Harding, 23 July 1998.

[40] T. S. Eliot to E. McKnight Kauffer, 6 Jan. 1930. Cited in Humphrey Carpenter, *W. H. Auden: A Biography* (London, 1981), 95.

religious views and convictions are feeble or limited and incapable of development, then his technical development is restricted.[41]

As we have seen, Eliot's 1933 BBC report worried that Auden might go to seed in frivolously clever 'dissipation'.[42] In 1935, Eliot described Auden to Virginia Woolf as 'a very nice rattled-brained boy'.[43] On the other hand, reviewing *Look, Stranger!* (1936) in the *Criterion* Adam Smith chose to accentuate the positive; praising Auden's accumulation of memorable lines and phrases:

[Auden] collects phrases, gestures, actions like a magpie; and his hoard always provides him with the effective word and image; . . . Metres and stanza-forms are collected and produced in the same way; not out of technical virtuosity, but because the situation demands a tone of voice which another poet has already produced.[44]

The previous month, F. R. Leavis published in *Scrutiny* a review of *Look, Stranger!* in which he finally lost patience with the 'irresponsible' and 'immature' elements in Auden's poetry.[45] Adam Smith also had misgivings about the flippancy with which Auden could blur the distinction between 'private faces' and 'public places'. It was a failing that she, like Leavis, felt could function 'irresponsibly'.[46]

Adam Smith's sensitivity to what she described as 'the relation between the public life of politics, government, revolution, war, and the private life of love, children, music, pictures and gaiety'[47] became a way of identifying the relative merits of the Auden group: a way of separating the liberal tendencies in the work of

---

[41]   T. S. Eliot to Herbert Read, 11 Dec. 1930. Cited in Carpenter, *Auden*, 137.

[42]   Eliot may have been irritated when John Hayward praised *The Orators* as 'the most valuable contribution to English poetry since *The Waste Land*' ('Books of the Quarter', *Criterion* (Oct. 1932), 134). 'Speech for a Prize Day' from *The Orators* was first published in the *Criterion* the previous year.

[43]   See *The Diary of Virginia Woolf, iv. 1931–1935* ed. Anne Olivier Bell and Andrew McNellie (London, 1982), 324.

[44]   'Books of the Quarter', *Criterion* (Jan. 1937), 331, 332.

[45]   See 'Mr. Auden's Talent', *Scrutiny* (Dec. 1936), 323–7. Auden had been an idiosyncratic reviewer for the *Criterion* and *Scrutiny* until the end of 1935, when he was obliged to accept the better financial rates offered by the *Listener*, the *New Statesman*, and the *Daily Telegraph*.

[46]   Janet Adam Smith's remarks were levelled against *On the Frontier*, a play written in collaboration with Christopher Isherwood ('Books of the Quarter', *Criterion* (Jan. 1939), 323).   [47]   'Books of the Quarter', *Criterion* (July 1938), 730.

MacNeice, Spender, and Allott from the revolutionary propaganda of Day Lewis and Madge—reversing, in the process, her former enthusiasm for these two poets. Some years later, Adam Smith reflected that by the mid-1930s Michael Roberts had come to believe: 'the politics of gesture and emotion, the whole rhetoric of the Left [was] an excuse for not taking the trouble to know, a refuge from hard thinking, and an escape from a situation's real complexity.'[48] Reviewing Madge's *The Disappearing Castle*, she located both a human and a poetic failure in his avowed communism.[49] Adam Smith, who had lost two brothers in the First World War, had little patience with adolescent warmongering. 'The value of a human life', she remarked in the *Criterion* in April 1938, 'is greater than that of any "cause".'[50] Reviewing Day Lewis's doom-laden *Overtures to Death* in the final *Criterion*, she ironically invoked Auden's *Spain*: 'one wonders whether the energy that once went into the patient search for the right inflection, the accurate image, has now been diverted to "the flat ephemeral pamphlet and the boring meeting." '[51]

It appears that Adam Smith's seriousness and integrity commanded widespread respect. In spite of the austerity of her *Criterion* reviews, she remained on friendly terms with Auden, Spender, Madge, and Gascoyne. Eliot also expressed the opinion that Michael Roberts was 'conscientious, scrupulous and responsible' and that Adam Smith was a truly admirable person,[52] a valuation reinforced by his decision not to send Roberts's *Poems* (1936) to Adam Smith for review.[53] In an obituary address, Karl Miller recalled Janet Adam Smith's 'gravity and scruple', characterizing her as an Edinburgh reviewer in an old Scots style.[54] Leavis's complaint that the reviewing pages of the *Criterion* had sold out to the Auden–Spender coterie was simply not true. The regular reviews

---

[48] See Adam Smith, 'Introduction', *The Collected Poems of Michael Roberts* (London, 1958), 25.   [49] See 'Books of the Quarter', *Criterion* (July 1937), 703–5.
[50] 'Books of the Quarter', *Criterion* (Apr. 1938), 523.
[51] 'Books of the Quarter', *Criterion* (Jan. 1939), 321.
[52] See 'Introduction', in Eason and Hamilton (eds.), *A Portrait of Michael Roberts*, p. ix. T. S. Eliot to John Hayward, 3 Nov. 1941. Cambridge (King's).
[53] See T. S. Eliot to Michael Roberts, 18 June 1936. Keele. The volume was sent to E. W. F. Tomlin after Hugh Gordon Porteus had been unavailable. Tomlin expressed his disappointment with Roberts's poetry ('Books of the Quarter', *Criterion* (Oct. 1936), 137–9).   [54] See *Janet Adam Smith Remembered* (London, 2000), 7–9.

of Roberts and Adam Smith represent the most fair-minded, thorough, and up-to-date engagement with contemporary poetry in the files of the *Criterion*. The cumulative effect of these reviews was to confirm and endorse the selection made in *The Faber Book of Modern Verse*. This is an observation of some interest given that the Faber anthology soon eclipsed Yeats's idiosyncratic *Oxford Book of Modern Verse*, also published in 1936, as the standard anthology of early twentieth-century English poetry. In the words of Anne Ridler, it 'formed the taste of a generation'.[55]

III

Eliot valued Michael Roberts chiefly as a cultural critic: a writer who scrutinized the cultural activities of English society from a viewpoint that was not incompatible with Anglican morality. The exercise of the moral imagination in the cause of social reconstruction was a potential point of contact between Christians and communists during the 1930s. As Roberts put it in a 1934 BBC broadcast: 'the essential quarrel is not between Christians and Communists, but between those who wish civilization to survive, and those who fight to retain their privilege for a few more years.'[56] Eliot, unlike the Revd Hewlett Johnson, the 'red' Dean of Canterbury, was not in favour of 'amiable bridge-builders' between Christianity and communism.[57] That said, Roberts's remarks in a special 1937 'English Number' of *Poetry* (Chicago)— co-edited with Auden—repays quotation:

Auden, Spender, and Madge are sometimes called communist poets, and Eliot a Christian poet, but their importance depends on the fact that they see more clearly than the ordinary communist or ordinary Christian. . . . the gulf which separates them from the ordinary politician is greater than that which separates the poets themselves. . . . The prevailing mood of Spender and Auden, as of Eliot, is one of grief and sympathy rather than anger or denunciation. It is in this sense that their poetry is political: they

[55] 'Introduction to the Second Edition', *The Faber Book of Modern Verse* (London, 1951), 35.

[56] Cited in *Michael Roberts, Selected Poems and Prose*, ed. Frederick Grubb (Manchester, 1980), 89. Cf. Spender: 'Even today a writer who is religious or a Communist has the advantage of not being an individualist rebel forced to create a system of beliefs of his own' (*New Country* (London, 1933), 71).

[57] See 'A Commentary', *Criterion* (Jan. 1936), 269.

have a clear idea of the kind of life which they wish to see in Europe, and they express the temper in which more and more Englishmen wish those changes to be made.[58]

After the Faber anthology, Roberts concentrated his efforts on the essays assembled under the title *The Modern Mind*: the fruits of what he called 'a long desultory reading in the history of religion, poetry and science'.[59] Eliot saw some of the essays in manuscript and, when the volume was rejected by Jonathan Cape, he secured publication by Faber. It is possible to sympathize with Cape's decision to turn down this highly ambitious attempt to explain why and how science had superseded Christianity as the ultimate arbiter of truth in Western civilization. Partly an attempt to rewrite A. N. Whitehead's *Science and the Modern World* (1926)[60] in terms of a finely balanced agnosticism, *The Modern Mind* was often contestable on points of detail. In *Scrutiny*, Michael Oakeshott complained of Roberts's tendency to overstate his case and the 'alarming and disconcerting tendency to wander from his thesis'.[61] The leading thread of *The Modern Mind* attempted to negotiate a path between the atheistic materialism of Hobbes and the dogmatic theology of Thomism.[62] Roberts's *via media* was dependent on a 'poetic' sensibility and on the religious traditions of the Anglican Church; of which he remarked that its 'dogma is nebulous and admits of personal interpretation'. He concluded: 'we need the living conception of religion that is expressed through poetry, and the personal humility that makes men turn to a Church.'[63]

Eliot increasingly turned to the Church—Catholic and Anglican—for many of his contributors to the *Criterion* during the late 1930s.[64] More than that, he carefully matched books

[58] 'Aspects of English Poetry', *Poetry* [Chicago] (Jan. 1937), 213–14.

[59] *The Modern Mind* (London, 1937), 8.

[60] Herbert Read described *Science and the Modern World* as 'the most important book published in the conjoint realms of science and philosophy since Descartes's *Discourse on Method*' ('Books of the Quarter', *Criterion* (June 1926), 581).

[61] 'The Modern Mind', *Scrutiny* (Sep. 1937), 208.

[62] Roberts's hostile account of Hobbes as a precursor of modern science showed the influence of Eliot's 'John Bramhall', *Theology* (July 1927), 13–16.

[63] *The Modern Mind*, 277.

[64] Among the clergymen who contributed to the *Criterion* were: Geoffrey Curtis; Martin D'Arcy; F. N. Davey; V. A. Demant; George Every; R. Newton Flew; Charles Harris; Frederic Hood; Cyril Hudson; Cyril Martindale; T. M. Parker; William Pick; Edward Quinn; Charles Smyth; Henry Swabey; and William Force Stead, the Chaplain of Worcester College, Oxford, who baptized Eliot into the Church of England in 1927.

dealing with the new scientific world-view to reviewers professing Christian faith. The terrain covered by *The Modern Mind* was, in fact, already familiar to readers of the *Criterion* from Roberts's miscellaneous reviews of books on science, philosophy, and theology. In a lengthy *Criterion* review, the poet and Anglican monk, George Every, welcomed *The Modern Mind* as a profound examination of the age: 'a thoroughly honest attempt to investigate the most important intellectual change in the history of the modern world.'[65] Every admired Roberts's search for authoritative values that could be applied in political, ethical, and literary spheres: a necessary antidote to what he described in 1939 as 'the dogmatism and triviality of scientific specialists upon things [*sic*] they know nothing about'.[66] A graduate of chemistry and mathematics from the Universities of London and Cambridge, Roberts's contributions are particularly helpful in ascertaining the *Criterion*'s response to the human implications of modern science. Roberts believed that the philosophical pragmatism underpinning scientific methodology revealed an inadequate conception of human life—just as he believed that the dismissal of metaphysics propounded by positivists in Cambridge or Vienna was inadequate 'to anyone with claims to have some knowledge of imaginative and spiritual truth'.[67] For Roberts, advances in scientific knowledge presented a profound challenge to received ethics, but he concluded: 'The solution of social problems requires a sober wisdom which is part of the heritage of Christianity, and it requires too, a vitality and a persistence more vigorous than anything likely to result from the philosophy of Wittgenstein and Carnap.'[68]

The English translation of Einstein's *Relativity: The Special and the General Theory* (1920), together with bestselling works of scientific exposition by Sir Arthur Eddington and Sir James Jeans, did much to popularize the implications and impositions of the 'new science'. Eliot's disapproval of this trend may be inferred from his decision to translate personally Charles Mauron's 'On Reading Einstein' for the *Criterion*: an article in which fashionable

---

[65] 'Books of the Quarter', *Criterion* (Oct. 1937), 129–33. On the strength of *The Modern Mind*, Every invited Roberts to lecture at Kelham (Janet Adam Smith, letter to Jason Harding, 19 Nov. 1998).

[66] 'The Claims of Politics', *Scrutiny* (Sep. 1939), 141–5.

[67] 'Books of the Quarter', *Criterion* (Jan. 1937), 377.   [68] Ibid. 380.

talk of 'relativist theories' was given short shrift.[69] Montgomery Belgion went even further asserting, with exceptional implausibility, that Einstein had probably 'never seriously attended to metaphysics' and was 'not a very interesting man'.[70] However, other *Criterion* contributors, such as Joseph Needham, editor of *Science, Religion and Reality* (1925), searched for a synthesis between science and Christianity. Moreover, the early poetry of Roberts's friend, William Empson, was a demonstration that science had not robbed the world of metaphysical wonder. Empson observed in the *Criterion*: 'It is likely, indeed, that the view of space taken by modern physics will eventually alter our notions of reality.'[71] In a 1932 broadcast talk, Eliot commented: 'it is not science that has destroyed religious belief, but our preference of unbelief that has made illegitimate use of science.'[72] Eliot, in common with Empson, could share Pascal's awe at the silence of astronomical immensities, but unlike Empson he did not believe that modern science had antiquated religion.

Roberts's transition from 'the communist attitude' to the Anglican Church was not a popular trajectory.[73] Adam Smith remarked: 'Michael's apparent switch of interest from politics to philosophy and religion was not along the usual line of development in the Thirties; it led to an increasingly isolated position and a good deal of misunderstanding.'[74] A sense of that isolation and misunderstanding can be gauged from the pages of *New Verse*, where Grigson lamented, with a false sense of concern, a 'lost' leader. George Every's *Criterion* review of *The Modern Mind* confirmed that Roberts was no longer the leader of a group. And yet, the 'apparent switch' in Roberts's allegiances can be explained in terms offered by Every:

At one time in the nineteen-thirties many of the younger contributors were attracted to Communism, but they continued to observe, in their work for

---

[69] See 'On Reading Einstein', *Criterion* (Oct. 1930), 23–31.

[70] 'Books of the Quarter', *Criterion* (July 1935), 711.

[71] 'Books of the Quarter', *Criterion* (Oct. 1930), 170–71.

[72] 'Religion and Science', *Listener* (23 March 1932), 429.

[73] See Eliot: 'I do not think that most of [Roberts's] contemporaries in the decade before the war were in a mood to be led in the direction in which his thought was moving' ('Introduction', in Eason and Hamilton (eds.), *A Portrait of Michael Roberts*, p. xii).   [74] 'Introduction', *Collected Poems of Michael Roberts*, 23.

The Criterion, a decent respect for the labours expended in the creation of a European tradition, and to many of them the place of Christianity in that tradition grew more personally significant as the years drew by.[75]

In fact, Roberts's 'isolated superiority' commended itself greatly to Eliot, who hailed *The Modern Mind* as a 'profound examination of the age'.[76]

In the years leading up to the Second World War, Roberts doggedly opposed the fatalism and cultural pessimism symbolized by Spengler's *The Decline of the West*. In *The Recovery of the West*, published by Faber in 1941, but begun around the time of the collapse of the *Criterion*, Roberts wrote: 'The decadence of Western Society in our own time, its loss of conviction and vitality, is largely due to the weakening of Christian faith.'[77] The preservation of a tradition of Christian European civilization was axiomatic to the *Criterion*. On the eve of war, Eliot informed John Betjeman that *The Recovery of the West* was an important book and that it was essential to keep Roberts alive for the post-war reconstruction.[78] Eliot's valedictory 'Last Words' made it clear that he did not believe that the *Criterion* could be continued under another editor. However, in a tender obituary essay, written following Roberts's premature death from leukaemia in 1948, he paid Roberts perhaps the largest tribute he could make:

He would have made an admirable editor of a review of ideas; indeed, had *The Criterion* continued, he was the only man junior to myself of whom I could think for the editorship.[79]

---

[75] 'The Way of Rejections', in March and Tambimuttu (eds.), *T. S. Eliot: A Symposium*, 186. Cf. Every: 'The difficulty is that so few of our "Communist" poets do believe. They are nearly all, from the strict Marxist point of view, heretics or sceptics. . . . Which then is impossible of belief, Marxism or Christianity? . . . it is significant that Christian poetry can still be written, and not only by Eliot, and that our 'emotive' poets are still sucking images, rhythms and vowel-combinations out of Eliot and Hopkins' ('Books of the Quarter', *Criterion* (Oct. 1935), 148).

[76] 'Introduction', in Eason and Hamilton (eds.), *A Portrait of Michael Roberts*, pp. xi, x.   [77] *The Recovery of the West* (London, 1941), 268.

[78] T. S. Eliot to John Betjeman, 18 Sept. 1939. Victoria.

[79] 'Michael Roberts', *New English Weekly* (13 Jan. 1949), 164.

PART III

Cultural Politics

9

A Religio-Political Organ

> For myself, a right political philosophy came more and more
> to imply a right theology—and right economics to depend
> upon right ethics: leading to emphases which somewhat
> stretched the original framework of a literary review.
>
> 'Last Words', *Criterion* (January 1939), 272

Recent critical commentary has too often assumed that the political
ideas formulated and debated in the *Criterion* can be dismissed as
predictably conservative, even proto-fascist. On the contrary, a
sympathetic consideration of the journal's treatment of political
affairs unearths Eliot's editorial determination not to oversimplify
difficult and complex areas of politico-cultural exchange. It is true
that the early volumes of the *Criterion* exhibited a somewhat
dandyish reluctance to enter the political arena. In 'The Idea of a
Literary Review' (January 1926), Eliot observed that a literary
review 'must protect its disinterestedness, must avoid the temptation ever to appeal to any social, political or theological prejudices'.[1] However, in his editorial Commentary for June 1927,
under the Maurrassien *reveille* 'Politique d'abord', he declared: 'It
is a trait of the present time that every "literary" review worth its
salt has a political interest: indeed that *only* in the literary reviews
which are not the conscientious organs of superannuated political
creeds, are there any living political ideas.'[2] Such an assertion
could only be made seriously at a time when the 'literary review',
taken in its broadest sense, was a powerful and influential forum
for politico-cultural criticism: albeit a step viewed by some
contemporary literary reviews as an abuse of function.[3]

[1] 'The Idea of a Literary Review', *Criterion* (Jan. 1926), 4.
[2] 'A Commentary', *Criterion* (June 1927), 283.
[3] 'The most natural step for a review to take, if it wishes to survive, is to adopt a
"political" attitude, . . . and, though we realise that such an attitude may be almost

Reassessment of the *Criterion*'s place within the thickets of political controversy calls for attention to the precise chronological dating of Eliot's editorial stand (or conspicuous lack of editorial stand) on what he called 'the great political and social issues of the day'.[4] In short, the vexed question of the *Criterion*'s policy on foreign affairs emerges only gradually from a careful reconstruction of the symposia organized by Eliot on the rival claims of fascism and communism in the late 1920s, and, after the onset of economic depression, discussion of the writings of Major Douglas and John Maynard Keynes. The larger picture that comes into focus from these details helps to show to what extent the *Criterion*'s contribution to politico-economic discourse was conditioned, following Eliot's entry into the Church of England in 1927, by a reactionary theological position—a position that is usefully brought into contrast with two contemporary weeklies, the *New Statesman* and the *New English Weekly*. It also helps the modern commentator to arrive at a temperate assessment of Bonamy Dobrée's complaint, made to Herbert Read in 1929, that the *Criterion* was a 'Religio-Political Organ'.[5]

I

In its initial belletristic incarnation, the *Criterion* did not interest itself overtly in politics; at least not beyond the occasional outbursts of pugnacious Toryism from Charles Whibley and his associates. A series of *Criterion* essays on great Tory patriarchs—Bolingbroke, Lord Chesterfield, Disraeli, and Lord Curzon—advocated the inherent strengths of monarchy, aristocracy, and the Anglican Church and the concomitant evils of liberal democracy, or more insidiously, the Russian Revolution. In October 1924, the staunchly Tory historian F. W. Bain, delivered a stern Burkean homily regarding the French Revolution, drawing attention to 'the sinister quality of 1789, which nineteenth-century Liberalism has studiously disguised, just as the sentimental democratic idealism

---

essential to the achievement of a sound economic status, we cannot consider it as less than an abuse of function' ('Valediction', *Calendar* (July 1927), 172).

  [4] 'A Commentary', *Criterion* (July 1933), 642.
  [5] Bonamy Dobrée to Herbert Read, 9 Apr. 1929. Victoria.

of today turns a blind eye on the Bolshevik atrocities in Russia'.[6] 'Crites'—Eliot's editorial *alter ego*—was scarcely more sympathetic towards Soviet Russia in the following issue: there was little doubt that Whibley's insistence on the value of inherited forms of traditional authority was representative of the *Criterion*'s political thinking at this time.[7] In December 1924, a circular drawn up for prospective subscribers claimed that the *Criterion*, although avoiding discussion of contemporary politics, expounded the philosophy of 'pure Toryism'.[8]

In his editorial 'Last Words', Eliot claimed it was only from 1926 that the lineaments of the post-war world became clearly visible. This year, of course, was the year of the General Strike, an event that laid bare bitter and entrenched class divisions in British society. Of more local interest, it was also the year in which he launched the *New Criterion*. Less constrained by the financial purse-strings of Lady Rothermere and no longer a moonlighting employee of Lloyds Bank, Eliot could now, should he chose, speak freely in his signed editorials on political and cultural topics. From 1926, the *Criterion* saw political commentary as within its province.[9] Eliot used the journal as a platform, occasionally a pulpit, to address the small, politically conservative audience he courted. The move signalled a return to the strenuous intellectual rectitude of the great Victorian reviews of general culture, journals that had facilitated discussion between public figures on the most important issues of the day: the format of the symposium apparently imposing a fair-minded or what Matthew Arnold called a 'disinterested' tribunal of enquiry. However, the idea of the literary periodical as a free forum of debate is a problematic one. Unavoidable pragmatic questions of editorial selection and arrangement neatly frame the question of Eliot's direction of the *Criterion* in arguably its most intriguing form. As a case in point, several recent commentators have viewed the journal's 'disinterested' treatment of, say, Italian

---

[6] '1789', *Criterion* (Oct. 1924), 51.
[7] 'Crites' [T. S. Eliot], 'A Commentary', *Criterion* (Jan. 1925), 161–3.
[8] The circular is among the papers of Vivien Eliot. Oxford.
[9] H. G. Dalway Turnbull called Aristotle, a little anachronistically, as a witness to testify that 'communism is "impossible"—a conclusion which modern experiments have abundantly verified' ('Aristotle on Democracy and Socialism', *Criterion* (Jan. 1926), 13).

fascism as evidence of a sinister complicity with morally culpable right-wing ideology.

In November 1927, Eliot spoke from the editorial platform of the *Criterion* with the sonority of the Victorian public moralist:

The man of letters of today is interested in a great many subjects—not because he has many interests, but because he finds that the study of his own subject leads him irresistibly to the study of others; and he must study the others if only to disentangle his own, to find out what he is really doing himself. Three events in the last ten years may be instanced: the Russian revolution (which has also directed our attention to the East), the transformation of Italy (which has directed our attention to our own forms of government), and the condemnation of the Action française by the Vatican. All these events compel us to consider the problem of Liberty and Authority, both in politics and in the organisation of speculative thought. Politics has become too serious a matter to be left to politicians.[10]

Such authoritative pronouncements may sound impressive, but they run the risk of appearing pompous if the implicit claim to authority is not accepted. What the non-specialist 'man of letters' or the *Criterion*, a non-technical 'literary review', had to contribute to political debate was not always clear. For example, although astute contemporaries realized that developments in Italy and Russia were of profound international importance, the Vatican condemnation of the French Royalist movement, Action française, was seen as a backwater event by many English observers. In 1928, Eliot published an article defending the movement's founder, Charles Maurras, against a pamphlet written by a Catholic apologist, Leo Ward. Invited to reply, Ward professed himself a friend who hoped the *Criterion* would not become 'a refuge where French philosophies go when they die'.[11] Ward was not alone in wondering at Eliot's nostalgia for the *ancien régime* and his public defence of the intolerant, chauvinist Maurras. A further 'rejoinder' from Ward was followed by an abrupt editorial injunction: 'The controversy must now be closed.' This did not, however, prevent Eliot translating the lengthy prologue to Maurras's 'Essay on Criticism' in the *Criterion* later that year; an example of the limits of his editorial impartiality. Eliot's public

[10] 'A Commentary', *Criterion* (Nov. 1927), 386.
[11] 'L'Action française', *Criterion* (June 1928), 84.

declaration of support for Maurras's idealized alliance of Church and State resonated throughout his editorship of the *Criterion* long after this tiresome controversy had ended.

The *Criterion* consolidated its position as a commentator on political theory with a symposium on the 'rival merits of fascism and communism'. Again, the *Criterion* sought to emulate the debates staged in the great Victorian reviews of political, theological, and cultural interests. However, the inertia of Eliot's solemn and cumbersome quarterly review meant that the *Criterion*'s forays into politics often appeared cursory or merely opportunistic.[12] What is more, the *Criterion* was not so much interested in politics as in views about politics: discussion was conducted at such a high-minded and theoretical level that the reader could be forgiven for forgetting the urgency of the practical political issues at stake. In June 1928, Eliot announced loftily: 'In the theory of politics, in the largest sense, the *Criterion* is interested so far as politics can be dissociated from party politics, from the passions or fantasies of the moment, and from problems of local and temporary importance.'[13] Put another way, Eliot's political philosophy was based upon an ecclesiastical conception of hierarchy.

Eliot's editorial control of the *Criterion* scrupulously avoided party affiliations and entailed maintaining some unusual associations. For example, 'dispassionate examination' of Italian fascism and Soviet communism led him to solicit articles from J. S. Barnes, Secretary-General of the International Centre of Fascist Studies at Lausanne, and from the Labour parliamentary candidate, A. L. Rowse, Fellow of All Souls College, Oxford. To stage the debate, Eliot contributed a review-article entitled 'The Literature of Fascism' dealing with a spate of recent books on the subject, including Barnes's *The Universal Aspects of Fascism* (a work that bore Il Duce's imprimatur). In July 1928, Eliot explained his motives to Rowse:

I have thought of dealing myself with the question of Fascism, and have recently worked through four or five books on the subject. The more I read about it the more uninteresting it seems, but it might be worth while

---

[12] See Desmond Hawkins: 'The rough-and-tumble of weekly journalism adds the topical sharpness of debate that a quarterly must lack' (*When I Was* (London, 1989), 177).   [13] 'A Commentary', *Criterion* (June 1928), 293.

to say even that. What I am trying to do is to find out whether there is any idea in Fascism at all; if not it might be at least worth while to say so. The books on the subject seem to be of two types. Those written by people who wish to prove either how virtuous or how wicked the régime has been; and those who wish to prove that Fascism is the realisation of a magnificent political ideal. The former have a certain scandalous interest, the latter are extremely dull. I only chatter about this in order to give you some notion of the possible series. The question is not to examine particular facts of government, but the importance of certain political ideas.[14]

Rather disappointingly for those critics who cite the title of the essay as evidence of Eliot's proto-fascism, the article amounted to an indictment of totalitarian government. In fact, oddly enough, in 'The Literature of Fascism' Eliot could sound at times like a social democrat: 'The modern question as popularly put is: "democracy is dead; what is to replace it?" whereas, it should be: "the frame of democracy has been destroyed: how can we, out of the materials at hand, build a new structure in which democracy can live?" '[15]

Eliot employed Rowse and Barnes to demarcate the antipodes of contemporary political debate, in order to clarify the *Criterion*'s position on the political field. On closer inspection, the political allegiances of Rowse and Barnes were far from clearly formulated. Rowse had suggested himself to Eliot after he had written to the *Criterion* to defend Harold Laski's primer *Communism*.[16] Rowse affirmed: 'The theories of Marxism, whether one agrees with them or not, have an undeniable present importance, and it is not unlikely that their influence upon our thought will increase in the future.'[17] In his subsequent *Criterion* article on communism, Rowse described *The Communist Manifesto* as 'one of the great classics of political thought', a profound diagnosis of class struggle, while at the same time he dismissed Eliot's monarchism and Anglicanism as 'completely irrelevant' to an understanding of contemporary politics.[18] However, Rowse was never a member

---

[14] Cited in A. L. Rowse, *A Cornishman Abroad* (London, 1976), 262–3.

[15] 'The Literature of Fascism', *Criterion* (Dec. 1928), 287.

[16] John Gould Fletcher had reviewed the volume unsympathetically. See 'Recent Books', *Criterion* (Sept. 1927), 261.

[17] 'Correspondence', *Criterion* (Dec. 1927), 542.

[18] See 'The Literature of Communism', *Criterion* (Apr. 1929), 422–36, and 'Marxism: A Reply', *Criterion* (Oct. 1929), 84–8.

of the Communist Party and he viewed recent developments in Stalinist Russia with some alarm. Similarly, Barnes may have been an ardent admirer of 'the genius of Mussolini' but his real intention was to show, in spite of the violent anticlericalism of fascist *squadristi* (who had attacked Catholic priests), the compatibility of fascism with Catholic doctrine.[19] In truth, the inherent strains and contradictions in the political positions espoused by Rowse and Barnes could do little to clarify the *Criterion*'s stance on contemporary issues.

It was understandable that Eliot should have taken an interest in Italian fascism at a time when Faber were publishing expositors, commentators, and opponents of Mussolini's government. Some recent critics seem reluctant to admit that Eliot publicly dissociated himself from fascism. Moreover, to castigate Eliot for his illiberal views may be to miss some of the political complexities that he struggled to accommodate in the *Criterion*. For example, it is inconsistent to criticize Eliot for soliciting the fascist opinions of Barnes, while simultaneously condoning the reasonableness of his endorsement of Rowse as an apologist for communism.[20] The real lesson of this symposium was its demonstration of the *Criterion*'s weak grasp of political realities. Eliot modestly informed Rowse that his essay on 'The Literature of Fascism' was 'very superficial' and 'beyond my competence'.[21] Eliot's judicial summing up of the case for fascism and communism in the *Criterion* certainly sounds like an exercise in captious sophistry:

I confess to a preference for fascism in practice, which I dare say most of my readers share; and I will not admit that this preference is itself wholly irrational. I believe that the fascist form of unreason is less remote from my own than is that of the communists, but that my form is a more reasonable form of unreason. But my chief purpose in venturing to criticise two authors [Barnes and Rowse] immeasurably more learned

---

[19] See J. S. Barnes, 'Fascism', *Criterion* (Apr. 1929), 445–59, and 'Fascism: A Reply', *Criterion* (Oct. 1929), 70–83. Barnes's position was perhaps given more credence after the 1929 Lateran Treaty between the Vatican and the Italian government.

[20] Rowse, although dismissive of Eliot as a political theorist, found him 'patient and courteous' as editor of the *Criterion*. See *A Cornishman Abroad*, 265. Frederick Tomlin recalled that Eliot described Rowse's *The Politics of the Younger Generation*, published by Faber, as a 'bad book'. See *T. S. Eliot: A Friendship* (London, 1988), 14, 19.   [21] See *A Cornishman Abroad*, 265, 266.

and competent than myself, is to affirm my previous contention that neither fascism nor communism is new or revolutionary as *idea*.[22]

The *Criterion*'s treatment of contemporary politics was often characterized by judgements that appear extremely unpersuasive today—for instance, Eliot's editorial dismissal of the 'brainless' 1929 General Election won by the Labour Party.[23]

In 1934, the Catholic historian, Christopher Dawson, offered an extended examination in the *Criterion* on the place of religion in the totalitarian state; an essay that could blithely overlook, by its refusal to go into detail, the assault on civil and religious liberty in Hitler's Germany. Nevertheless, Eliot agreed with Dawson that Christian faith should underlie all cultural and political institutions. If Eliot expressed a preference for fascism over political radicalism, he also made it clear that he found fascism less 'digestible' than Maurras's harmonious vision of Church and State.[24] Eliot repeatedly inveighed against the 'Russian religion' of communism in his *Criterion* Commentaries throughout the 1930s.[25] No doubt, his repetitive hammering on this point did much to alienate many left-wing intellectuals.[26] That said, one young communist, A. L. Morton, a regular reviewer for the *Criterion* in the 1930s, recalled: 'I should add that during all the years of my association with the *Criterion* I had complete freedom to express in it a viewpoint which [Eliot] must have thought entirely mistaken.'[27] The *Criterion*, of course, was never indiscriminately catholic and it is natural to wonder what influence, if any, Eliot's brand of reactionary Anglicanism had on his readership.[28]

---

[22] 'Mr. Barnes and Mr. Rowse', *Criterion* (July 1929), 690–1.

[23] 'A Commentary', *Criterion* (July 1929), 578–9.

[24] Eliot confided to Herbert Read that fascism could never be grafted on to the royalist, Anglo-Catholic stock (T. S. Eliot to Herbert Read, 19 Feb. 1934. Victoria).

[25] Eliot's most concentrated version of this argument appeared in a BBC broadcast published as 'Christianity and Communism', *Listener* (16 Mar. 1932), 382–3.

[26] See Desmond Hawkins: 'The most powerful group of younger writers [in London] have not much in common with Eliot, and there is little public support for any literary review which is not nominally anti-fascist' ('London Letter', *Partisan Review* (Summer 1939), 89). Hawkins was the *Criterion*'s fiction chronicler from 1936 until 1939.

[27] See 'T. S. Eliot—A Personal View', *Zeitschrift für Anglistik und Amerikanistik* (Leipzig, 1966), 288. Morton contributed 24 book reviews to the *Criterion*.

[28] See Spender: 'In his role of political commentator in the *Criterion* [Eliot] must have baffled readers who did not realise that his mind was moving along lines laid down by Charles Maurras' (*The Thirties and After* (London 1978), 200).

II

The proper study of mankind is, for the time being, economics.

F. S. Flint, *Criterion* (October 1937), 1

Eliot introduced economics as a feature of his *Criterion* Commentaries in January 1931, when he claimed that economic articles in the *Referee*, or works advocating Major Douglas's 'Social Credit' reforms, had confirmed his belief that the present economic system did not work, but he added: 'I can never understand enough to form any opinion as to whether the particular prescription or nostrum proffered is right.'[29] In July 1932 he declared that economics was 'no longer to be ignored by literary critics'.[30] The following January, the *Criterion* published a critique by the French social theorists Robert Aron and Arnaud Dandieu, editors of the periodical *L'Ordre nouveau*, of the dehumanizing effects of a mechanical economic system on man's creative faculties.[31] The same issue also carried a batch review by Geoffrey Biddulph attacking the remedies of a host of professional economists; including Gustav Cassel of Stockholm University and the Treasury official Ralph Hawtrey (an economic adviser to the Bank of England). Biddulph concluded bitterly: 'The revolting senselessness of such proceedings in a world suffering not from poverty but from abundance, makes one feel that a society that submits to the conventions of its bankers, and tolerates their moralising is not fitted to survive.'[32] Chronic world-wide unemployment and the paradox of 'poverty amidst plenty', exacerbated by the lack of consensus among professional economists, had led to a crisis of faith in classical economic theory.

By 1933, Eliot's voluminous correspondent, Ezra Pound, was becoming increasingly insistent that the economic theories of Major Douglas were the correct remedy for an unjust economic system that cheated artists of the leisure time their 'cultural heritage' had

[29] 'A Commentary', *Criterion* (Jan. 1931), 309.

[30] 'A Commentary', *Criterion* (July 1932), 676.

[31] See Robert Aron and Arnaud Dandieu, 'Back to Flesh and Blood: A Political Programme', *Criterion* (Jan. 1933), 185–99. At Montgomery Belgion's prompting, Eliot noted the premature death of Dandieu, aged 35, in his Commentary (Jan. 1934) as 'a loss to the *Criterion* as well as to the intellectual life of Paris'.

[32] 'Books of the Quarter', *Criterion* (Jan. 1933), 323.

earned them. In April 1933, Faber published Pound's *ABC of Economics*, described by one biographer as 'a set of off-beat thoughts on economic and social matters'.³³ This was followed in July 1933 by a lengthy *Criterion* article 'Murder by Capital'. In Pound's words, 'Mr. Eliot's august organ' had permitted him to 'say a few words on Society at large, and on the unlikelihood of genius getting a break UNTIL the whole economic order were so changed that EVERY MAN would get a break quite good enough for the first-rate artist or writer'.³⁴ The article had been accepted for the *Criterion* during Eliot's absence on a lecture tour of the United States—a period of great personal difficulty, including his permanent separation from his wife.

On his return, Eliot informed I. A. Richards that he was anticipating a rough review by Pound of the Page-Barbour Lectures delivered at the University of Virginia, collected as *After Strange Gods: A Primer of Modern Heresy*.³⁵ In his second lecture, Eliot had been critical of Pound's rejection of Christianity and his support of economic panaceas.³⁶ Pound's review appeared in the *New English Weekly*, a small circulation sixpenny weekly launched by Alfred Orage in April 1932. It was hardly surprising that Pound's review—provocatively entitled 'Mr. Eliot's Mare's Nest'—dismissed Eliot's advocacy of Christian orthodoxy as an 'irrelevance'. Pound contrasted Dante's punishment of usurers in the third *girone* of the *Inferno* with the 'ethical weakness' of modern-day higher ecclesiastics, asserting: 'when religion was real the church concerned itself with vital phenomena in ECONOMICS.'³⁷ A week later, Eliot wrote to Orage to express his dissatisfaction

---

³³ Humphrey Carpenter, *A Serious Character: A Life of Ezra Pound* (London, 1988), 494. See Pound: 'I am not proceeding according to Aristotelian logic but according to the ideogramic method of first heaping together the necessary components of thought' ('ABC of Economics', in *Selected Prose, 1909–1965*, ed. William Cookson (London, 1973), 209).

³⁴ Ezra Pound, 'Mr. Eliot's Quandaries', *New English Weekly* (29 Mar. 1934), 559. See Ezra Pound, 'Murder by Capital', *Criterion* (July 1933), 585–92.

³⁵ T. S. Eliot to I. A. Richards, 24 Feb. 1934. Cambridge (Magdalene).

³⁶ See *After Strange Gods* (London, 1934), 41–3.

³⁷ See 'Mr. Eliot's Mare's Nest', *New English Weekly* (8 Mar. 1934), 500. Pound exaggerated Dante's concern with usury in his review article on Laurence Binyon's translation of the *Inferno* ('Hell', *Criterion* (Apr. 1934), 382–96). It was Pound's *Cantos*, of course, that were preoccupied with the evil of 'usura'.

with Pound's treatment of *After Strange Gods*—understandable given Pound's tangential treatment of its subject-matter.[38]

Orage sent the letter to Pound in Rapallo, sparking a prolonged controversy on the relative merits of religion and economics in the pages of the *New English Weekly*—a valuable source of free copy for this non-paying periodical.[39] On 29 March, Pound struck again: 'Mr. Eliot's book is pernicious in that it distracts the reader from a vital problem (economic justice); it implies that we need more religion, but does not specify the nature of that religion.'[40] Eliot countered:

It is only a step from asserting (what appears to be true) that the economic problem must be solved if civilisation is to survive, to asserting (what I dispute) that all other problems may or ought to be neglected until the solution of the economic problem. And from this point it is only one step more into complete Secularism. The political alternatives which we are offered as alternatives to the present rotten state of affairs both seem to me wholly secular. The reason why I have been able to support the *New English Weekly* is that the doctrines it advocates do not appear to be necessarily and exclusively secular.[41]

It is not clear how the doctrine of Social Credit, propounded with proselytizing zeal in Orage's editorial 'Notes of the Week' and in Alfred Newsome's pseudonymous 'Credit Forum', was not exclusively secular.[42] At any rate, Pound's facetious review of Eliot's Norton Lectures at Harvard, *The Use of Poetry and the Use of Criticism*, revived his public debate with 'the dean of English Criticism and Editor of Britain's Brightest Quarterly'.[43] There was certainly an element of sarcasm in Pound's back-handed tribute, for readers of the *New English Weekly* would have recalled his earlier wish that Eliot did not read the *Criterion*

---

[38] Pound told Charles Olson that he had not read *After Strange Gods* with care. See Carpenter, *A Serious Character*, 502.

[39] The controversy has been documented in Christina Stough's 'The Skirmish of Pound and Eliot in *The New English Weekly*: A Glimpse at Their Later Literary Relationship', *Journal of Modern Literature* (1983), 231–46.

[40] 'Mr. Eliot's Quandaries', 559.

[41] 'Modern Heresies', *New English Weekly* (3 May 1934), 71.

[42] Eliot claimed that he read the political and economic sections of the *New English Weekly* every Wednesday morning. See 'A. R. Orage', *New English Weekly* (15 Nov. 1934), 100.

[43] 'What Price the Muses Now', *New English Weekly* (24 May 1934), 130.

on account of its unsavoury circle of contributors.[44] Pound concluded his review by remarking that Eliot's lack of vigour in his lecture on 'The Modern Mind' could be ascribed to editorial fatigue:

It is extremely easy for an editor to acquire the habit of reading mainly or exclusively the stuff submitted to him to edit, and so, gradually to circumscribe his horizon to what contending contributors think he is likely to publish, or to stuff boosted by snobs in their circles.[45]

There was a hint of exasperation behind Eliot's gentle reproof, in a letter signed 'Your outraged, POSSUM'—an in-house joke presumably designed to placate Pound and end the debate.[46] Aside from the use of controversy to furnish free copy for the *New English Weekly* and, largely unwanted, free publicity for Eliot's works, the skirmish provides some pointers towards the *Criterion*'s stance on economic issues in the 1930s that repay extended analysis. In doing so, it is instructive to situate the *Criterion* in relation to other 'Douglasite' periodical networks.

David Bradshaw has suggested that 'Eliot was a committed advocate of Social Credit, not a writer who made the odd reference to the theory in his literary journalism'.[47] And yet, the evidence he assembles does not demonstrate that Eliot had anything but a passing acquaintance with Douglas or more than a partial sympathy with Social Credit. In fact, Eliot's involvement with Douglasite periodical networks requires a considerably more careful and scrupulous parsing of the available material than performed by Bradshaw. Eliot met Douglas twice: once with Pound in March 1920 and again in November 1931 in the

[44] See 'Mr. Eliot's Quandaries', 558–9. See also Ezra Pound to T. S. Eliot, 28 Mar. 1935: 'Waal, anyhow, I have read mos' ov yr. muggyzeen fer onct and wish I cd. git at the bastids with a acid cleaner' (*Selected Letters of Ezra Pound, 1907–1941*, ed. D. D. Paige (New York, 1950), 272).   [45] 'What Price the Muses Now', 132.

[46] [T. S. Eliot], 'The Use of Poetry', *New English Weekly* (14 June 1934), 215. Pound had the last word, reiterating the primacy of economics over religion in 'Ecclesiastical History', *New English Weekly* (5 July 1934), 272–3. Recounting the controversy to Frank Morley, Pound explained: 'I cant go on shadow boxin with the Possum, I socked him three, in hope of sellin his works, and all you can get out of him is "Portrait of the Possum as a Young Possum, labled Mat Arnold".' Cited in Stough, 'The Skirmish of Pound and Eliot', 246.

[47] 'T. S. Eliot and the Major', *TLS* (5 July 1996), 14.

company of Hugh MacDiarmid.[48] Although Eliot liked Douglas personally, he found his *Economic Democracy* 'fearfully difficult and obscurely written'.[49] In October 1933, Eliot discussed Douglas in his *Criterion* Commentary. Rebuking Pound for imagining that he was 'wholly unacquainted with the person or the writings of Major Douglas'—odd given that Pound had introduced him to both—Eliot commented:

Nor can Mr. Pound justly suppose that I and perhaps several other contributors to the *Criterion*, are anything but friendly to the theory [Social Credit]. Perhaps there is a more convinced acceptance of the diagnosis than the remedy; but it is easier for the lay mind to distinguish *between* diagnoses of a malady of which we are all aware, than, between schemes any one of which may ignore important considerations which we have not been trained to look for. I hope that Major Douglas is right from top to bottom and copper-plated; but whether he is right or wrong does not matter a fig to my argument for the priority of ethics over politics.[50]

If Pound sought an economic solution for the current state of public affairs, then Eliot felt 'inclined to approach public affairs from the point of view of a moralist'.[51]

The writings that Bradshaw adduces to demonstrate Eliot's commitment to Douglas are extremely thin. The first, an article published in *New Britain* (a vehicle for Frederick Soddy's radical credit reform proposals[52]), declared that the Christian project of social amelioration could not be left to 'Professor Soddy, or Major Douglas, or anyone else'.[53] The second, a letter to the journal *Social Credit*, actually undermines Bradshaw's thesis, since Eliot claimed that he did not 'pretend that I understand Major Douglas's theory yet'.[54] For Bradshaw to conclude from these asides that Douglas and Soddy provide the 'source' and 'context' for Eliot's anti-Semitic sentence regarding the undesirability of 'free-thinking

---

[48] See Alan Bold, *MacDiarmid* (London, 1988), 264.

[49] T. S. Eliot to Sydney Schiff, 24 Mar. 1920. *Letters*, 376.

[50] 'A Commentary', *Criterion* (Oct. 1933), 119–20.

[51] In the Preface to *After Strange Gods*, Eliot had claimed to ascend the platform as a moralist.

[52] Frederick Soddy, Nobel Laureate for Chemistry in 1921, was a founding member of the Economic Freedom League. See Soddy, 'The New Britain Movement', *Oxford Magazine* (7 June 1934).

[53] 'In Sincerity and Earnestness', *New Britain* (25 July 1934), 274.

[54] 'Letter', *Social Credit* (27 Aug. 1934).

Jews' in *After Strange Gods*, is really to misread that context wilfully. For however gravely one judges Eliot's remark, it was without question a statement founded on religio-cultural—the importance of 'unity of religious background'—and not economic grounds.[55] There is no evidence to suggest that Eliot shared Douglas's or Soddy's paranoiac fantasies of an international conspiracy of Jewish financiers. The two works Bradshaw cites as source-material for Eliot's anti-Semitism—Douglas's *Social Credit* and Soddy's *Wealth, Virtual Wealth and Debt*—were dismissed in the *Criterion* as respectively 'an extravagant and pretentious book' and 'a dangerous half-truth which begs the real difficulties'.[56] Where else would Eliot espouse his Douglasite anti-Semitism if not in the *Criterion*? In 1936, Pound complained to the poet Joseph Gordon Macleod, a former *Criterion* contributor, that Eliot would only print him when he was 'harmless'.[57] That was hardly surprising given Pound's increasingly virulent diatribes against 'usury', an evil associated in his mind with a crude stereotype of Judaism. It is a depressing fact that Pound's obituary notice of the *Criterion*, highly critical of Eliot's 'theological verbiage', appeared in Oswald Mosley's anti-Semitic *British Union Quarterly*.[58] In 1940, Eliot set a correspondent straight: 'As for Mr. Pound, I have already made it clear that I do not associate myself with any of his opinions about Jews.'[59]

Although the remedy of Social Credit was never wholeheartedly administered by the *Criterion*, in January 1935 the economist R. McNair Wilson (recommended to Eliot by Pound[60]), puffed

[55] See *After Strange Gods*, 18–20. For lucid discussions of this notorious passage, see Christopher Ricks, *T. S. Eliot and Prejudice* (London, 1988), 40–54, and Anthony Julius, *T. S. Eliot: Anti-Semitism and Literary Form* (Cambridge, 1996), 150–62.

[56] See J. McAlpine, 'Books of the Quarter', *Criterion* (Apr. 1925), 472, and (June 1928), 429.

[57] Ezra Pound to Joseph Gordon Macleod, 28 Mar. 1936. *Selected Letters of Ezra Pound*, 279.

[58] See 'The *Criterion* Passes', *British Union Quarterly* (Apr.–June 1939), 60–72. Eliot thanked Pound for his notice (T. S. Eliot to Ezra Pound, 9 Sept. 1939. Yale). He was less appreciative to other correspondents. See T. S. Eliot to John Hayward, 14 Sept. 1939. Cambridge (King's).

[59] T. S. Eliot to J. V. Healy, 19 June 1940. Cited in Ricks, *T. S. Eliot and Prejudice*, 54.

[60] Wilson's appearance in the *Criterion* was conditional upon Bonamy Dobrée's favourable reception of his economics primer *Promise to Pay*. See T. S. Eliot to Bonamy Dobrée, 23 Mar. 1934. Leeds. In 1939, Pound described Wilson as a 'Christian Monarchy man' (*Selected Prose*, 269).

a series of evangelical Social Credit pamphlets published by Stanley Nott:

The service of Major Douglas to the cause of monetary reform is of so signal a character that none who hope to see reform accomplished can refrain from paying tribute. Thanks to his brilliant and searching analyses of the existing financial system, millions of men and women in all parts of the world have been brought face to face with the supreme political and economic issue of this time and have learnt that, in the absence of national control of money, national control in almost any form is impossible.[61]

This was the zenith of the *Criterion*'s flirtation with Social Credit. And yet, almost immediately its star began to wane. By this time, Pound had written to Eliot offering to summarize the economic theories of Silvio Gesell for the *Criterion*. In 'The Individual in His Milieu', Pound attempted to supplement Douglas's Social Credit with Gesell's idea of stamp-script.[62] The article caused Eliot the usual editorial consternation, in respect of Pound's inability or refusal to write clearly and soberly on a technical subject for readers of the *Criterion*. Eliot complained: 'I asked you to write an article which would explain this subject to people who had never heard of it; yet you write as if your readers knew about it already, but had failed to understand it.'[63] Nevertheless, Pound's essay closed with a statement that was in harmony with the *Criterion*'s approach to economics: 'You can not make good economics out of bad ethics.'[64]

Blanket use of the term 'Douglasite', then, overlooks important schisms and splinter groups within the movement. When Orage died unexpectedly on 6 November 1934, throwing the *New English Weekly* into disarray, Eliot was approached by one group of Social Creditors to help stave off a takeover bid by another group, led by the Serbian writer Dmitri Mitrinovic.[65] Eliot's sympathies

---

[61] 'Books of the Quarter', *Criterion* (Jan. 1935), 342.

[62] Silvio Gesell's 'stamp-script' was a stamped money designed to discourage hoarding. Small stamps had to be purchased monthly and attached to the money to preserve its value. See Tim Redman, *Ezra Pound and Italian Fascism* (Cambridge, 1991), 122–52.   [63] See 'Ezra Pound', *Poetry* [Chicago] (Sept. 1946), 326–38.

[64] 'The Individual in His Milieu', *Criterion* (Oct. 1935), 45.

[65] The *Criterion* printed two obituaries of Orage, see 'A Commentary' (Jan. 1935), 260–4, and Ezra Pound, 'In the Wounds' (Apr. 1935), 391–407.

lay not with Mitrinovic but with the members of a Christian sociology discussion group that met fortnightly at the Chandos Restaurant in St Martin's Lane. The so-called 'Chandos group' unofficially led by Maurice Reckitt, the editor of *Christendom: A Journal of Christian Sociology*,[66] included the journalists Travers Symons and Philip Mairet (editors of the quarterly *Purpose*—a curious admixture of Adlerian psychology and Social Credit), the American psychologist Alan Porter (an occasional *Criterion* reviewer), and the Revd V. A. Demant, Director of Research at the Christian Social Council.[67] On 10 November, Symons introduced Mairet to Eliot, in order that Mairet (hitherto Orage's assistant editor on the *New English Weekly*) could ask for advice and support.[68] Eliot agreed to join the editorial committee in an advisory capacity and on 15 November he informed Dobrée that the *New English Weekly* would continue under Mairet's editorship.[69] A few months later, Eliot solicited an article from I. A. Richards in an attempt to bolster the literary side of the paper.[70] From 1935, Eliot generously contributed poems and a miscellaneous page of 'Views and Reviews' to the *New English Weekly* and was seconded by his *Criterion* lieutenants.

Moving in the other direction, the *Criterion* benefited from its association with the *New English Weekly*. Apart from Mairet, Reckitt, and Demant, the *Criterion* recruited Montgomery Butchart, Clifford Dyment, Rolf Gardiner, Ashley Sampson, Michael Sayers, Hugh Gordon Porteus and his wife Zenka Bartek, Desmond Hawkins, and Kenneth Barlow from the *New English Weekly*. Mairet recalled:

most of the best contributors to the weekly [*New English Weekly*] also wrote for the *Criterion*—and as a rule they wrote for it better, not only,

---

[66] Eliot met Reckitt at the 1933 Anglo-Catholic Summer School at Keble College, Oxford. He reviewed Reckitt's *Christian Sociology for Today* favourably in the *Criterion* (July 1934), 710. See also Maurice Reckitt, 'The Chandos in Retrospect', (Jan. 1966). Sussex.

[67] Eliot had praised Demant's *This Unemployment* and *God, Man and Society* in his *Criterion* Commentaries (Jan. 1932), 271–3, and (Jan. 1934), 276–7. He acknowledged a debt to Demant in *The Idea of a Christian Society* (London, 1939), 67–8.

[68] See Philip Mairet, 'Memories of T. S. E.', in Nevile Braybrooke (ed.), *T. S. Eliot: A Symposium for His Seventieth Birthday* (London, 1958), 36–44, and 'T. S. Eliot as Editor', *Philbeach Quarterly* (Summer 1965), 5–6.

[69] T. S. Eliot to Bonamy Dobrée, 15 Nov. 1934. Leeds.

[70] See T. S. Eliot to I. A. Richards, 25 Jan. 1935. Cambridge (Magdalene).

I think, because it was a quarterly, and therefore worthy of more durable work, but because they were writing for Eliot.[71]

These writers and intellectuals were drawn from all sections of the political spectrum—from those sympathetic to Christian socialism (Demant, Reckitt, and Mairet), to those with leanings towards fascism (Gardiner, Butchart, and Porteus[72]). The real common denominator was their antipathy to unregulated indus-trialism and laissez-faire capitalism, an opposition supported by Eliot's public writings in the late 1930s.

Eliot's commitment to Anglican assemblies and discussion groups has not received the scholarly attention it deserves.[73] In 1935, he urged the Assembly of the Church of England to consider 'the fundamental moral laws founded on Christian theology' when examining social and economic problems.[74] His adherence to Douglas's economic reforms, it is clear, could never be more than partial and passing—economic theories were no substitute for the doctrines of an Anglican moralist. The whole thrust of Eliot's close engagement with Christian sociological groups was predicated upon the assumption that economic and political philosophy must derive its values from Christian ethics.[75] In that sense, Eliot and Pound could nod ruefully when Henry Swabey argued that the Anglican Church might have upheld the doctrine of the medieval Catholic Church regarding usury had Lancelot Andrewes become Archbishop of Canterbury.[76]

---

[71] Mairet, 'Memories of T. S. E.', 39.

[72] In correspondence, Mairet referred to Montgomery Butchart, co-editor of the quarterly *Townsman*, as a 'fascist'. See Philip Mairet to Maurice Reckitt, 18 Oct. 1936. Sussex. Butchart reviewed Pound's *Jefferson and/or Mussolini* in the *Criterion* (Jan. 1936), 323–6. In the *Criterion* Hugh Gordon Porteus commented: 'To give here a sympathetic appraisal of Fascism today, or to accord it the attention it deserves, would be to put the *Criterion* on the black list ... That is surely a disquietening [*sic*] feature of our intellectual life' ((Oct. 1937), 194). Porteus later claimed that the term 'Fascism' was as neutral as the term 'syndicalism' during the 1930s. See 'Letters to the Editor', *TLS* (2 May 1968), 464.

[73] For an admirable attempt to redress this imbalance, see Stefan Collini, 'The European Modernist as Anglican Moralist', in Mark S. Micale and Robert L. Dietle (eds.), *Enlightenment, Passion, Modernity: Historical Essays in European Thought and Culture* (Stanford, Calif., 2000), 207–29.

[74] 'Douglas in the Church Assembly', *New English Weekly* (14 Feb. 1935), 383.

[75] Cf. 'A Commentary', *Criterion* (Jan. 1934), 276.

[76] See Henry Swabey, 'The English Church and Money', *Criterion* (July 1937), 619–37. On 3 Nov. 1939, Pound told a correspondent that Swabey, a theology student

The *Criterion* ultimately lost interest in Social Credit. The last extended discussion of the theory came in 1937, when F. S. Flint gave an analysis, buttressed by algebraic formulae, of the logical failings of the Douglas system.[77] Pound detested Flint's criticism, but even he refrained from mentioning Douglas in his January 1938 *Criterion* notes 'For a New Paideuma'.[78] Almost inevitably, Eliot publicly distanced himself from Social Credit, on religious grounds, in his April 1938 Commentary:

[Social Credit] seems to me constantly in danger of petrifying in a form fifteen or twenty years old. . . . It is most important that we should have heretical theories: but they become futile when they fall into the ortho-doxy of heresy, and out of touch with the facts.[79]

In his editorial 'Last Words' Eliot repeated his belief that 'concen-tration upon technical economics' alone could never bring about social cohesion.

III

Apart from Douglas, one other economist received a measure of approval in the pages of the *Criterion*: John Maynard Keynes, the leading critic of the monetary and fiscal policy pursued by the British government during the inter-war period.[80] In 1920, Eliot was certainly more enthusiastic about Keynes's *The Economic Consequences of the Peace* than Douglas's *Economic Democracy* (surprising given Eliot's duties at Lloyds Bank relating to pre-war German debts).[81] In 1927, an anonymous short notice in the *Criterion* hailed Keynes's *The End of Laissez-Faire* as a 'masterly summary of political thought'.[82] In the early 1930s, the *Criterion* published articles on Keynes's *Essays in Persuasion* (1931) and

---

at Durham University, had 'set out to teach father Eliot a few about Lancelot Andrewes' (*Selected Letters of Ezra Pound*, 328). Pound had suggested the topic to Swabey.

[77] 'The Plain Man and the Economists', *Criterion* (Oct. 1937), 1–18. The article expanded criticisms Flint had made in letters to the *Criterion* published in Jan. 1935 (292) and Apr. 1935 (474). Flint had studied Fabian economics as a Treasury clerk.

[78] 'For a New Paideuma', *Criterion* (Jan. 1938), 205–13.

[79] 'A Commentary', *Criterion* (Apr. 1938), 484.

[80] For details see Robert Skidelsky, *John Maynard Keynes: The Economist as Saviour, 1920–1937* (London, 1992).   [81] See *Letters*, 353.

[82] 'Short Notices', *Criterion* (Jan. 1927), 154.

Essays in Biography (1933) by two left-wing intellectuals, A. J. Penty and A. L. Rowse, who paid testimony to his 'alert mind' and 'distinction of mind' respectively.[83] In 1933, the *Criterion* commissioned a book review on economics from the Oxford 'Keynesian' Roy Harrod. Interestingly, during the *New English Weekly* controversy with Pound, Eliot had discussed the topics of religion, morality, and economics with Keynes—a response to the latter's praise of *After Strange Gods*—although Eliot pointed out that he had avoided technical aspects of economics in his Virginia lectures since he did not feel competent to speak with authority on the subject.[84]

The *Criterion*'s muted approval of Keynes was in sharp contrast to the *New English Weekly*'s censure of the 'egregious Mr. Keynes'.[85] The source of the *New English Weekly*'s hostility was not difficult to locate, given Keynes's disparaging remark in a 1934 lecture on the 'underworld' of Marx, Gesell, and Douglas.[86] That Keynes initially considered Douglas something of a crank can be inferred from a passage in Pound's *Cantos* recounting a meeting between the two economists that apparently took place in 1920. According to Pound, Keynes defended himself rather lamely in Douglas's presence as 'an orthodox Economist'.[87] Keynes was certainly no orthodox economist by the time he published *The General Theory of Employment, Interest and Money* (1936), a work that 'fell among the economists of the day with a very big bang'.[88] In October 1936, the American Social Credit

---

[83] See Arthur Penty, 'The Philosophy of Mr. Keynes', *Criterion* (Apr. 1932), 397; A. L. Rowse, 'Books of the Quarter', *Criterion* (July 1933), 674. In 1936, Rowse claimed that Keynesian economics was coextensive with Labour Party monetary policy. See *Mr. Keynes and the Labour Movement* (London, 1936).

[84] T. S. Eliot to John Maynard Keynes, 5 Apr. 1934. Cambridge (King's). In her diary entry for 19 Apr. 1934, Virginia Woolf records that Keynes and Eliot discussed *After Strange Gods* at Tavistock Square. (*The Diary of Virginia Woolf*, iv. 1931–1935, ed. Anne Olivier Bell and Andrew McNellie (London, 1982), 208).

[85] [Alfred Orage], 'Notes of the Week', *New English Weekly* (19 July 1934), 315.

[86] Cited in Skidelsky, *John Maynard Keynes*, 511.

[87] Keynes is thinly disguised as Mr Bukos ('The economist consulted of nations'), in *The Cantos* (London, 1987), 102. Pound retold the story to H. G. Wells, 3 Feb. 1940 (*Letters of Ezra Pound*, ed. Paige, 337). See also Pound: 'until [Keynes] makes definite public acknowledgement of the value of C. H. Douglas, I shall be compelled either to regard him as a saphead or to believe that his writings arise from motives lying deeper in the hinterland of his consciousness than courtesy can permit me to penetrate' ('ABC of Economics', 232).

[88] Donald Moggridge, *Keynes* (London, 1976), 114.

supporter, Montgomery Butchart, reviewing *The General Theory* in the *Criterion*, commented: 'The high praise accorded this volume by the Press is deserved.'[89] Butchart was swayed, no doubt, by the fact that Keynes had referred to Douglas and his acolytes in an appendix of *The General Theory* as a 'brave army of heretics'.[90] In his 1946 *New English Weekly* obituary, Eliot claimed that Keynes had told him that he thought Douglas's proposals were 'quite good'.[91]

It was clear from that obituary that Eliot did not possess a technical understanding of Keynesian economics. He did, however, describe his acquaintance as 'an economist of a very different type', a 'very exceptional intelligence', and he praised Keynes's 'unusual combination of speculative genius and practical ability'. It should not be forgotten that Keynes was a highly cultivated Bloomsbury intellectual who conceived of political economy as a pragmatic moral science founded on practical action. Keynes was a prolific and highly talented professional journalist who could place his articles in a number of influential periodicals.[92] In 1931, he oversaw the merger of the *Nation and Athenaeum* with a rival weekly, the *New Statesman*. The Agreement for Amalgamation stated the policy of the paper would be that of an independent organ of the left, without special attachment to any political party.[93] By 1934 the *New Statesman and Nation* was a paying proposition. The impecunious *New English Weekly* frequently made fun of the business interests of the *New Statesman's* board of directors (including Keynes and the Rowntree family); its popular competitions and crossword puzzles; above all, the financial dependence of the paper on advertising revenue.[94] Critics have suggested that the *New Statesman's* left-wing ideology was

---

[89] 'Books of the Quarter', *Criterion* (Oct. 1936), 177.

[90] *The Collected Writings of John Maynard Keynes* (London, 1971), vii. 371. E. W. F. Tomlin referred to Keynes as a 'partial ally' of Social Credit in the *Criterion* (Jan. 1937), 364.

[91] 'John Maynard Keynes', *New English Weekly* (16 May 1946), 47, 48.

[92] In 1922, the *Manchester Guardian* paid Keynes £4,000 for a dozen articles. See Skidelsky, *John Maynard Keynes*, 27.

[93] Agreement for Amalgamation of the *New Statesman and Nation*. Keynes Papers. Cambridge (King's).

[94] In a typical 42-page issue of the *New Statesman*, 14 pages (or one-third of the paper) was devoted to advertising. In May 1939, the *New Statesman's* business manager, John Roberts, calculated that the weekly made a net profit of £9 on every page of advertising—a net yearly profit of £6,570 and a gross advertising revenue of £15,000.

compromised by financial considerations.[95] Whatever the truth, sales of the *New Statesman* doubled throughout the 1930s, from around 14,500 at the time of the merger in 1931, to approximately 29,000 in 1939—making it unquestionably the leading British intellectual weekly of the decade.

Under the direction of Kingsley Martin, the combative Cambridge-educated journalist whom Keynes installed as editor in 1931, the *New Statesman* pursued a course of radical socialism. However, by 1936, Martin's anti-fascist 'Popular Front' policy on foreign politics was placing an increasing strain on Keynes's involvement with the paper. Eliot observed: '[Keynes] could hardly have endorsed all the views of the weekly paper he had done such a great deal to maintain.'[96] There is little doubt that Eliot harboured an extreme dislike of the weekly nostrums propounded in Martin's *New Statesman* leader 'London Diary'. In 1934, Eliot informed Pound that he did not want to dirty his hands on the *New Statesman*.[97] In his memoir, Martin revealed: 'T. S. Eliot wrote a note declining some assignment: he is the only exception I can remember.'[98] Partly by virtue of his personal relations with Keynes and other Bloomsbury members, Eliot followed developments in the political and literary sections of the *New Statesman*,[99] although he never enjoyed the cordial relations with the journal that he maintained with its right-wing weekly rival, the *Spectator*.[100]

---

[95] George Orwell bemoaned 'papers that have the mentality of a whore, like the *New Statesman*'. Cited in Edward Hyams, *The New Statesman* (London, 1963), 140. It should also be pointed out that Orwell disliked the *Criterion*'s snobbishness.

[96] 'John Maynard Keynes', 47.

[97] T. S. Eliot to Ezra Pound, 19 Dec. 1934. Yale.

[98] See *Editor* (London, 1968), 43–4. See also Herbert Read: '[Eliot] had a positive dislike for the weekly critical journals and boasted that he had never contributed to *The New Statesman*' ('T.S.E.—A Memoir', in Allan Tate (ed.), *T. S. Eliot: The Man and His Work* (London, 1967), 28). In point of fact, Eliot had contributed to the *New Statesman* in 1916–17 during the literary editorship of J. C. Squire.

[99] Eliot introduced Desmond MacCarthy to the young poet Robert Waller. MacCarthy recruited Waller as a *New Statesman* reviewer in 1936. However, he withdrew after little over a year complaining that Martin was a 'gasbag' and that the lack of a coherent policy between the political and literary sections rendered the *New Statesman* 'schizophrenic'. See Waller, *The Pilgrimage of Eros* (London, 1992), 150–2.

[100] In 1934, Derek Verschoyle, the *Spectator*'s literary editor, contributed a book review to the *Criterion*. The following year the *Spectator* declared that the *Criterion* 'continues to preserve its supremacy among English literary periodicals' ((1 Nov. 1935), 746).

The cause of this state of affairs can be examined in relation to Eliot's editorial advocacy, during the crisis-ridden 1930s, of (what he termed with reference to Jacques Maritain) 'the just impartiality of the Christian philosopher'.[101] In January 1936, Eliot canvassed three pamphlets discussing the Italian invasion of Abyssinia. The Commentary is noteworthy in revealing Eliot's distate for the political pronouncements of the self-styled 'intellectual' (a distaste signalled by his recourse to Julien Benda's use of the apparently less offensive term 'clerc'):

The Criterion has never undertaken, but has rather avoided the discussion of topical political issues, however extensive. There are enough other periodicals, of every shade of opinion, which exist primarily for such discussion: discussion which in any case can be more adequately conducted in journals appearing at more frequent intervals. . . . But whenever any collection of intellectuals, of clercs, takes upon itself to issue a manifesto at some moment of crisis, then I think that it is within our province to discuss, not so much the crisis itself, as the opinions of the intellectuals about it.[102]

The rhetorical manoeuvre being made here is the cultural critic's adoption of the moral high ground: the engaged intellectual risks a partial judgement from the darkling plain, whereas the Christian philosopher uses his moral imagination to scrutinize the political bearing of any possible intervention. In his Criterion Commentary, Eliot transcended the positions of the Abyssinian pamphleteers to assert: 'All men are equal before God; if they cannot all be equal in this world, yet our moral obligation towards inferiors is exactly the same as that towards our equals.'[103] How exactly this elevated morality might have impinged upon the Italian army in Abyssinia was left unclear.

On the question of the Spanish Civil War, a more troubling dilemma to most European observers, both Eliot and Keynes supported the non-interventionist stance adopted by the British government.[104] In his January 1937 Commentary Eliot refused the starkly Manichaean terms of the 'irresponsible zealots' who

[101] See 'A Commentary', Criterion (Oct. 1938), 58.
[102] 'A Commentary', Criterion (Jan. 1936), 265.   [103] Ibid. 268.
[104] See John Maynard Keynes, 'British Foreign Policy', New Statesman and Nation (10 July 1937). Keynes's belief in non-intervention was reinforced by the death of Julian Bell on 18 July 1937.

worded a *Left Review* questionnaire, *Authors Take Sides on The Spanish Civil War*. Eliot pointed out that the *Criterion* was decidedly not 'compelled' to 'take sides' and claimed that the press had been responsible for a shameful 'deterioration of political thinking' during the crisis, grossly oversimplifying complex issues for doctrinaire aims.[105] 'One might think, after perusing a paper like *The New Statesman*', Eliot remarked caustically, 'that the elected Government of Spain represented an enlightened Liberalism.' Eliot's own reflections on the crisis, owing something to Irving Babbitt, were highly idiosyncratic:

But so long as we are not compelled in our interest to take sides, I do not see why we should do so on insufficient knowledge: and even any eventual partisanship should be held with reservations, humility and misgiving. That balance of mind which a few highly-civilized individuals, such as Arjuna, the hero of the *Bhagavad Gita*, can maintain in action, is difficult for most of us even as observers, and, as I say, is not encouraged by the greater part of the Press.[106]

In 1977, Denis Donoghue, with one eye on the troubles in Northern Ireland, described Eliot's position as 'facile in the assumption of a perspective far beyond the fray'.[107] And yet, neutrality was a tenable, even sensible position, for non-Spanish commentators on the Spanish Civil War. It was true that the *Criterion*'s detachment contrasted sharply with the *New Statesman*'s staunchly pro-Republican reporting of the war, but it is not entirely evident why Martin's deliberate editorial policy of *suppressio veri* was a more honourable position than Eliot's 'just impartiality'.[108]

---

[105] In the *Left Review* questionnaire, C. Day Lewis described the conflict as 'quite simply as a battle between light and darkness'. For a discussion of the *Criterion* and *Authors Take Sides on The Spanish War*, see Dominic Rowland, 'T. S. Eliot, *The Criterion*, and Literary Controversy, 1922–1939', Ph.D. thesis (London, 1997). Rowland's chapter is a useful corrective to those modern critics who, following Valentine Cunningham, persist in maintaining that the *Criterion* was tacitly pro-Franco. Stan Smith wilfully distorts Eliot's Jan. 1937 Commentary to accommodate a fascist charge in *The Origins of Modernism* (London, 1994), 27.

[106] 'A Commentary', *Criterion* (Jan. 1937), 289–90.

[107] 'Eliot and the *Criterion*', in David Newton-de Molina (ed.), *The Literary Criticism of T. S. Eliot* (London, 1977), 26.

[108] Martin refused to publish George Orwell's articles drawing attention to communist persecution of various Republican factions. See Kingsley Martin to George Orwell, 29 July 1937. Cited in Bernard Crick, *George Orwell: A Life* (London, 1980), 341–2.

In fact, Martin's blinkered and propagandist anti-fascism, together with his credulous acceptance of the evidence of Stalin's Moscow show trials, precipitated a rift with Keynes.[109] In November 1937, Keynes wrote to Martin to say that he felt increasingly unhappy with the *New Statesman*'s coverage of contemporary political events, exemplified, above all, by Martin's confused editorials.[110] After the German annexation of Austria in March 1938, Keynes launched a withering attack on the British government from the *New Statesman*. It closed with the passionate appeal: 'If we still recognise the difference, not merely between peace and war, but between good and evil and between right and wrong, we need to rouse up and shake ourselves and offer leadership.'[111] Keynes's practical and constructive response to foreign affairs (he circulated copies of his article, in advance of publication, to various influential public figures—including Winston Churchill and Harold Nicolson) could hardly be further from Eliot's defeatist and world-weary 'there seems no hope in contemporary politics at all' uttered in his Commentary for October 1938.[112] It was Eliot's 'depression of spirits' following the Munich agreement that brought the *Criterion* to a close.[113] In that sense, the *Criterion* ultimately did a great deal to sustain what George Watson has called 'The Myth of Catastrophe' that characterized the London literary world during the 1930s. On the other hand, according to Watson, Keynes, 'the most widely acclaimed economist of the age, was offering reasons for supposing the woes of the West might be remediable'.[114]

In 'Last Words' Eliot expressed his 'general sympathy' with non-profit, small circulation periodicals such as the *New English*

[109] See J. M. Keynes to Kingsley Martin, 25 July 1937. Cambridge (King's).
[110] J. M. Keynes to Kingsley Martin, 7 Nov. 1937. Cambridge (King's).
[111] See 'A Positive Peace Programme', *New Statesman and Nation* (25 Mar. 1938).
[112] 'A Commentary', *Criterion* (Oct. 1938), 60. Eliot confessed that he was 'deeply shaken' by the Munich agreement: 'The feeling which was new and unexpected was a feeling of humiliation, which seemed to demand an act of personal contrition, of humility, repentance and amendment; what had happened was something in which one was deeply implicated and responsible' (*The Idea of a Christian Society*, 64).
[113] See 'Last Words', *Criterion* (Jan. 1939), 269–75.
[114] See *Politics and Literature in Modern Britain* (London, 1977), 106.

Weekly—'an asylum to non-conformists of all descriptions'.[115] He surmised dolefully:

the continuity of culture may have to be maintained by a very small number of people indeed—and these not necessarily the best equipped with worldly advantages. It will not be the large organs of opinion or the old periodicals; it must be the small and obscure papers and reviews, those which hardly are read by anyone but their own contributors, that will keep critical thought alive, and encourage authors of original talent.[116]

Viewed against the background of a sharply polarized intelligentsia, the *Criterion*, overwhelmed by the politico-economic crisis—stretching, as Eliot conceded, the original framework of a literary review—resembled a ponderous Victorian interloper. With the prospect of war, the apparent collapse of liberal democracy, and following his rejection of fascism and communism, Eliot put his faith in the millennial programme of the notional idea of a Christian society. Expounding that social system to an audience of Cambridge dons in March 1939, he recapitulated much of the *Criterion*'s indictment of the free-market capitalist economy:

the realisation of a Christian society, must lead us inevitably to face such problems as the hypertrophy of the motive of Profit into a social ideal, the distinction between the *use* of natural resources and their exploitation, the use of labour and its exploitation, the advantages unfairly accruing to the trader in contrast to the primary producer, the misdirection of the financial machine, the iniquity of usury, and other features of a commercial society which must be scrutinised on Christian principles.[117]

An imposition of 'Christian principles' was Eliot's response, perhaps his retreat, from the sectarian discontent of politico-economic debate in the inter-war period.

---

[115] 'A Commentary', *Criterion* (Jan. 1937), 293.
[116] 'Last Words', 274. See also Eliot: 'when I enumerate the periodicals that I read regularly, and the opinions of which I take seriously, I find that with the exception of *The Times* they are all periodicals of, I imagine, considerably smaller circulation than either *The Spectator* or *The New Statesman*' ('A Commentary', *Criterion* (July 1938), 687). [117] *The Idea of a Christian Society*, 33.

Defence of the West

Recovering from the effects of nervous exhaustion in Switzerland in December 1921, Eliot, who read German fluently, purchased a copy of Hermann Hesse's *Blick ins Chaos* (1921). The notes appended to the 1922 Boni & Liveright edition of *The Waste Land* included a citation from this book:

Schon ist halb Europa, schon ist zumindest der halbe Osten Europas auf dem Wege zum Chaos, fährt betrunken in heiligem Wahn am Abgrund entlang und singt dazu, singt betrunken und hymnisch wie Dmitri Karamasoff sang. Über diese Lieder lacht der Bürger beleidigt, der Heilige und Seher hört sie mit Tränen.[1]

(Already half of Europe, already at least half of Eastern Europe, is on the way to Chaos, drives drunkenly in holy delusion along the edge of the abyss, singing drunkenly, singing hymns, as Dmitri Karamazov sang. The offended bourgeois laughs at the songs; the saint and seer hear them with tears.)

Hesse's forebodings were understandable given the humiliating cycle of inflation, economic depression, and unemployment that Germany was passing through in the wake of the punitive Versailles Treaty. In March 1922, Eliot wrote to Hesse: 'Je trouve votre *Blick ins Chaos* d'un sérieux qui n'est pas encore arrivé en Angleterre, et je voudrais en répandre la réputation.'[2] The similarities between Eliot's and Hesse's visions of breakdown in post-war Europe were cemented in the *Criterion*: the opening number published *The Waste Land*'s lament for the 'Falling towers' of civilization alongside Hesse's gloomy survey of 'Recent German Poetry'. Although Hesse did not name any of his poetic contemporaries he drew a general conclusion: 'These poets feel, or seem to feel, that there

---

[1] Hermann Hesse, *Blick ins Chaos* (Bern, 1921), 20. T. S. Eliot's autographed copy is now in the Modern Archive Centre, King's College, Cambridge.

[2] T. S. Eliot to Hermann Hesse, 13 Mar. 1922. *Letters*, 510.

must first be disintegration and chaos, the bitter way must first be gone to the end, before new settings, new forms, and new affinities are created.'³ It was a noticeable feature of the 'bitter way' to 'new settings' that both the apocalyptic last section of *The Waste Land* and Hesse's *Siddharta*, also published in 1922, gestured towards Eastern mysticism as a remedy for the spiritual ills of the West.⁴

A month after the publication of *The Waste Land*, Eliot described the poem to Richard Aldington as 'a thing of the past'.⁵ By 1931 he would expressly deny that the poem represented the 'disillusionment of a generation', informing Thomas MacGreevy that it constituted nothing more than a personal grumble against life.⁶ After a meeting in May 1922 at Montagnola, near the lake of Lugano, Eliot did not see the reclusive Hesse again and their correspondence lapsed. Nevertheless the brief acquaintance was decisive in the direction the *Criterion* was to take; that is, a concerted movement away from the profound cultural pessimism of post-war 'disintegration and chaos' towards an attempt to establish a pan-European ideal of Latinate 'classicism'. In a 1956 retrospective Eliot went so far as to say that the beginning of his 'adult life' could be dated as 'the period in my life which is marked by *The Waste Land*, and the foundation of the *Criterion*, and the development of relations with men of letters in the several countries of Europe'.⁷ Recent scholarship has placed too much emphasis on Eliot's links with the American Southern Agrarians; few critics have explored his avowed intention to use the *Criterion* to nourish intellectual exchange between 'an international fraternity of men of letters, within Europe'.⁸

I

The *Criterion* enabled Eliot to establish fruitful contacts with like-minded European men of letters. An important connection

---

³ 'Recent German Poetry', *Criterion* (Oct. 1922), 90.
⁴ See Craig Raine, '*The Waste Land* as a Buddhist Poem', *TLS* (4 May 1973), 503–5.   ⁵ T. S. Eliot to Richard Aldington, 15 Nov. 1922. *Letters*, 506.
⁶ See *Thoughts After Lambeth* (London, 1931), 10. T. S. Eliot to Thomas MacGreevy, 14 Feb., 1931. Dublin.
⁷ 'Brief über Ernst Robert Curtius', *Freundesgabe für Ernst Robert Curtius* (Bern, 1956), 25.   ⁸ *Notes Towards the Definition of Culture* (London, 1948), 118.

was made on the recommendation of Hesse. In July 1922, Ernst Robert Curtius received a letter at Marburg from an unknown editor inviting him to contribute to a forthcoming English quarterly review. Eliot described the journal's credo: 'Its great aim is to raise the standard of thought and writing in this country by both international and historical comparison.'[9] Curtius was an exemplary exponent of comparative and historical criticism. Born in German-occupied Alsace and a graduate of Romance philology at the University of Strasbourg, he had come to prominence as an expert on contemporary French literature. His essays on Rolland, Gide, Claudel, Péguy, and others in *Die literarischen Wegbereiter des neuen Frankreich* (1919) had been praised by Hesse as effecting a much-needed post-war rapprochement between French and German intellectuals.[10] Eliot, who took a keen interest in contemporary French thought, possessed a copy of this book. As a visitor to Paul Desjardins's celebrated summer *Décades* at the abbey church in Pontigny—again followed with interest by Eliot[11]—and a friend of leading French *hommes des letters*, André Gide, Charles du Bos, and Valéry Larbaud,[12] Curtius represented an important recruit for the new internationalist quarterly review.

Eliot assured Curtius that he would find the readership of the *Criterion* congenial. Curtius, in spite of the disapproval of his German Romanist colleagues, found periodical publication the most stimulating outlet for his research. He was scathing about the subjugation of journalistic *Literaturkritik* by academic *Literaturwissenschaft*: 'The newspaper article and periodical article is an indispensable form of the modern spirit, and whoever looks down on it from pedantry hasn't the faintest idea of what is going on.'[13] He contributed essays on Balzac and Proust to the *Criterion*, essays praised by René Wellek as fine examples of his literary criticism, characterizing a writer's *œuvre* through an

---

[9] *Letters*, 551. Cf. Eliot: 'We cannot determine the true status and significance of the significant writers in our language, without the aid of foreign critics with a European point of view' ('Brief über Ernst Robert Curtius', 27).

[10] See Hesse, 'Über die neuere französische Literatur', *Vivos voco* (Oct. 1919), 76–7.

[11] See 'A Commentary', *Criterion* (Nov. 1927), 385–7. If not for illness, Eliot would have attended the 1924 *Entretiens* in Pontigny.

[12] See *La Correspondence de Ernst Robert Curtius avec André Gide, Charles du Bos et Valéry Larbaud*, ed. Herbert and Jane Dieckmann (Frankfurt, 1980).

[13] *Essays on European Literature*, trans. Michael Kowal (Princeton, 1973), 307.

imaginative but learned exposition of leading motifs and themes.[14] Not only did Eliot introduce Curtius's pioneering work on French literature to the English-speaking world, he set the stage for the appearance of an extract from C. K. Scott-Moncrieff's ongoing translation of À la recherche du temps perdu in the Criterion shortly after Proust's death.[15] In point of fact, the first two volumes of the Criterion published work by Hesse, Larbaud, Curtius, Proust, original contributions from Luigi Pirandello, Lucien Lévy-Bruhl, Ramón Gómez de la Serna, Julien Benda, Antonio Marichalar, Paul Valéry, Hugo von Hofmannsthal, Gerhart Hauptmann, and C. P. Cavafy—a declaration of the quarterly's aspiration to repudiate the damaging nationalism of First World War propaganda and thereby to valorize what Eliot would refer to in the Criterion as 'the mind of all Europe'.[16]

The Criterion's role as a vital conduit of European intellectual currents was sustained after 1923 in the reviews of 'Foreign Periodicals'. Richard Aldington recommended his friends, the civil servants F. S. Flint and Alec Randall, as reviewers of French and German periodicals, respectively.[17] After graduating from London University, Randall had taught at Tübingen until the outbreak of the First World War, at which point he joined Charles Masterman's War Propaganda Bureau at Wellington House.[18] From 1920 onward, Randall combined a career as a Foreign Office diplomat with work as a freelance reviewer of German literature (most notably for The Times and the Times Literary Supplement). Eliot allowed Randall, in common with all the

---

[14] See 'Ernst Robert Curtius', in A History of Literary Criticism, vii (New Haven, 1991), 97–113.

[15] In July 1922, Eliot had written to Sydney Schiff, a friend and translator of Proust, asking for an introduction. See Letters, 537. Unfortunately, Proust did not respond to Eliot's enquiry. See also Jean-Yves Tadié, Marcel Proust (Paris, 1996), 812–14.

[16] 'A Commentary', Criterion (Nov. 1927), 387. The phrase, of course, is redolent of Eliot's formulation 'the mind of Europe' in 'Tradition and the Individual Talent' (1919).

[17] Incidentally, the appearance of the Russian-born translator John Cournos (Johann Gregorievich Korshone) as the reviewer of Russian periodicals led Aldington, who had been embroiled in a menage à trois involving Cournos, to sever his connection with the Criterion. For details see Richard Aldington to Ezra Pound, 22 Aug. 1927. Texas.

[18] See Alec Randall in Alister Kershaw and Fréderic-Jacqueo Temple (eds.), Richard Aldington: An Intimate Portrait (Carbondale, Ill., 1965), 110–21.

other *Criterion* reviewers of foreign journals, complete freedom to suggest new periodicals for review. Randall's surveys of a wide variety of German-speaking periodicals bear witness to the besetting problems and the plight of German intellectuals throughout the inter-war years.

Foreign distribution of the *Criterion* was extremely difficult. Nevertheless, the journal maintained a tiny but influential circulation in Europe. Eliot believed that his 'revue des revues' section was 'necessary for the transmission of ideas' and as a local forum for international thought. He spoke with feeling about the importance of establishing close links with European reviews, especially those magazines commanding a similar standing in their own country: 'their co-operation should continually stimulate that circulation of influence of thought and sensibility between nation and nation in Europe, which fertilises and renovates from abroad the literature of each one of them'.[19] He recalled: 'the *Criterion* was only one of a number of reviews similar in character and purpose, in France, Germany, Switzerland, Italy, Spain and elsewhere; and my own interest in making my contemporaries in other countries known in England, responded to the interests of the editors and contributors of these other reviews'.[20] Foremost amongst these reviews was the French monthly, the *Nouvelle Revue française*, in many ways Eliot's template for the *Criterion* and a journal justly praised for its coverage of English, German, and Russian literature. Eliot proudly informed Curtius that he was the English correspondent of the *Nouvelle Revue française*. It was his personal connection with this journal that helped to secure work from the editor Jacques Rivière,[21] from Valéry Larbaud, Charles du Bos, and the regular columnist Ramon Fernandez.

The *Criterion* also maintained affiliations with two German-language periodicals of high standing: *Die Neue Rundschau* and *Neue Schweizer Rundschau*. *Die Neue Rundschau* the monthly house-magazine of the Berlin publisher, Samuel Fischer (sponsor of the work of Hesse, Gerhart Hauptmann, and Thomas Mann),

---

[19] *Notes Towards the Definition of Culture*, 116.
[20] 'Brief über Ernst Robert Curtius', 26.
[21] For Eliot's obituary reminiscences of Jacques Rivière, see 'Rencontre', *Nouvelle Revue française* (1 Apr. 1925), 657–8 and 'A Commentary', *Criterion* (Apr. 1925), 344.

carried Rudolf Kayser's bulletin 'Europäische Rundschau', detailing topical literary events in England, France, Italy, and Russia. In 1922 the highly cultivated Swiss literary journalist, Max Rychner, took over the editorship of the Zürich monthly *Wissen und Leben*, transforming it into the internationalist *Neue Schweizer Rundschau*. The *Criterion* also developed close links, via Giovanni Battista Angioletti, with the modernist Milanese review *Il Convegno* and from October 1923, through Antonio Marichalar, with a new Madrid periodical, *La Revista de Occidente*, edited by José Ortega y Gasset. Looking back on the heady optimism and cosmopolitanism sweeping Europe in the 1920s, Curtius suggested that the co-operation of like-minded European periodicals transcended national and political differences: 'A Europe of the mind—above politics, in spite of all politics—was very much alive. This Europe lived not only in books and periodicals but also in personal relations.'[22]

II

Curtius's personal relations with leading German scholars—Paul Jacobsthal, Wilhelm Worringer, Max Scheler, and Friedrich Gundolf—secured the *Criterion* some of its most distinguished contributions. The essays by these writers had a strong bearing on what Eliot referred to in his April 1926 Commentary as 'the idea of a common culture of western Europe'.[23] Eliot hoped that a common cultural patrimony of Graeco-Roman 'classicism' might be used as a principle of order and authority in the reconstruction of post-war Europe. In his lengthy article on responses to classical antiquity since Winckelmann's *Geschichte der Kunst des Alterums* (1764), Jacobsthal wrote: 'one of the essential components in the history of Western art is the perpetual adjustment of relations with the antique inheritance—expressed at times in the wordless achievement of artists, but in other epochs of enhanced self-consciousness accompanied by a literature that throws light into the deepest problems of life'.[24] Notwithstanding the philhellenism

[22] *Essays on European Literature*, 170.
[23] 'A Commentary', *Criterion* (Apr. 1926), 222.
[24] 'Ancient Art Since Winckelmann', *Criterion* (July 1925), 543.

of Goethe, Schiller, Hegel, Hölderlin, Heine, Nietzsche, and Stefan George—although each writer celebrated different aspects and epochs of classical Greece—Jacobsthal discerned a modern-day devaluation of classical aesthetics. For instance, Worringer's influential thesis *Abstraktion und Einfühlung* (1908)—taken by many art critics as a manifesto for Expressionism—had championed the elemental, life-denying 'abstraction' (*Abstraktion*) of Egyptian and Byzantine art at the expense of a Western tradition of sensuous, humanist 'feeling into' (*Einfühlung*) art which could trace a genealogy from classical Greece.

In his 1927 Munich lecture to the Goethe Fellowship, reprinted in the *Criterion* as 'Art Questions of the Day', Worringer pronounced the funeral rites of 'studio Expressionism' as the death-knell of European art.[25] Similarly, Max Scheler, in one of his forays into 'philosophical anthropology' remarked with admirable scientific impartiality: 'A crisis in Europe is really not quite a sign that humanity is departing this life! ... Even if the famed "Culture of the West" should bury its creators in an overplus of "civilization"—that would be no great matter to the life of mankind.'[26] Eliot would not have agreed, although he deeply regretted that Scheler's untimely death in 1928 ruled out further contributions to the *Criterion*.[27] For Scheler, a thinker steeped in Catholic philosophy, focused attention upon what Eliot described at length in his August 1927 Commentary as 'The European Idea':

Not how Europe can be 'freed,' but how Europe can be organised, is the question of the day.

One of the ideas which characterises our age may be called The European Idea. It is remarkable first because of the variety of its appearances; it may take the form of a meditation on the decay of European civilization by Paul Valéry, or of a philosophy of history such as that of Oswald Spengler, or it may appear allied with an intense nationalism as in the work of Henri Massis. It is remarkable second in that it is primarily an appeal to reason rather than an emotional summons to international brotherhood. It has no obligation to the thought of Romain Rolland, to nineteenth-century socialism, or to the humanitarian sentiments out of which the League of Nations arose; and it has as yet no direct connection

---

[25] See 'Art Questions of the Day', *Criterion* (Aug. 1927), 101–17.
[26] 'Future of Man', *Criterion* (Feb. 1928), 100–16.
[27] See 'A Commentary', *Criterion* (Apr. 1926), 222–3, and (Sep. 1928), 190.

with the League and no perceptible influence upon it. It owes its origin to a new feeling of insecurity and danger; it goes to prove that the most important event of the War was the Russian Revolution. For the Russian Revolution has made men conscious of the position of Western Europe as (in Valéry's words) a small and isolated cape on the western side of the Asiatic continent. And this awareness seems to be giving rise to a new European consciousness. It is a hopeful sign that a small number of intelligent persons are aware of the necessity to harmonize the interests, and therefore to harmonize first the ideas, of the civilized countries of Western Europe. We are beginning to hear the reaffirmation of the European tradition. It will be helpful, certainly, if people will begin by believing that there is a European tradition; for they may then proceed to analyse its constituents in the various nations of Europe; and proceed finally to the further formation of such a tradition.[28]

Eliot's gravitas underlined the urgency of the defence of Western civilization; his grandiloquence underscored the importance of his own work in the cause of the European 'tradition'.

It is worth examining in a little more detail the sources of Eliot's cultural pessimism. Discussing the post-war 'spiritual crisis' of European civilization in a 'Letter from France' (1919), Paul Valéry observed: 'From an immense terrace of Elsinore which extends from Basle to Cologne, and touches the sands of Nieuport, the marshes of the Somme, the chalk of Champagne, and the granite of Alsace, the Hamlet of Europe now looks upon millions of ghosts.'[29] It is hard to believe that Eliot did not read or was not deeply moved by Valéry's plangent elegy for the 'ghosts' of Europe. Under the auspices of the *Criterion*, Eliot sponsored new English translations of his poetry and prose and published several critical essays on his work.[30] In 1946 Eliot claimed that Valéry was 'a figure symbolic of the Europe of our time'.[31] He had also read in Oswald Spengler's rambling and unsystematic 'comparative morphology of cultures', *Der Untergang des Abendlandes* (two volumes, 1918 and 1922), a bleak diagnosis of the life-cycle of Western civilization in terms of a biological organism approaching

---

[28] 'A Commentary', *Criterion* (Aug. 1927), 97–9.
[29] 'Letters from France', *Athenaeum* (11 Apr. 1919), 184.
[30] Wardle's translation of *Le Serpent* was published in 1924 by Cobden-Sanderson with an introduction by Eliot. See also *Letters*, 562.
[31] 'Leçon de Valéry', *Listener* (9 Jan. 1947), 72.

exhaustion and extinction. The conclusion of Spengler's influential bestseller, namely that the history of Western Europe was nearing the end, was a powerful and pervasive presence in Western Europe. The *Criterion* noticed the appearance of C. F. Atkinson's authorized English translation, *The Decline of the West*, as well as Spengler's subsequent political pamphlets.[32] The *Criterion*'s spirited defence of European culture, however, repudiated the pessimism and fatalism of Spengler's philosophy of history, just as Eliot would eventually characterize Valéry as 'a profoundly destructive mind, even nihilistic'.[33]

The case of Henri Massis's polemical essay 'Défense de l'Occident', serialized in the *Revue universelle* in 1925, was more problematical. Eliot chose to publish two long extracts from Flint's translation for Faber. The tendentious and alarmist keynote was struck in the opening sentence: 'The future of Western civilisation, indeed the future of mankind, is today in jeopardy.'[34] If Massis were to be believed, the cornerstone of Western culture—personality, stability, authority, tradition—was under threat from an intellectual invasion from the East. Properly understood, Massis's cultural politics were really a defence of the Catholic Church as *la religion de l'ordre*: part of a 'spiritual war' waged against Soviet communism.[35] Germany's pivotal cultural and geographical position, allied with Massis's intense French nationalism, made her a prime object of attack. Citing an article by Curtius on Asiatic influences on the current intellectual life of Germany,[36] and pointing to recent work by Hesse, Spengler, and Count Hermann Keyserling, Massis asserted that post-war Germany, in her hour of distress, had succumbed to the 'germs of a destructive Asiaticism'.[37] More than that, Massis sought to exclude Germany from the 'European unity' afforded by Graeco-Latin culture:

Graeco-Latin culture is not Germany's own proper possession, the foundation of her humanity; it is an acquisition of her learned men, her

[32] For a discussion of the *Criterion* and Spengler, see Jeo-Yong Noh, 'T. S. Eliot and the *Criterion*: Aspects of Literary and Political Toryism', Thesis (Oxford, D.Phil. 1991).
[33] 'Leçon de Valéry', 72.
[34] Massis, 'Defence of the West', *Criterion* (Apr. 1926), 224.
[35] See Geoffrey Sainsbury: 'we must not forget that the West that [Massis] is defending is the Catholic Church' ('Books of the Quarter', *Adelphi* (Dec. 1927), 163).
[36] See Ernst Robert Curtius, 'Les Influences asiatiques dans la vie intellectuelle de l'Allemagne', *Revue de Genève* (1920), 890.   [37] 'Defence of the West', 232.

philologists.... The Graeco-Latin culture is not a fundamental asset of civilization for the German, since he has not shared its past to the point of becoming identified with it.[38]

Massis's chauvinistic *causerie* received a series of stern rebuttals in the *Criterion*. An Indian correspondent, Vasudeo Metta, the Islamic writer, Sirdar Ikbal Ali Shah, and John Gould Fletcher, all pointed to the profound influence of Eastern art, philosophy, and religion on Massis's 'Latin inheritance'. In a letter to the *Criterion* which Massis complained exhibited 'deplorable manners', Fletcher, a poet deeply versed in Eastern mysticism, attacked the binary ethnological and ontological assumptions underpinning Massis's East–West dichotomy. Fletcher criticized the 'disease' of 'Mediterraneanism' whereby one supposes 'that the Greeks were alone enlightened, that Graeco-Roman culture is the only classic culture, that Italy and France are the great centres of culture, that every other race and nation, Eastern and Western, is *per se* barbarian'.[39] In a subsequent *Criterion* essay published in June 1928, Fletcher argued for a harmonious colloquy or synthesis of East and West.[40] The *Criterion*'s 'line' on the 'idea of Europe', however, was qualified and complicated by several contributions. In the same issue as Fletcher's essay, Kenneth Codrington, a lecturer on Indian art at London University, reviewed Flint's translation of Massis, *Defence of the West*. Codrington rejected the idea of a synthesis between East and West as 'degradation'.[41]

Eliot confided to Alec Randall that, in spite of differences, his own position was closer to Massis than Fletcher.[42] Characteristically, Eliot recommended Massis to readers of the *Criterion*.[43] Fletcher later complained of a strain of 'Hellenic paranoia' pervading the '*Criterion* gang', but he still praised Eliot's editorial spirit of open-mindedness:

As an editor, I found him to be practically ideal, willing for opinions to be mooted that ran contrary to his own avowed toryism, so long as those

---

[38] Ibid. 236, 237.   [39] 'Letter', *Criterion* (Oct. 1926), 748.
[40] 'East and West', *Criterion* (June 1928), 20–34.
[41] 'Books of the Quarter', *Criterion* (June 1928), 148. Cf. Eliot: 'I do not believe that a Christian can fully appreciate Buddhist art, or vice versa' ('Poetry and Propaganda', *Bookman* (Feb. 1930), 601).
[42] T. S. Eliot to Alec Randall, 14 Aug. 1928. Tulsa.
[43] Eliot mentioned 'our friend Massis' in 'A Commentary', *Criterion* (Apr. 1934), 451.

opinions were not merely emotional prejudices, but were backed up by something resembling intellectual judgement. In a way, this refusal on his part to insist on any general agreement among his contributors led to his undoing: it made the contributors themselves less a coherent body of doctrine, than a number of assembled but divergent minds, each approaching a problem from a limited angle motivated by some intense intellectual attraction or antipathy.[44]

Contemporary critics accused the *Criterion* of vagueness, even confusion; Eliot's editorial policy left a lot to individual choice and did not presuppose, thankfully, a 'coherent body of doctrine'.

Curtius's contribution to the 'idea of Europe' was crucial. In November 1927 the *Criterion* published 'Restoration of the Reason' in which Curtius argued that the 'classical' revival sweeping Europe represented a necessary counterpoise to the 'spiritual anarchy' of democracy:

The intellectual conscience of the European *élite* must of itself come to the rescue here, before some revolutionary Moloch sets fire to our libraries or a new Attila devastates our fields. . . . There exists a hidden aristocracy of Europe. . . . we should form a phalanx, as Aeneas the *penates* of Troy, to set them up and do them honour upon the new soil that holds the promise of future greatness. . . . On their shoulders rests the responsibility for the preservation, the recovery and the renovation of Europe.[45]

There is little doubt that Eliot and Curtius saw themselves as members of this intellectual aristocracy: self-elected custodians and guardians of the European tradition. The use of the martial metaphor 'phalanx'—a term employed by Eliot to describe the organization of the Criterion group[46]—suggests the embattled nature of the undertaking; nothing less than the rebuilding of a Virgilian *penates* on the 'waste land' of post-war Europe. The project possessed an odd kind of grandeur; all the same it was a losing battle.

In Alexandria during the Hellenistic period, the poets composed in a style that was allusive, witty, and strikingly obscure— evidence to some observers of the fragmentation and impending

---

[44] *Life is My Song* (New York, 1937), 308.
[45] 'Restoration of the Reason', *Criterion* (Nov. 1927), 391, 394, 396. The article was reprinted from *Neue Schweizer Rundschau* and translated from the German by Curtius's friend, William Stewart, a Romanist at the University of Bristol.
[46] See Allen Tate (ed.), *T. S. Eliot: The Man and His Work* (London, 1967), 20.

collapse of classical Greek civilization. Curtius believed that *The Waste Land*, a poem he translated into German in 1927, was 'Alexandrian': 'a lament for all the misery and fear of this age.'[47] But if 1927 was the high watermark of Curtius's collaboration on the *Criterion*, a journal he described as 'in a class by itself among the literary periodicals of the globe',[48] then Eliot's public declaration of reaction (classicism, royalism, Anglo-Catholicism) in the preface to *For Lancelot Andrewes* heralded an unmistakable cooling in their relationship. In an article published in the scholarly monthly review, *Die Literatur*, in 1929 (and not reprinted in English), Curtius spelt out their critical differences. Calling Eliot 'der Führer conservativer Geistespolitik' in England, he proceeded to dismantle Eliot's tripartite declaration. Curtius noted that Eliot's 'classicism' had more in common with reactionary French political thought than the civilizations of Greece and Rome; his 'royalism'—an irrelevance in contemporary English political debate—made little sense outside of the French nationalism of Maurras's *Camelots du roi*; finally his Anglo-Catholic *via media* and his essays on the Anglican bishops, Lancelot Andrewes and John Bramhall, signalled to Curtius a regrettable shrinkage and parochialism in his interests as a critic, a defection from literary criticism to lay theology, and worse, a retreat from 'europäischer Universalgeschichte' ('European universal-history').[49]

Curtius did not appear in the *Criterion* after 1927. He did not write the series of essays on English authors or the half-yearly 'German Chronicle' that Eliot attempted to persuade him to contribute.[50] He did, however, recommend his friend, the Swiss essayist and literary historian, Max Rychner, editor of *Neue Schweizer Rundschau*.[51] Rychner had met Curtius at Marburg in 1923 and they soon recognized shared interests and a mutual esteem—'wie jeder rechte Mensch in Frankreich verliebt und von Deutschland erfüllt und für Europa geboren' ('like every true man in love with France, filled with [thoughts of] Germany and

---

[47] *Essays on European Literature*, 369.   [48] Ibid. 356.
[49] 'T. S. Eliot als Kritiker', *Die Literatur* (Oct. 1929), 11–15.
[50] Eliot attempted to persuade Curtius to write articles on James, Conrad, Kipling, Strachey, Lewis, Woolf, and Forster. See T. S. Eliot to Ernst Robert Curtius, 22 Jan. 1926; 19 Dec. 1929; 30 Jan. 1930. Bonn.
[51] T. S. Eliot to Ernst Robert Curtius, 15 Feb. 1926. Bonn.

born for Europe').[52] The 'German Chronicles' submitted by
Rychner (and translated into English by Marjorie Gabain[53]) often
acknowledged a debt to Curtius: their personal ties bore some of
the characteristics of a master and pupil relationship. Following
Curtius, Rychner's first chronicle (April 1926) challenged
Massis's assertion that Graeco-Latin culture was not Germany's
legitimate possession:

There is then a spiritual Germany which is convinced that it belongs to
the domain of the former 'imperium romanum', and that its ancestors
had their place within the 'limes'. On this soil the feeling of cultural
continuity is so firmly stamped that it cannot be washed away by any
new current of radicalism and hostility to tradition. Conservative
powers in the best sense are not in danger in Germany.[54]

All this is deduced on the basis of Rychner's penchant for
generalizations grounded on racial-national 'type', particularly
when a question of a Germano-Latin inheritance was at stake. In
his Criterion obituary article on Rainer Maria Rilke, Rychner
skirted the frankly esoteric nature of his poetic meditations,
choosing instead to cite his Prague birthplace and his translations
of Valéry as an instance of a German-Latin-Slav Ausgleich
(balance). As Rychner put it: 'The nature of his gift, his outlook
on life, and certain of his inclinations were European.'[55] Eliot was
immune to the growing cult of Rilke, believing instead that Stefan
George was a more important poet.[56] It was a comparison that
Rychner rationalized—on the occasion of George's reception of
the 1927 Frankfurt Goethe Prize—in terms of the Rhinelander's
closer proximity to the 'imperium romanum'. Describing George
as the greatest German lyric poet since Hölderlin, Rychner

---

[52] Cited by Claudia Mertz-Rychner, 'Ein Briefwechsel: Ernst Robert Curtius—
Max Rychner', Merkur (1969), 371.
[53] Marjorie Gabain (b. 1891), French-born actress and writer on child psychology,
educated in Düsseldorf and at Newnham College, Cambridge.
[54] 'German Chronicle', Criterion (Apr. 1926), 726–32.
[55] 'German Chronicle', Criterion (May 1927), 241–6. See also Michael Hofmann:
'How could he [Rilke] be a European? He was a man out of time and a man out of
place. Who could claim Rilke as a fellow-citizen or a contemporary? . . . Rilke cannot
be called European because he never committed himself to anything beyond himself
and his poetry' ('A Man Out of Time and Place', TLS (22 July 1988)).
[56] T. S. Eliot to Ernst Robert Curtius, 28 Feb. 1928. Bonn. Samuel Beckett gave an
unenthusiastic review of J. B. Leishman's translations of Rilke. See 'Books of the
Quarter', Criterion (July 1934), 705.

emphasized the operative and creative force of the Latin inheritance on German history and literature:

By birth and descent George is a Catholic, a son of the Rhine, whose 'Roman atmosphere' he extols. The buildings of the colonies of the Roman Empire were among his earliest youthful impressions; the vines of the Rhine, of which he sings, were planted by the Roman colonists.[57]

In short, George stood as living proof of the vitality of Germany's classicism.

III

Curtius had been a youthful member of the George-*Kreis*, but he came to contrast George's dictatorial role in German intellectual life unfavourably with the Austrian man of letters, Hugo von Hofmannsthal. As a young poet, Hofmannsthal had absorbed the aestheticism of decadent *fin de siècle* Vienna, but the First World War awakened a new socio-political dimension to his work; in particular, an awareness of the Habsburg Empire as a *Praeceptor Europae*, the great melting-pot and frontierland of Western civilization. In his 1916 essay, 'Die Idea Europa', Hofmannsthal declared:

He who says Austria really says: a thousand years of struggle for Europe, a thousand-years of faith in Europe.

   For us, Germans and Slavs and Latins dwelling on the soil of two Roman Empires, chosen to bear a common destiny and inheritance—for us Europe is truly the basic colour of the planet, for us Europe will be the colour of the stars when from an unclouded sky the stars will again shine above us.[58]

The collapse of the Habsburg Monarchy in 1918 modified his position. Hofmannsthal brooded on the social disintegration and spiritual dereliction of post-war Europe. His cultural politics were advanced in *Neue Deutsche Beiträge*, which serialized *Der Turm* (1925), a visionary but despairing prose-drama interpretable as an allegory of the melancholy predicament of the

---

[57] 'German Chronicle', *Criterion* (Dec. 1927), 534–41.
[58] Cited in Brian Coghlan, *Hofmannsthal's Festival Dramas* (Cambridge, 1964).

Austrian Republic.[59] In a 1927 lecture entitled 'Das Schrifttum als geistiger Raum der Nation' ('Literature as the Spiritual Space of the Nation') Hofmannsthal proclaimed the cause of the paradoxical 'conservative revolution': nostalgia for the *status quo ante* of old imperial Catholic Austria. This monastic evasion of contemporary social reality continued up until his death in July 1929: he was buried in the habit of a tertiary of the Franciscan Order.

Eliot printed a generous obituary notice in the *Criterion*:

Pray for the soul of Hugo von Hofmannsthal. We mention him particularly because he supported and contributed to the *Criterion*. Hofmannsthal who is not long dead, was a fine poet and fine prose writer. He was, during his lifetime, the leading man of letters in Vienna. Not only by his own work, but by his patronage, his influence, and the periodicals which he affected, one of the great European men of letters.[60]

Hofmannsthal's single contribution to the *Criterion*, secured by Scofield Thayer of the *Dial*,[61] was an evocative 'intellectual pilgrimage' to Greece, an extraordinary attempt to inhabit the spiritual world of the ancients—reflections generated by sunlight on broken columns.[62] Eliot considered reprinting Curtius's obituary essay on Hofmannsthal in *Neue Schweizer Rundschau*.[63] In the end, the job of celebrating the life and work of Hofmannsthal in the *Criterion* went to Rychner's 'German Chronicle': 'He was a European for whom Europe with its twenty centuries of growth was a comprehensive whole exhibiting a thousand shades of inner differentiation, and the secret laws of whose crystallization lay open to his piercing glance.'[64] More revealingly still, some years later Curtius weighed Hofmannsthal in the balance with George:

Romanic-German substance, as an ancestral heritage, became alive again in George's poetry. But the Viennese, Hofmannsthal, also bore the

---

[59] In his 'Note' on Michael Hamburger's 1963 translation of *Der Turm*, Eliot refers to the work as a 'difficult' and 'strange play'. Eliot saw the play as an expression of Christian hope. See Hugo von Hofmannsthal, *Selected Plays and Libretti* (London, 1964), pp. lxxiii–lxxiv.   [60] 'A Commentary', *Criterion* (Oct. 1929), 5.
[61] Hofmannsthal had contributed a 'Vienna Letter' to the *Dial* in 1922. In Oct. 1933, the *Criterion* printed reminiscences of Hofmannsthal by Marta Karlweis (Frau Jakob Wassermann).   [62] See 'Greece', *Criterion* (Oct. 1923), 95–102.
[63] Curtius, 'Hofmannsthals deutsche Sendung', *Neue Schweizer Rundschau* (Aug. 1929), 583. Curtius also contributed an essay to a special Hofmannsthal commemorative number of *Die Neue Rundschau* (Nov. 1929).
[64] See 'German Chronicle', *Criterion* (July 1930), 710–17.

heritage of the Imperium and acknowledged it. Both poets felt that they were related to Rome by blood, that is, through the strength of their native soil, in the Rhineland as in the Danube basin. From these roots there sprang for both poets a love of the ancient Roman world, but also for the languages and literatures of the Romanic nations. In the work of both men the conflict not only between Greek and Roman but between Classical and German culture is resolved. The Roman continuity of the European form of mind was once more made a possession of consciousness.[65]

The talismanic significance of Hofmannsthal for the *Criterion* was a matter of the 'conservative revolution'.[66] In his 1929 essay on Eliot, Curtius cited Hofmannsthal's lecture, adding:

Schicksalsbesorgt und mit allweisem Überblick deutet er den Lauf der Jahrhunderte und kündet er eine 'Konservative Revolution' als die Signatur der kommenden Zeiten. Ein bedächtiger deutscher Sinn edelster Ahnenschaft kennzeichnet den Ton seiner Rede.[67]

(Worried by fate and displaying his wise overview of things he reads the course of centuries and announces a 'conservative revolution' as the typical feature of the coming times. A thoughtful German sense of noble descent marks the tone of his speech.)

Hofmannsthal's 'conservative revolution' was clerical and reactionary: a mythology encapsulating Austria's socio-political ambitions. The oppressed and messianic figure of Prince Sigismund in *Der Turm* embodies some of these idealized values, although his tragic fate may well be a comment on the *realpolitik* of inter-war Europe. At any rate, Hofmannsthal's 'conservative revolution' was a rearguard struggle fought along the banks of the Rhine and the Danube and with Vienna, the *cor et scutum imperii* or the heart and shield of the Holy Roman Empire, at its core.

On Curtius's lips the 'conservative revolution' sounded eminently *bürgerlich*. In a series of articles published in *Die Neue Rundschau* and *Neue Schweizer Rundschau* and collected in the volume *Deutscher Geist in Gefahr* (1932), Curtius attempted to reform a humanist model of education inherited from Wilhelm

---

[65] *Essays on European Literature*, 22.
[66] In his obituary for the *Neue Schweizer Rundschau* Curtius bracketed Hofmannsthal, Eliot, and Maurras together in the cause of the 'conservative revolution'.
[67] 'T. S. Eliot als Kritiker', 12.

von Humboldt as a necessary counterbalance to the cultural nihilism espoused by Hitler's National Socialist movement. Eliot praised chapter 5 of Curtius's book in the *Criterion* as 'one of the best and most reasonable expositions of a "humanist" attitude that I have ever read'.[68] Rychner's 'German Chronicle' for July 1932 expounded Nazism's crude race consciousness and Wagnerian 'cult of the irrational' against which Curtius levelled his critique:

> Against them [Curtius] defends humanism, 'a humanism of initiative', that preserves the eternal forces and symbols and is not merely a humanism or erudition. . . . This new humanism will have a different form from that which it had in the nineteenth century. It must arise spontaneously and cannot grow out of any educational programme. It will be brought about by a new type of human being . . . Curtius calls to him in this year of 1932, the year of Goethe's centenary. He is the spiritual, not the 'intellectual' man. Through him is made manifest ever and anew the oneness of the things of heaven and the things of the earth within depths of human experience.[69]

Deutscher Geist in Gefahr directed a flashlight on an impending crisis of classical humanism.

Unfortunately, Curtius's Goethean optimism was hopelessly out of touch with the campaign of terror that brought Hitler to power in January 1933.[70] The ensuing National Socialist revolution or *Gleichschaltung* (co-ordination) in the summer of 1933 effectively silenced him—the editors of *Die Neue Rundschau*, *Neue Schweizer Rundschau*, *Die Literatur*, and *Europäische Revue*, suspected of opposition or lukewarmness towards National Socialism, were dismissed from their posts in a sweeping Nazification of the arts and press, leaving Curtius without a platform for his periodical essays.[71] As Alec Randall put it in October 1933: 'The Nazi purge had a fairly prompt influence on

---

[68] 'A Commentary', *Criterion* (Oct. 1932), 74.

[69] 'German Chronicle', *Criterion* (July 1932), 709.

[70] Consider the epigraph to *Deutscher Geist in Gefahr* taken from Hölderlin: 'Wo aber Gefahrist, wächst das Rettende auch' ('But where there is danger, salvation springs forth').

[71] In 1929, the *Criterion* collaborated with *Europäische Revue*, *Nouvelle Revue française*, *Revista de Occidente*, and the long-established Milanese journal *Nuova antologia* on a short story competition. Ernst Wiechart's winning entry (chosen by Curtius, Thomas Mann, and Max Clauss) was published in the *Criterion* (Jan. 1930). Wiechart became a respected novelist and dramatist in Nazi Germany.

German periodicals and books generally.'[72] In common with all German university teachers, Curtius was compelled to join the National Socialist Teachers' League and to teach only subjects sanctioned by the Third Reich. Besides, *Deutscher Geist in Gefahr* rendered Curtius a *persona non grata* in Nazi Germany. Eliot, who met Curtius in London in the summer of 1934, feared for the personal safety of his friend. After German troops re-entered the Rhineland in 1936, Curtius's opportunities for free speech and foreign travel were restricted: an SS officer holding the rank of a 'visiting' associate professor at the University of Bonn was assigned to write reports on him.[73] Curtius retreated to the professional obscurity of his research into the Latin Middle Ages, his 'intellectual alibi', as he put it, during the Nazi era.

Rychner, writing from Cologne 1932–6, and Randall, writing from Copenhagen 1935–8, documented in the *Criterion* the rising tide of Nazi anti-intellectualism, including the persecution of Jewish writers. Given the *Criterion*'s record on these matters it is remarkable that recent critics have stigmatized the journal by suggesting that Eliot was sympathetic to the aims and methods of Nazism.[74] A more adequate characterization of Eliot's editorial policy would have to take into account essays published in the *Criterion* during the period in which war with Germany seemed imminent. As has already been noted, in July 1938 Eliot published the Revd Edward Quinn's long essay on 'Christian Politics' containing an explicit condemnation of the racial theories of National Socialism in the light of Christian teaching.[75] Moreover, the leading article in the final issue of the *Criterion* was by a German

---

[72] 'German Periodicals', *Criterion* (Oct. 1933), 173.

[73] Wolf-Dieter Lange in conversation with Jason Harding, 14 Apr. 1998. Bonn.

[74] John Gross accuses the *Criterion* of a creepy 'tenderness' towards Nazism, but he does not cite any evidence in support of his assertion (*The Rise and Fall of the Man of Letters* (London, 1969), 254). Similarly, in *T. S. Eliot, Anti-Semitism and Literary Form* (London, 1996), Anthony Julius overlooks several articles in the *Criterion* drawing attention to Nazi anti-Semitism. It is unfortunate that he should quote out of context a remark on 'Jewish propaganda' by Alec Randall—a former propaganda writer—in order to demonstrate the *Criterion*'s hostility to Jews, while ignoring Randall's praise of Ernst Toller, Lion Feuchtwanger, and Jakob Wassermann, not to mention his celebration of the 'remarkable contributions to German thought and science' made by German-Jewish intellectuals. See 'Books of the Quarter' and 'German Periodicals', *Criterion* (Oct. 1934), 168–75.

[75] 'Christian Politics', *Criterion* (July 1938), 627.

Jew, Friedrich Gundolf, a writer whose works were banned as 'degenerate' in Germany.[76] On 14 January 1939, Curtius wrote a letter of condolence to Eliot, expressing his deep sympathy with the editor's depression, expressed in his 'Last Words', that: 'The "European mind", which one had mistakenly thought might be renewed and fortified, disappeared from view.'[77]

It is natural to wonder why Curtius, unlike Thomas Mann, chose not to leave Nazi Germany. Alec Randall observed in the *Criterion* that Mann 'was among the first who grasped the implications of the new [National Socialist] philosophy'.[78] As early as 1931 Eliot had published Mann's appeal to the citizens of Berlin in the aftermath of massive gains for Hitler at the recent German elections. Mann posed some important questions:

Can a people, old and ripe and highly cultivated, with many demands on life, with a long emotional and intellectual experience behind it: a people who possess a classical literature that is lofty and cosmopolitan, a romantic literature of the profoundest and most subtle; who have Goethe, Schopenhauer, Nietzsche, and in their blood the noble malady of Tristan music—can such a people conform, even after ten thousand banishings and purificatory executions, to the wish image of a primitive, pure-blooded, blue-eyed simplicity, artless in mind and heart, that smiles and submits and claps its heels together?[79]

If Curtius chose not to emigrate it was because he believed that in his role as a university teacher he could still influence German

---

[76] Eliot cited Gundolf, Scheler, and Curtius in support of his contention that: 'It is greatly to the credit of the intellectuals of post-war Germany, living in a country which has been more politics-ridden than any other in Western Europe, and in an atmosphere which one might suppose most discouraging to dispassionate thought, that they have been able to produce so much that is first rate' ('A Commentary', *Criterion* (Oct. 1932), 73).

[77] 'Last Words', *Criterion* (Jan. 1939), 272. In his 1946 broadcast to Germany, Eliot spoke of 'the gradual closing down of the mental frontiers of Europe' (*Notes Towards the Definition of Culture*, 116). The 'closing down' of the *Criterion*'s links with European periodicals was gradual but far reaching. In 1933 the editorial boards of *Die Neue Rundschau* and *Neue Schweizer Rundschau* were removed. In 1936 Ortega y Gasset's exile from the Spanish Civil War brought *Revista de Occidente* to an end. *Il Convegno* closed in 1939. The *Nouvelle Revue française*, under the editorship of Drieu La Rochelle, survived the fall of France, ceasing publication, temporarily, in 1943.

[78] 'Books of the Quarter', *Criterion* (Apr. 1934), 478.

[79] 'An Appeal to Reason', *Criterion* (Apr. 1931), 399–411. See also Mann's criticism of the Hitler Youth in 'Freud's Position in the History of Modern Thought', *Criterion* (July 1933), 549–70. Both articles were translated by Helen Lowe-Porter (1877–1963). Eliot had been introduced to Mann's work by Curtius.

students. He was mistaken and his decision has courted mis-understanding and hostility: Mann later commented upon the 'intellectual atrophy' he discerned in Curtius's post-war writing.[80] And yet, there is an undeniable consanguinity in both writers' belief in 'akademische Freiheit' ('academic freedom'), in their desire to keep literature free from ideological dogmatism.

In July 1945, Stephen Spender visited a bitterly disillusioned Curtius in Bonn.[81] After their conversation, Spender pondered in print the reasons why Curtius had not joined the exodus of German intellectuals:

Since 1933, I have often wondered why Curtius didn't leave Germany. I think really the reason was a passion for continuity, a rootedness in his environment which made him almost immovable. He had modelled his life on the idea of Goethe who boasted that during the Napoleonic struggle he had been a mighty cliff towering above and indifferent to the waters raging hundreds of feet beneath him. If he always detested the Nazis he also had little sympathy for the Left, and the movement to leave Germany was for the most part a Leftwards one. Above all, he may well have felt that it was his duty, as a non-political figure, to stay in Germany, in order to be an example before the young people of the continuity of a wiser and greater German tradition.[82]

Curtius was deeply offended by Spender's speculative inferences and one may wonder how well the young English poet understood the atmosphere of fear and menace in totalitarian Germany. All the same, Spender correctly understood the importance of Goethe to Curtius's conception of the European cultural tradition.[83] The valuation was not without ramifications for the *Criterion*.

IV

Sainte-Beuve, in his celebrated *causerie* 'Qu'est-ce qu'un classique?' (1850), formulated an important question for modern industrial

[80] Thomas Mann to Hermann Hesse, 25 Nov. 1947. *Briefe, 1937–1947* (Frankfurt, 1963), 569.
[81] Curtius met Spender during the Weimar Republic. Enamoured of Spender, Curtius translated his poems for *Neue Schweizer Rundschau* (Aug. 1930). Spender praised the translations in a letter to Curtius, dated 13 Aug. 1930. Private collection.
[82] 'Rhineland Journal', *Horizon* (Dec. 1945), 398.
[83] Curtius described Goethe as 'die grösste Gestalt des deutschen Geistes' ('the greatest figure of the German spirit-intellect'). See *Deutscher Geist in Gefahr* (Stuttgart, 1932).

society: namely, how to select and classify a secular literary 'canon' to teach in our institutions of learning. What constitutes the intrinsic merit of a literary work? What gives it a sense of timeless value, an essence of permanence in an ephemeral and increasingly materialistic world? Such questions preoccupy the existential historicism that James Longenbach has termed the 'modernist poetics of history', a strange atemporal historiography where 'history is not conceived on the model of a linear or cyclical pattern of events, but a palimpsest in which the present is actually made up of remnants of the entire past'.[84] Palimpsest is a useful word to employ in relation to Curtius's neo-religious idea of topoi. Both Eliot and Curtius rejected literary historical 'archaeology' in favour of a full recognition of the transhistorical modernity of 'tradition' or 'topology'; taken up in the cause of a politically and culturally conservative response to threatened anarchy. Having said that, substantive differences in their respective national backgrounds ultimately undermined a common aspiration to unify the cultural traditions of Christian Europe.

In Germany during the inter-war period there was a busy trade in Goethe scholarship that grew to almost industrial proportions. In the course of his own research into the literature of the Latin Middle Ages, Curtius came to view Goethe as the heir and the crowning achievement of a classical tradition of rhetoric, an epigone poet, 'the thesaurus of European tradition':[85] '[Goethe] is something more and something other than a German poet. He is solidary [solidarisch] with the spiritual heritage of Europe [Geisteserbe Europas]. He stands in the line of Homer, Sophocles, Plato, Aristotle, Virgil, Dante, and Shakespeare.'[86] In 1931, Gundolf confidently asserted in the *Criterion*: 'all men of judgement recognize Dante, Shakespeare and Goethe as grand-masters of their craft.'[87] It is not clear that the bound volumes of the *Criterion* uphold that judgement.[88] Eliot was consistently condescending towards Goethe throughout his editorship of the *Criterion*. In

---

[84] *Modernist Poetics of History* (Cambridge, 1987), 168.
[85] *Essays on European Literature*, 493.   [86] Ibid. 90–1.
[87] 'Eduard Mörike', *Criterion* (July 1931), 682–708.
[88] The *Criterion* contained several entries on Dante, including extracts from Laurence Binyon's translation of *Purgatorio*, and an impressive roll call of the latest Shakespearean scholarship. By contrast, there was nothing more substantial on Goethe than a single short book notice by Stephen Spender. See also Eliot: 'Dante and Shakespeare divide the modern world between them; there is no third' (*Dante* (London, 1929), 51).

1933 he told a lecture audience at Harvard: 'Of Goethe perhaps it is truer to say that he dabbled in both philosophy and poetry and made no great success of either.'[89] Hans Hennecke's warmly appreciative 1936 essay on Eliot in *Europäische Revue* praised the *Criterion* for its intelligent coverage of political, religious, cultural, and economic matters, and then balked when it came to the sentence: 'kennte Eliot nur die deutsche Dichtung nicht so beklagenswert wenig!' ('if only Eliot didn't know German poetry so regrettably little!').[90]

In fact, Eliot's antipathy to Goethe struck a blow at the unity of European culture that the *Criterion* had worked so hard to promote. For Curtius, Eliot's dismissal of Goethe represented not only the exclusion of the nation's greatest poet from the European pantheon, 'but also the exclusion of Germany her language and her culture'.[91] It is a revelation to realize that the *Criterion*'s treatment of German literature and letters does not compare favourably with reputedly more insular journals.[92] That, of course, illumines the canalization of European culture implicit in the *Criterion*'s veneration of a Latin-Christian inheritance. It is possible to argue that Eliot's initially dynamic conception of the 'historical sense' hardened during the 1930s into the dogmatic assertions of *After Strange Gods* and his wartime address to the Virgil Society, entitled 'What is a Classic?' where he dismissed Goethe as 'unrepresentative of the whole European tradition, and, like our own nineteenth-century authors, a little provincial'.[93]

[89] *The Use of Poetry and the Use of Criticism* (London, 1949), 99. Eliot wrote to Curtius about his prejudice against Goethe, expressed in denigratory remarks in 'The Function of Criticism', in the *Criterion* (Oct. 1923) and in a review of two English studies of *Faust* for the *Nation and Athenaeum* (12 Jan. 1929).

[90] See Hans Hennecke, 'T. S. Eliot', *Dichtung und Dasein* (Berlin, 1950), 185. Eliot's copy, inscribed by Hennecke, is now in the Modern Archive Centre, King's College, Cambridge.

[91] 'T. S. Eliot and Germany', in Richard March and Tambimuttu (eds.), *T. S. Eliot: A Symposium* (London, 1948), 122.

[92] Eliot professed to dislike the 'emotional obliquities which render German metaphysics monstrous' ('A Commentary', *Criterion* (Oct. 1924), 1). The *Criterion* did not contain a single contribution, editorial, or book review devoted to the work of Schiller, Lessing, Novalis, Schlegel, Hegel, Heine, Schopenhauer, Nietzsche, Brecht, Heidegger, or Benjamin. Curtius and Edwin Muir offered articles on Hölderlin, a poet undergoing a revival of fortunes in Germany, but they did not appear.

[93] See 'What is a Classic?' in *On Poetry and Poets* (London, 1957), 67. Eliot's view diplomatically softened on his acceptance of the Hanseatic Goethe Prize in 1955, when he praised Dante, Shakespeare, and Goethe as 'great Europeans'.

On the contrary, Eliot's celebration of Virgil as *the* 'criterion' of Western literature followed Sainte-Beuve in valuing Virgil as the classic of a perpetually renewed Latin tradition.[94] Eliot was greatly influenced during the mid-1930s by the German Catholic philosopher, Theodor Haecker, who updated a strand of medieval textual commentary that celebrated Virgil as the author of the messianic Fourth Eclogue, essentially an *anima naturaliter christiana*. In Haecker's words, Virgil was the father of Western civilization; an exemplary figure who smoothed the passage between the Roman Empire and the Holy Roman Empire—the *imperium sine fine*.[95] In 1934 Arthur Wheen, a member of the Criterion group, translated Haecker's *Vergil, Vater des Abendlandes* into English. The Revd William Force Stead reviewed it in the *Criterion* as a salutary book for the times: 'the book deserves to be read for its vigorous attack upon our modern chaos and its attractive picture of Virgil and his ordered world with the divine decree above and *pietas* within'.[96] But the Virgilian imperial theme goes deeper. According to Frank Kermode: 'in all the years of the *Criterion* he [T. S. Eliot] struggled to make our mind, provincial and vernacular though it is, part of the mind of Europe; of which mind Virgil was *figura* and founder'.[97] Eliot's élitist and imperialist cultural politics found a number of fellow-travellers among Germany's leading bourgeois humanists—Hofmannsthal, Gundolf, Curtius. What they shared was a mission to preserve Europe's cultural heritage at a time of spiritual aridity, communism, fascism, nazism, and the spectre of war.

It was the papal myth of Rome in her universalism, the *urbs aeterna*, that came to symbolize—with a degree of nostalgia bordering upon despair—the order and continuity that the *Criterion*

---

[94] 'Sainte-Beuve was not merely a "man of letters" . . . he had a devouring[,] an insatiable interest in human nature in books, and was forever brooding over problems which are perhaps insoluble. The permanent and the changing in humanity; the problems of religious faith and doubt; the problems of the mind, the flesh and the spirit' ('A Commentary', *Criterion* (July 1931), 716).

[95] Eliot praised *Vergil, Vater des Abendlandes* in 'Religion and Literature' (1935) as 'an example of literary criticism given greater significance by theological interests' (*Essays Ancient and Modern* (London, 1936), 93). In 1946, he described Haecker, a contributor to the *Criterion*, as a 'great critic and good European' (*Notes Towards the Definition of Culture*, 116).

[96] 'Books of the Quarter', *Criterion* (July 1935), 681.

[97] *The Classic* (London, 1975), 42.

sought in the face of historical dissolution. As Eliot put it in his
Commentary for April 1926:

The Old Roman Empire is an European idea.... The general idea is
found in the continuity of the impulse of Rome to the present day. It
suggests Authority and Tradition ... It is an idea which comprehends
Hooker and Laud as much as (or to some of us more than) it implies
St. Ignatius or Cardinal Newman. It is in fact the European idea—the
idea of a common culture of Western Europe.[98]

Seventeenth-century Anglicanism and pagan Rome bear a dubious relation and do not very obviously walk hand in hand. It was
a mythologizing conflation often practised by Eliot. In an
unsigned *Criterion* editorial, that Curtius was fond of quoting, he
even pronounced that England was a 'Latin' country:

The fact is, of course, that *all* European civilisations are equally dependent upon Greece and Rome—so far as they are civilisations at all. If we
were indeed beyond the sphere of influence of Greece and Rome, and
could produce a civilisation independent of them, well and good; we
have no prejudice against non-European civilisations. .... [But] If everything derived from Rome were withdrawn—everything we have from
Norman-French society, from the Church, from Humanism, from every
channel direct and indirect, what would be left? A few Teutonic roots
and husks. England is a 'Latin' country.[99]

Curtius once declared that he would be prepared to perish in the
struggle for the 'civilisation of old Europe'.[100] His redoubtable
labours in this cause have been variously described as a 'giant
going down to defeat' (Arthur R. Evans) and as 'belonging to a
past irrevocably gone' (René Wellek). Much the same may be said
of the *Criterion*. The attempt to mobilize a cohort of European
periodicals in the defence of a Virgilian *penates*, for all the heroic
grandeur attached to such a project, seems a curiously misguided
undertaking. The *Criterion*, with its exiguous circulation, elegiac
tone, and lack of *realpolitik*, could never have established the
validity of the 'European idea' for those beyond the ambit of its
Latinate *catholica traditio*. In a goodwill message for the launch
of the *London Magazine* in 1954, Eliot conceded that the time for

[98] 'A Commentary', *Criterion* (Apr. 1926), 222.
[99] 'Notes', *Criterion* (Oct. 1923), 104–5.
[100] *Essays on European Literature*, 167.

a quarterly review like the *Criterion* had passed. Nevertheless, he took the opportunity to reiterate the indispensable service provided by an international literary magazine.[101] We breathe a different intellectual air today. From the vantage point of a globalized, electronic print media world it is not necessary to endorse the myth of catastrophe that enveloped the fall of the *Criterion*. In *East Coker* (1940), Eliot wrote of 'Twenty years largely wasted, the years of *l'entre deux guerres*'. Still, we can consider with profit the *Criterion*'s struggle to 'recover what has been lost' in times that were unpropitious.

---

[101] 'A Message', *London Magazine* (Feb. 1954), 16. The draft typescript is now in the Modern Archive Centre, King's College, Cambridge.

Afterword

The critical reputation of T. S. Eliot must inevitably play an important part in all retrospective valuations of the *Criterion*. The analytical focus of this work, however, has been less concerned with examining substantive issues relating to Eliot's 'intellectual development' than with an attempt to resituate the *Criterion* back within the complicated periodical networks in which he worked. Of course, his Commentaries should be accorded a special significance in any assesment of the *Criterion*, but that does not mean that they can be extracted from their journalistic context and read like the carefully chosen contents of *Selected Essays*. Recent critics have consistently judged Eliot's views and pronouncements on the literary-cultural events of the inter-war period as stolid and reactionary. It is hoped that this study has gone at least some way to account for the belief, widely held in London literary circles, that the *Criterion* Commentaries were often an eloquent and authoritative response to contemporary issues. Eliot's involvement in public intellectual controversy could also be skilful and well judged, just as the self-professed 'depression of spirits' that brought the *Criterion* to an end in 1939 bears testimony to an honourable engagement with complex and difficult areas of politico-cultural exchange.

Eliot believed that the *Criterion* possessed a definite character and cohesion. However, the journal did not attempt to express a single editorial 'line' or to reflect the impress of one person's point of view. The pattern of the changing roles of Herbert Read and Bonamy Dobrée on the *Criterion* clearly demonstrates that regular contributors did not always need to follow instructions from Eliot. Furthermore, as his agonistic relations with the Auden generation indicate, rather than coerce or browbeat contributors, Eliot preferred to put his trust in younger critics, like Michael Roberts and Janet Adam Smith, who shared a basic sympathy with his Church–State Anglicanism. That said, Eliot's use of Montgomery Belgion as a 'useful irritant' also showed that he was not above tipping the scales of weighty intellectual matters. Examination of Eliot's habitually oblique, ambivalent, even inconsistent attitude towards his regular contributors is certainly important in reconstructing the overall profile of the *Criterion*.

One of the challenges that this book offers to existing scholarship is to question certain current assumptions about the *Criterion*. For example, this study has tried to resist the temptation to let a bland recourse to words like 'fascism' or 'anti-Semitism', or an equally misguided intention to exonerate Eliot, determine the agenda of discussion. The conclusions furnished by this study— regarding the identity of the *Criterion* or Eliot's role as editor— are not easily torn from the detailed and intricate arguments contained in each chapter. However, if one were to offer a summary sketch of the *Criterion*'s engagement with the milieu of inter-war literary journalism, it would have to highlight Eliot's foundational desire to stitch together into some kind of unity the Latin-Christian elements of the otherwise diverse cultures of Western Europe, an undertaking modified by his Anglican *via media* during the 1930s. Eliot's social thinking has appeared either dangerous or simply irrelevant to many contemporary critics, and yet it is important not to forget that one may be simultaneously politically conservative and culturally broadminded. From the appearance of *The Waste Land* onward, the *Criterion* published numerous essays, reviews, and original creative contributions that have had a significant impact on the literary history of the twentieth century. If the circulation was always small, the *Criterion* really did become something of an establishment journal—it did, as Michael Levenson suggested at the outset of this study, represent the institutional consolidation of a revolutionary artistic moment, and for that reason alone Eliot was right to describe his journal as a valuable record of intellectual thought between the wars.

In the past decade, the appearance of scholarly editions of Eliot's Clark Lectures and of the early poetic notebooks, prepared with the co-operation of the Eliot estate, give grounds for optimism about the future. In his important recent volume, *Eliot's Dark Angel*, Ronald Schuchard noted that countless works on Eliot sink to the bottom of the sea of print because they have severed all connections to a wealth of unpublished material. He went on to predict a brave new world of modernist scholarship:

And I say confidently to young scholars that we are now at the threshold of a new age for the study of all modernist literature, that there is no richer time to be a modernist teacher and scholar, and that many of the riches are yet to be found in the untapped archives and in the unexamined histories of modernist texts.[1]

It does seem that there is a nascent interest in the milieu of interwar literary journalism—witnessed, above all, by the compilation of the *TLS* Centenary Archive. It will be fascinating to discover how this fresh attention to the undergrowth of journalistic reviewing may alter our conception of the *Criterion*'s place and significance in the intellectual history of the twentieth century.

[1]   Ronald Schuchard, *Eliot's Dark Angel*, (Oxford, 1999) 216.

Select Bibliography

ACKROYD, PETER, *T. S. Eliot* (London: Hamish Hamilton, 1984).

ADAMSKI, DANIEL, 'Letters', *London Review of Books*, 18: 12 (20 June 1996), 5.

AGHA, SHAHID ALI, *T. S. Eliot as Editor* (Ann Arbor: UMI Research Press, 1986).

AIKEN, CONRAD, *Ushant, an Essay* (Boston: Little Brown, 1952).

—— *Selected Letters of Conrad Aiken*, ed. Joseph Killorin (New Haven: Yale University Press, 1978).

ALDINGTON, RICHARD, *Stepping Heavenward* (London: Chatto & Windus, 1931).

—— *Life for Life's Sake* (New York: Viking, 1941).

Anon., 'Current Literature', *Spectator* (11 Nov. 1935), 746.

Anon., 'The New Criterion', *Nation* [New York] (22 Oct. 1926), 259.

ASHER, KENNETH, *T. S. Eliot and Ideology* (Cambridge: Cambridge University Press, 1995).

AUDEN, W. H., *The Complete Works of W. H. Auden, i. 1926–38*, ed. Edward Mendelson (Princeton: Princeton University Press, 1996).

BAGGULEY, PHILIP, *Harlequin in Whitehall: A Life of Humbert Wolfe* (London: Nyala, 1997).

BEACHCROFT, T. O., 'Letter', *TLS* (2 May 1968), 464.

BELGION, MONTGOMERY, *Our Present Philosophy of Life* (London: Faber & Faber, 1929).

—— *The Human Parrot* (Oxford: Oxford University Press, 1931).

—— *News From the French* (London: Faber & Faber, 1938).

—— *Reading for Profit* (Harmondsworth: Penguin, 1945).

BENNETT, ARNOLD, *The Journal of Arnold Bennett, iii. 1921–1928* (New York: Viking, 1943).

BERGONZI, BERNARD, *T. S. Eliot* (London: Macmillan, 1972).

BLOOMFIELD, B. C. (ed.), *An Author Index to Selected British 'Little Magazines', 1930–1939* (London: Mansell, 1985).

BOARDMAN, GWENN R., 'T. S. Eliot and the Mystery of Fanny Marlow', *Modern Fiction Studies*, 7 (Summer 1961), 99–105.

BOLD, ALAN. (ed.), *The Letters of Hugh MacDiarmid* (London: Hamilton, 1984).

—— *MacDiarmid* (London: Murray, 1988).

BRADBURY, MALCOLM, 'Literary Periodicals and Little Reviews and their Relation to Modern English Literature', MA thesis (London, 1955).

—— 'The Criterion: A Literary Review in Retrospect', London Magazine, 5: 2 (Feb. 1958), 41–54.

—— The Social Context of Modern English Literature (Oxford: Basil Blackwell, 1971).

BRADSHAW, DAVID, 'T. S. Eliot and Anti-Semitism', TLS 4866 (5 July 1996), 14–16.

BRAYBROOKE, NEVILLE (ed.), T. S. Eliot: A Symposium for His Seventieth Birthday (New York: Farrar, Strauss & Cudahy, 1958).

BROWER, REUBEN, VENDLER, HELEN, and HOLLANDER, JOHN (eds.), I. A. Richards: Essays in His Honor (New York: Oxford University Press, 1973).

BUNTING, BASIL, 'English Poetry Today', Poetry [Chicago] (Feb. 1932), 266.

BUSH, RONALD, T. S. Eliot: A Study in Character and Style (New York: Oxford University Press, 1983).

BUTTER, P. H. (ed.), Selected Letters of Edwin Muir (London: Hogarth Press, 1974).

CAESAR, ADRIAN, Dividing Lines: Poetry, Class and Ideology in the 1930s (Manchester: Manchester University Press, 1991).

CARPENTER, HUMPHREY, W. H. Auden: A Biography (London: George Allen & Unwin, 1981).

—— A Serious Character: A Life of Ezra Pound (London: Faber & Faber, 1988).

CARSWELL, JOHN, Lives and Letters: A. R. Orage, Beatrice Hastings, Katherine Mansfield, John Middleton Murry, S. S. Koteliansky, 1906–1957 (London: Faber & Faber, 1978).

CHILD, HAROLD [Anon.], 'Periodicals: The Criterion', TLS 1084 (26 Oct. 1922), 690.

COGHLAN, BRIAN, Hofmannsthal's Festival Dramas (Cambridge: Cambridge University Press, 1964).

COLLINI, STEFAN, 'The European Modernist as Anglican Moralist', in Mark S. Micale and Robert L. Dietle (eds.), Enlightenment, Passion, Modernity: Historical Essays in European Thought and Culture (Stanford, Calif.: Stanford University Press, 2000), 207–29.

CONSTABLE, JOHN (ed.), I. A. Richards and his Critics: Selected Reviews and Critical Articles (London: Routledge, 2001).

COWLING, MAURICE, Religion and Public Doctrine in Modern England (Cambridge: Cambridge University Press, 1980).

CRANE, HART, The Complete Poems and Selected Letters and Prose of Hart Crane (London: Oxford University Press, 1968).

CRICK, BERNARD, George Orwell: A Life (London: Secker & Warburg, 1980).

CUNNINGHAM, VALENTINE, British Writers of the Thirties (Oxford: Oxford University Press, 1988).

CURTIUS, ERNST ROBERT, *Essays on European Literature*, trans. Michael Kowal (Princeton: Princeton University Press, 1973).

DAVIES, VANESSA, 'A Diet of Dead Crow: Aspects of French Culture in the *Criterion* (1922–39)', in Ceri Crossley and Ian Small (eds.), *Imagining France: Studies in Anglo-French Cultural Relations* (London: Macmillan, 1988), 124–34.

DAY-LEWIS, SEAN, C. *Day-Lewis: An English Literary Life* (London: Weidenfeld, 1980).

DIECKMANN, HERBERT, and DIECKMANN, JANE (eds.), *La Correspondence de Ernst Robert Curtius avec André Gide, Charles du Bos et Valéry Larbaud* (Frankfurt: Klostermann, 1980).

DONOGHUE, DENIS, 'Criteria Omnia', *Cambridge Review*, 89A, 2164 (9 Feb. 1968), 257–60.

—— 'Eliot and the *Criterion*', in David Newton-de Molina (ed.), *The Literary Criticism of T. S. Eliot* (London: Athlone Press, 1977), 20–41.

DUNCAN, RONALD, *All Men Are Islands* (London: Rupert Hart-Davis, 1964).

EASON, T. W., and HAMILTON, R. (eds.), *A Portrait of Michael Roberts* (London: College of St Mark and St John, 1949).

ELIOT, T. S., *For Lancelot Andrewes* (London: Faber and Gwyer, 1928).

—— *The Use of Poetry and the Use of Criticism* (London: Faber & Faber, 1933).

—— *After Strange Gods* (London: Faber & Faber, 1934).

—— *Essays Ancient and Modern* (London: Faber & Faber, 1936).

—— *The Idea of a Christian Society* (London: Faber & Faber, 1939).

—— *Notes Towards the Definition of Culture* (London: Faber & Faber, 1948).

—— 'A Letter from T. S. Eliot, O.M.', *Catacomb*, 1: 1 (Summer 1950), 367–8.

—— *Selected Essays* (London: Faber & Faber, 1951).

—— 'A Message', *London Magazine*, 1: 1 (Feb. 1954), 15–16.

—— *On Poetry and Poets* (London: Faber & Faber, 1957).

—— *Selected Prose*, ed. Frank Kermode (London: Faber & Faber, 1975).

—— *The Letters of T. S. Eliot, i. 1898–1922*, ed. Valerie Eliot (London: Faber & Faber, 1988).

—— *The Varieties of Metaphysical Poetry: The Clark Lectures and the Turnbull Lectures* ed. Ronald Schuchard (London: Faber & Faber, 1993).

ELIOT, VALERIE (ed.), *'The Waste Land': A Facsimile and Transcript of the Original Drafts* (London: Faber & Faber, 1971).

—— 'Letters', *TLS* 4861 (31 May 1996), 17.

ELLIS, DAVID, *D. H. Lawrence: Dying Game, 1922–1930* (Cambridge: Cambridge University Press, 1998).

FLETCHER, JOHN GOULD, *Life Is My Song* (New York: Farrar & Rinehart, 1937).

GALLUP, DONALD, *T. S. Eliot: A Bibliography* (London: Faber & Faber, 1969).

—— 'T. S. Eliot and Ezra Pound: Collaborators in Letters', *Atlantic Monthly*, 225: 1 (Jan. 1970), 48–62.

GOLDIE, DAVID, *A Critical Difference: T. S. Eliot and John Middleton Murry in English Literary Criticism, 1919–1928* (Oxford: Clarendon Press, 1998).

GOODWAY, DAVID (ed.), *Herbert Read Reassessed* (Liverpool: Liverpool University Press, 1988).

GRAVES, ROBERT, *In Broken Images: Selected Letters of Robert Graves, 1914–1946*, ed. Paul O'Prey (London: Hutchinson, 1982).

GRIGSON, GEOFFREY (ed.), *The Arts Today* (London: John Lane, 1935).

—— 'Criterion and London Mercury', *New Verse*, NS 1: 2 (Winter 1939), 62.

—— (ed.), *New Verse: An Anthology* (London: Faber & Faber, 1939).

—— *The Crest on the Silver* (London: The Cresset Press, 1950).

—— 'A Conversation with Geoffrey Grigson', *Review*, 22 (June 1970), 15–26.

—— 'Viewpoint', *TLS* (8 Feb. 1980), 141.

—— *Recollections: Mainly of Writers and Artists* (London: Chatto/Hogarth, 1984).

GROSS, JOHN, *The Rise and Fall of the Man of Letters* (London: Weidenfeld & Nicolson, 1969).

HAFFENDEN, JOHN (ed.), *Auden: The Critical Heritage* (London: Routledge, 1983).

HAMILTON, IAN, *The Little Magazines: A Study of Six Editors* (London: Weidenfeld and Nicolson, 1976).

HARDING, JASON, '*Experiment* in Cambridge: A Manifesto of Young England', *Cambridge Quarterly*, 27: 4 (Dec. 1998), 287–309.

—— 'Doubting Thomist', *Cambridge Quarterly*, 29: 2 (June 2000), 184–9.

HÄUSERMANN, HANS WALTER, 'Das Ende einer europäischen Zeitschrift: *The Criterion*', *Der Kleine Bund*, 20: 6 (1939), 44–6.

HAWKINS, DESMOND, 'London Letter', *Partisan Review*, 6 (Summer 1939), 89.

—— *When I Was* (London: Macmillan, 1989).

HEALEY, R. M. (ed.), *Grigson at Eighty* (Cambridge: Rampant Lion Press, 1985).

HENNECKE, HANS, *Dichtung und Dasein* (Berlin: Karl Henssel, 1950).

HESSE, HERMANN, *Blick ins Chaos* (Bern: Seldwyla, 1921).

HOBDAY, CHARLES, *Edgell Rickword: A Poet at War* (Manchester: Carcanet, 1989).

HOFFMAN, FREDERICK J., ALLEN, CHARLES, and ULRICH, CAROLYN, *The Little Magazine: A History and Bibliography* (Princeton: Princeton University Press, 1946).

HOGGART, RICHARD, *Speaking to Each Other*, ii (Harmondsworth: Penguin, 1973).

HOLROYD, MICHAEL, *Lytton Strachey: A Biography, ii. 1910–1932* (London: Heinemann, 1968).

HOWARTH, HERBERT, *Notes on Some Figures behind T. S. Eliot* (London: Chatto & Windus, 1965).

HYAMS, EDWARD, *The New Statesman* (London: Longmans, 1963).

HYNES, SAMUEL, *The Auden Generation* (London: The Bodley Head, 1976).

JENKINS, ISLWYN, *Idris Davies* (Cardiff: University of Wales Press, 1972).

JULIUS, ANTHONY, *T. S. Eliot, Anti-Semitism and Literary Form* (Cambridge: Cambridge University Press, 1996).

KENNER, HUGH, *The Invisible Poet: T. S. Eliot* (London: Allen, 1960).

KERMODE, FRANK, 'The Calendar of Modern Letters', *New Statesman* (2 Sept. 1966), 320.

—— *The Classic* (London: Faber & Faber, 1975).

KERSHAW, ALISTER, and TEMPLE, FRÉDÉRIC-JACQUES (eds.), *Richard Aldington: An Intimate Portrait* (Carbondale and Edwardsville, Ill.: Southern Illinois University Press, 1965).

KEYNES, JOHN MAYNARD, *The Collected Writings of John Maynard Keynes* (London, 1971).

KING, JAMES, *The Last Modern: A Life of Herbert Read* (London: Weidenfeld and Nicolson, 1990).

KNIGHTS, L. C., 'Remembering *Scrutiny*', *Sewanee Review*, 89 (Fall 1981), 560–85.

KOJECKY, ROGER, *T. S. Eliot's Social Criticism* (London: Faber & Faber, 1971).

KRELLER, PAUL, 'Definitions of Classicism and Romanticism: Argumentative Strategies in the Eliot–Murry Debate (1923–1927)', *Yeats Eliot Review*, 13: 3–4 (Fall 1995), 63–70.

LAWRENCE, D. H., *The Letters of D. H. Lawrence, iv. June 1921–March 1924*, ed. Warren Roberts, James T. Boulton, and Elizabeth Mansfield (Cambridge: Cambridge University Press, 1987).

—— *The Letters of D. H. Lawrence, vii. November 1928–February 1930*, ed. Keith Sagar and James T. Boulton (Cambridge: Cambridge University Press, 1993).

—— *The Letters of D. H. Lawrence, v. March 1924–March 1927*, ed. James T. Boulton and Lindeth Vasey (Cambridge: Cambridge University Press, 1989).

—— *The Letters of D. H. Lawrence, vi. March 1927–November 1928*, ed. James T. Boulton, Margaret H. Boulton, and Gerald M. Lacy (Cambridge: Cambridge University Press, 1991).

LEA, F. A., *The Life of John Middleton Murry* (London: Oxford University Press, 1959).

LEAVIS, F. R., 'The Relationship of Journalism to Literature', Ph.D. thesis (Cambridge, 1924).

—— 'A Reply to the Condescending', *Cambridge Review*, 50: 1230 (8 Feb. 1929), 254–6.

—— *Mass Civilisation and Minority Culture* (Cambridge: The Minority Press, 1930).

—— *New Bearings in English Poetry* (London: Chatto & Windus, 1932).

—— (ed.), *Towards Standards of Criticism* (London: Wishart, 1933).

—— (ed.), *Determinations* (London: Chatto & Windus, 1934).

—— *Revaluation: Tradition and Development in Modern Poetry* (London: Chatto & Windus, 1936).

—— *'Anna Karenina' and Other Essays* (London: Chatto & Windus, 1967).

LEAVIS, Q. D., *Fiction and the Reading Public* (London: Chatto & Windus, 1932).

LEE, HERMIONE, *Viriginia Woolf* (London: Vintage, 1997).

LEHMANN, JOHN, *The Whispering Gallery* (London: Longmans, 1955).

LERNER, LAURENCE, 'The Life and Death of *Scrutiny*', *London Magazine* (Jan. 1955).

LEVENSON, MICHAEL, *A Genealogy of Modernism* (Cambridge: Cambridge University Press, 1984).

LEWIS, PERCY WYNDHAM, *The Apes of God* (London: Nash & Grayson, 1930).

—— *Men Without Art* (London: Cassell, 1934).

LONGENBACH, JAMES, *Modernist Poetics of History* (Cambridge: Cambridge University Press, 1987).

LUCAS, JOHN, *The Radical Twenties* (Nottingham: Five Leaves, 1997).

M., D., 'The Criterion', *Cambridge Review*, 52 (30 Oct. 1931), 74.

MACGREEVY, THOMAS, *Thomas Stearns Eliot* (London: Chatto & Windus, 1931).

MCKENZIE, D. F., *Bibliography and the Sociology of Texts* (London: The British Library, 1986).

MACKILLOP, IAN, *F. R. Leavis: A Life in Criticism* (London: Allen Lane, 1995).

MAIRET, PHILIP, 'T. S. Eliot as Editor', *Philbeach Quarterly* (Summer 1965), 5–6.

MANN, THOMAS, *Briefe, 1937–1947* (Frankfurt: S. Fischer, 1963).

MARCH, RICHARD, and TAMBIMUTTU (eds.), *T. S. Eliot: A Symposium from Conrad Aiken and Others* (London: Editions Poetry, 1948).

MARGOLIS, JOHN D., *T. S. Eliot's Intellectual Development, 1922–1939* (Chicago: Chicago University Press, 1972).

MARTIN, KINGSLEY, *Editor: A Second Volume of Autobiography, 1931–45* (London: Hutchinson, 1968).

MARTIN, WALLACE, *'The New Age' Under Orage* (Manchester: Manchester University Press, 1967).

MENAND, LOUIS, *Discovering Modernism: T. S. Eliot and his Context* (Oxford: Oxford University Press, 1987).

MERTZ-RYCHNER, CLAUDIA. (ed.), 'Ein Briefwechsel: Ernst Robert Curtius—Max Rychner', *Merkur*, 23 (1969), 371–82.

MEYERS, JEFFREY, *A Biography of Wyndham Lewis* (London: Routledge, 1980).

MOGGRIDGE, DONALD, *Keynes* (London: Macmillan, 1976).

MOODY, A. DAVID, *Thomas Stearns Eliot: Poet* (Cambridge: Cambridge University Press, 1979).

MOODY, PHILIPPA, 'T. S. Eliot and the Failure of *The Criterion*', *Melbourne Critical Review*, 2 (1959), 29–37.

MORRISH, P. S., 'Bonamy Dobrée, Theatre Critic of *The Nation and Athenaeum*', *Notes and Queries*, 29 (1982), 344–5.

MORTON, A. L. 'T. S. Eliot—A Personal View', *Zeitschrift für Anglistik und Amerikanistik* (Leipzig: Veb, 1966), 282–91.

MUIR, EDWIN, *An Autobiography* (London: The Hogarth Press, 1954).

MULHERN, FRANCIS, *The Moment of 'Scrutiny'* (London: New Left Books, 1979).

MURRY, JOHN MIDDLETON, *Defending Romanticism: Selected Essays of John Middleton Murry*, ed. Malcolm Woodfield (Bristol: The Bristol Press, 1989).

NOH, JEO-YONG, 'T. S. Eliot and *The Criterion*: Aspects of Literary and Political Toryism', D.Phil. thesis (Oxford, 1991).

O'DONOVAN, BRIGID, 'The Love Song of T. S. Eliot's Secretary', *Confrontation* (Fall–Winter 1975), 3–8.

PAIGE, D. D. (ed.), *The Selected Letters of Ezra Pound 1907–1941* (New York: Harcourt, Brace & Co., 1950).

PAULIN, TOM, *Writing to the Moment* (London: Faber & Faber, 1996).

PETER, JOHN, 'Eliot and the *Criterion*', in Graham Martin (ed.), *Eliot in Perspective* (London: Macmillan, 1970), 252–66.

PORTEUS, HUGH GORDON, 'Avant Garde', *New English Weekly*, 10 (29 Oct. 1936), 54–5.

—— 'Letter', *TLS* (2 May 1968), 464.

POUND, EZRA, 'Criterionism', *Hound and Horn*, 4: 1 (Oct.–Dec. 1930), 113–16.

—— 'The *Criterion* Passes. Notes on the Solitudes and Depressions of my Esteemed and Distinguished Contemporary, Mr. Thos. Stearns Eliot', *British Union Quarterly*, 3: 2 (Apr.–June 1939), 60–72.

—— *Selected Prose, 1909–1965*, ed. William Cookson, (London: Faber & Faber, 1973).

RAINE, CRAIG, 'The Waste Land as a Buddhist Poem', TLS (4 May 1973), 503–5.

RAINE, KATHLEEN, The Land Unknown (London: Hamish Hamilton, 1975).

READ, HERBERT, Reason and Romanticism (London: Faber & Faber, 1926).

—— English Prose Style (London: G. Bell & Sons, 1928).

—— Form in Modern Poetry (London: Sheed & Ward, 1932).

—— (ed.), Surrealism (London: Faber & Faber, 1936).

—— Poetry and Anarchism (London: Faber & Faber, 1938).

—— Selected Writings: Poetry and Criticism, with a foreword by Allen Tate (London: Faber & Faber, 1963).

REDMAN, TIM, Ezra Pound and Italian Fascism (Cambridge: Cambridge University Press, 1991).

RICHARDS, I. A., Principles of Literary Criticism (London: Kegan Paul, 1925).

—— Selected Letters of I. A. Richards, ed. John Constable (Oxford: Clarendon Press, 1990).

RICKS, CHRISTOPHER, T. S. Eliot and Prejudice (London: Faber & Faber, 1988).

RICKWORD, EDGELL, Essays and Opinions, 1921–1931, ed. Alan Young (Manchester: Carcanet, 1974).

RIDING, LAURA, Anarchism is Not Enough (London: Jonathan Cape, 1928).

RIDLER, ANNE (ed.), A Little Book of Modern Verse, preface by T. S. Eliot (London: Faber & Faber, 1942).

—— 'Working for T. S. Eliot: A Personal Reminiscence', Poetry Review, 73: 1 (Mar. 1983), 46–9.

ROBERTS, MICHAEL (ed.), New Signatures (London: Hogarth Press, 1932).

—— (ed.), New Country (London: Hogarth Press, 1933).

—— Critique of Poetry (London: Jonathan Cape, 1934).

—— (ed.), The Faber Book of Modern Verse (London: Faber & Faber, 1936).

—— The Modern Mind (London: Faber & Faber, 1937).

—— The Recovery of the West (London: Faber & Faber, 1941).

—— Collected Poems of Michael Roberts (London: Faber & Faber, 1958).

—— Selected Poems and Prose, ed. Frederick Grubb (Manchester: Carcanet, 1980).

ROSE, W. K. (ed.), The Letters of Wyndham Lewis (London: Methuen, 1963).

ROWLAND, DOMINIC, 'T. S. Eliot, The Criterion, and Literary Controversy, 1922–1939', Ph.D. thesis (London, 1997).

ROWSE, A. L., *A Cornishman at Oxford* (London: Jonathan Cape, 1965).
—— *A Cornishman Abroad* (London: Jonathan Cape, 1976).
RYCHNER, MAX, and BOEHLICH, WALTER (eds.), *Freundesgabe für Ernst Robert Curtius* (Bern: Francke, 1956).
RYLANDS, GEORGE, 'Recollections', *Paris Review*, 108 (1988), 108–36.
SCHUCHARD, RONALD, *Eliot's Dark Angel: Intersections of Life and Art*, (Oxford: Oxford University Press, 1999).
SCHWARTZ, DELMORE, 'The Criterion: 1922–1939', *Kenyon Review*, 1: 4 (Autumn 1939), 437–49.
SCOTT, CHRISTINA, *A Historian and His World: A Life of Christopher Dawson, 1889–1970* (London: Sheed & Ward, 1984).
SCOTT-JAMES, ROLFE-ARNOLD, 'Mr. T. S. Eliot and "The Criterion"' *London Mercury*, 39: 232 (Feb. 1939), 380–1.
SENCOURT, ROBERT, *T. S. Eliot: A Memoir*, ed. Donald Adamson (London: Garnstone Press, 1971).
SHARMA, L. R., *The T. S. Eliot–Middleton Murry Debate* (Allahabad: Silver Birch, 1994).
SINGH, G. S., 'Il *Criterion* di T. S. Eliot', *Il Verri: Rivista di Letteratura*, 9 (1978), 145–57.
—— *F. R. Leavis: A Literary Biography* (London: Duckworth, 1995).
SIRE, H. J. A., *Father Martin D'Arcy: Philosopher of Christian Love* (London, 1997).
SITWELL, EDITH, *Aspects of Modern Poetry* (London: Duckworth, 1934).
SKELTON, ROBIN (ed.), *Herbert Read: A Memorial Symposium* (London: Methuen, 1970).
SKIDELSKY, ROBERT, *John Maynard Keynes: The Economist as Saviour, 1920–1937* (London: Macmillan, 1992).
SMITH, JANET ADAM, 'T. S. Eliot and *The Listener*', *Listener* (21 Jan. 1965), 105.
SMITH, STAN, *The Origins of Modernism* (London: Harvester, 1994).
SPENDER, STEPHEN, *World Within World* (London: Hamish Hamilton, 1951).
—— *Eliot* (London: Fontana, 1975).
—— *The Thirties and After* (London: Collins, 1978).
—— *Journals 1939–1983*, ed. John Goldsmith (London: Faber and Faber, 1985).
SQUIRE, J. C., 'Editorial', *London Mercury*, 16 (June 1927), 117.
—— 'Editorial', *London Mercury*, 19 (Jan. 1929), 237.
STALLWORTHY, JON, *Louis MacNeice* (London: Faber & Faber, 1995).
STEWART, JEAN, 'Recollections of Pontigny', *London Magazine*, 1: 10 (Nov. 1954), 70.
STOUGH, CHRISTINA, 'The Skirmish of Pound and Eliot in *The New English Weekly*: A Glimpse at Their Later Literary Relationship', *Journal of Modern Literature* (1983), 231–46.

Symons, Julian, 'The Cri', *London Magazine*, NS 7: 8 (Nov. 1967), 19–23.

Tate, Allen (ed.), *T. S. Eliot: The Man and His Work* (London: Chatto & Windus, 1967).

—— *Memories and Essays Old and New: 1926–1974* (Manchester: Carcanet, 1976).

Thatcher, David S., 'Richard Aldington's Letters to Herbert Read', *Malahat Review*, 15 (July 1970), 5–44.

Thompson, Denys (ed.), *The Leavises* (Cambridge: Cambridge University Press, 1984).

Tillyard, E. M. W., *The Muse Unchained* (London: Bowes & Bowes, 1958).

Tolley, A. T., *The Poetry of the Thirties* (London: Gollancz, 1975).

Tomlin, E. W. F., 'The Criterion', *Townsman*, 2: 6 (Apr. 1939), 13–15.

—— *T. S. Eliot: A Friendship* (London: Routledge, 1988).

Treece, Henry (ed.), *Herbert Read: An Introduction to His Work by Various Hands* (London: Faber & Faber, 1944).

Waller, Robert, *The Pilgrimage of Eros* (London: Antony Rowe, 1992).

Watson, George, *Politics and Literature in Modern Britain* (London: Macmillan, 1977).

—— 'The Cambridge Lectures of T. S. Eliot', *Sewanee Review* (Fall 1991).

Weber, Brom (ed.), *Letters of Hart Crane, 1916–1932* (Berkeley: University of California Press, 1965).

Wellek, René, *A History of Literary Criticism, vii.* (New Haven: Yale University Press, 1991).

White, T. H., 'Crites', *Granta* (12 Oct. 1928), 25.

Willey, Basil, *Cambridge and Other Memories, 1920–1953* (London: Chatto & Windus, 1968).

Woolf, Virginia, *The Diary of Virginia Woolf, iii. 1925–1930*, ed. Anne Olivier Bell and Andrew McNeillie (London: The Hogarth Press, 1980).

—— *The Diary of Virginia Woolf, iv. 1931–1935*, ed. Anne Olivier Bell and Andrew McNellie (London: The Hogarth Press, 1982).

Young, Alan, and Schmidt, Michael, 'A Conversation with Edgell Rickword', *Poetry Nation*, 1 (1973), 73–89.

Zabel, Morton Dauwen, 'Recent Magazines', *Poetry* [Chicago] (Apr. 1936), 53–4.

—— 'News Notes', *Poetry* [Chicago] (Mar. 1939), 342.

Index